D0508469

HIKING &
BACKPACKING

HILLSBORO PUBLIC LIBRARIES
Hillsboro, OR
Member of Washington County
COOPERATIVE LIBRARY SERVICES

FUELED BY
FALCONGUIDES

KNACK™

HIKING & BACKPACKING

A Complete Illustrated Guide

BUCK TILTON

PHOTOGRAPHS BY STEPHEN GORMAN

KNACK™
MAKE IT EASY

Guilford, Connecticut
Member of The Globe Pequot Press

HILLSBORO PUBLIC LIBRARIES
Hillsboro, OR
Member of Washington County
COOPERATIVE LIBRARY SERVICES

To buy books in quantity for corporate use
or incentives, call **(800) 962–0973**
or e-mail **premiums@GlobePequot.com.**

Copyright © 2009 by Morris Book Publishing, LLC

ALL RIGHTS RESERVED. No part of this book may be reproduced or transmitted in any form by any means, electronic or mechanical, including photocopying and recording, or by any information storage and retrieval system, except as may be expressly permitted in writing from the publisher. Requests for permission should be addressed to The Globe Pequot Press, Attn: Rights and Permissions Department, P.O. Box 480, Guilford, CT 06437.

Knack is a registered trademark of Morris Publishing Group, LLC, and is used with express permission.

Falcon and FalconGuides are registered trademarks of Morris Book Publishing, LLC
Editor in Chief: Maureen Graney
Editor: Katie Benoit
Cover Design: Paul Beatrice, Bret Kerr
Text Design: Paul Beatrice
Layout: Kim Burdick
Cover photos by Stephen Gorman except photo left © Maksym Gorpenyuk/Shutterstock
All interior photos by Stephen Gorman with the exception of p. 41(left): Falk Kienas/shutterstock; p. 60(left): Falk Kienas/shutterstock; p. 63 (left): © Pat Goltz | Dreamstime.com; p. 63 (right): © Vaide Seskauskiene | Dreamstime.com; p. 86 (left), p. 87, p. 88 (right), p. 90 (left), p. 93 (right), p. 101(left), p. 103(right): Courtesy of the U.S. Geological Survey; p. 106 (left): Alessandro Contadini/istockphoto; p. 107(right): Steve Cukrov/shutterstock; p. 139(left): Steve Cukrov/shutterstock; p. 143(right): Jonathan Davies/istockphoto; p. 148(left): Jonathan Davies/istockphoto; p. 149(right): © James Phelps | Dreamstime.com; p. 160(left): © Brightdawn | Dreamstime.com; p. 162(left): © Virgil Dombroski | Dreamstime.com; p. 162(right): © Stephen Bonk | Dreamstime.com; p. 163(left): © David Schrader | Dreamstime.com; p. 163(right): photos.com; p. 164(left): © Wojciech Wojcik | Dreamstime.com; p. 164(right): © Musat Christian | Dreamstime.com; p. 165(left): © Kobby Dagan | Dreamstime.com; p. 165(right): Kevin Herrin/istockphoto; p. 166(right): David Dohnal/shutterstock; p. 167(left): Lev Ezhov/istockphoto; p. 167(right): Sebastian Kaulitzki/shutterstock; p. 168(left): © Photomyeye | Dreamstime.com; p. 168(right): Clint Spencer/ istockphoto; p. 169(left) Courtesy of Joe Belnap, Big H Products, Inc.; p. 170(left): © Johnbell | Dreamstime.com; p. 170(right): Jake Holmes/istockphoto; p. 171(left): photos.com; p. 171(right): Dave Rodriguez/istockphoto; p. 172 (right): Suzann Julien/istockphoto; p. 173(left): Richard Fitzer/shutterstock; p. 174(right): John Pitcher/istockphoto; p. 176(left): ryasick/shutterstock; p. 176(right): Michel de Nijs/istockphoto; p. 177(right): Zoran Ivanovic/istockphoto; p. 178(right): Alexey Fursov/istockphoto; p. 179(left): Darla Hallmark/shutterstock; p. 179(right): Margo vanLeeuwen/istockphoto; p. 180(left): © Elisalocci | Dreamstime.com; p. 180(right): © Ivan Mikhaylov | Dreamstime.com; p. 181(left): © Nedim Jukić | Dreamstime.com; p. 181(right): Laurie Knight/istockphoto; p. 182(left): © Addict | Dreamstime.com; p. 182(right): Iurii Konoval/shutterstock; p. 183(left): © Aleksey Puris | Dreamstime.com; p. 183(right): © Joellen Armstrong | Dreamstime.com; p. 196(left): Christophe Testi/istockphoto; p. 196(right): Artem Efimov/shutterstock; p. 197(left): Maria Bobrova/shutterstock; p. 198(left): Rainer Schmidt/shutterstock; p. 198(right): © Jim Mills | Dreamstime.com; p. 200(right): Nathan Holland/shutterstock; p. 201(left): Cheryl Casey/shutterstock; p. 201 (right): B.G. Smith/shutterstock; p. 202(right): George Peters/istockphoto; p. 204(left): Jeanette Zehentmayer/istockphoto; p. 205(left): Richard Clark/istockphoto; p. 223(left): Dmitry Rukhlenko/shutterstock; Photos pages 17(left), 43(right), and 20(left) courtesy of Cascade Designs; Photo page 174(left) courtesy of Judy Sinclair; Photo page 57(right) courtesy of Backpackers Party; Photos pages 3(left), 4(right), and 57(right) courtesy of Big Agnes; Photos pages 17(right), 21(right), & 86(left) courtesy of Brunton; Photos pages 1(left), 3(right), 12(right), and 91(left) courtesy of Coleman; Photo page 31(right) courtesy of Marmot; Photo page 2(right) courtesy of Eureka.

Library of Congress Cataloging-in-Publication Data is available on file.
ISBN 978-1-59921-400-9   4/23 6679 08/09

The following manufacturers/names appearing in Knack Hiking & Backpacking are trademarks: Ace, Band-Aid, Crazy Creek Chairs, Crocs, Egg Beaters, Gore-Tex, Lexan, M&Ms, Old Bay, Oreos, Outback Oven, Pilot Bread, Pilot Crackers, Rice Krispies, Sam Splint, Thermos, Wheat Thins, Wheatsworth

The information in this book is true and complete to the best of our knowledge. All recommendations are made without guarantee on the part of the author or The Globe Pequot Press. The author and The Globe Pequot Press disclaim any liability in connection with the use of this information.

Printed in China

10 9 8 7 6 5 4 3 2 1

Dedication

For Kathleen Hart Tilton. As a companion on any path that leads anywhere at any time, I choose her.

Acknowledgments

Most writers, I think, have embraced the new age of publishing. A few older writers, like me, have been dragged kicking and screaming, and cursing, into the electronic world of creating a book. I cannot imagine a more patient and talented dragger of kickers and screamers than Katie Benoit at Globe Pequot Press. Thank you, Katie, and thanks to Maureen Graney, editor in chief at Globe Pequot, for always understanding and offering excellent help. And one more thanks: to Max Phelps at Globe Pequot, who brought us all together and keeps making things happen and embodies all that's really great about being a human being.

CONTENTS

INTRODUCTION: GOING OUT THERE

Out there: the deeply shaded forest trail, the steep switchbacks ascending a mountain pass, the hot white meanderings between spiny cacti, the fantastic sandstone walls reigning over slim canyons, the gray beaches where sea otters bob offshore watching.

You don't have to go out there, out where your feet carry you everywhere, out where everything you need burdens your back (unless you forgot to pack it). Out there no thermostats are found, no TV or electronic games, or memory-foam beds, or restaurants that bring your favorite dishes to a spotlessly clean and properly set table.

My first backpacking trip, when I shouldered all I thought I should shoulder and left the car far behind, was into the Olympic National Forest in the state of Washington. The thing I called a "backpack" was a canvas bag attached somehow to two slats of wood that hung from my aching upper body on two canvas straps. The tube tent I slept in consisted of a single wall of waterproof red nylon on which every drop of moisture from out of my body condensed and dripped back down onto my body—and then rain began to fall. The mosquitoes were bad, the food was bad, the blister on my right heel was bad, and I came out two days later in the wrong place and had to sleep beside the road and walk another 5 miles to find a phone.

Why did I ever take a second backpacking trip?

You find something out there that defies explanation and can be only feebly described. It's part peace, part quiet, part wonder, part reaching way down inside and touching some gene that relates you to an ancient ancestor who was as much intertwined with the natural world as any tree, stone, or babbling brook. It's part the aroma of sap in piney woods. It's part an orange-red sunset that cuts a sharp swath beneath low clouds. It's part the heartbreaking trill of a canyon wren. It's part a sip of

phones and computers and the daily pileup of bills in the mailbox. Related to that, it can give you time to think things through without distractions. It can give you concentrated, valuable time with people you treasure. You get to see places that fewer and fewer people know firsthand—the mountains behind the mountains, where the rivers begin, one of the last habitats of the rare Missouri bladderpod (but, yes, that's sort of philosophical). Most importantly, it's fun. And in the words of the ineffable Dr. Seuss, ". . . fun is good."

What about that miserable first trip of mine? We'll get back to that soon.

"Hiking," in the context of this book, refers to going out for a walk, following a trail or, if you know how, walking off-trail. You have a small pack on your back with a few necessities and maybe a couple of luxuries. And you'll be home in time to sleep in your own comfy bed. You could call someone involved in this activity a "day hiker" as opposed to a "backpacker." When you see the word "backpacking," it means your pack is bigger and filled with enough gear and clothing to safely allow you to spend at least one night away from home but not in a motel. In this book, the information about hiking and backpacking is intertwined, like your genes and your ancient an-

coffee flavored with wood smoke. And it's part waking up to a fresh morning after a dreamless sleep in a place you can pretend no one has ever woken up in before.

Maybe Edward Abbey got it in a few words: "Wilderness is not a luxury but a necessity of the human spirit."

Or maybe you don't care about that philosophical stuff. There are other reasons to go out there: It is an excellent way to exercise. Plus it's a form of exercise you're already pretty good at. You've been walking for how many years now? It reduces stress, not only because you're exercising but also because the exercise carries you away from cestor's genes. What you need to know to be a great day hiker overlaps much of what you need to know to be a great backpacker, and most day hikers are also or soon will be backpackers anyway.

What you hold in your hands is, you could say, the result of my first backpacking trip. Despite the misery, I was utterly fascinated. I wanted to go back, and next time I wanted to do it right. I didn't—do it all right, I mean—but I did do it better the second time. And even better the third. It is sort of amazing, and certainly ironic, that you can do so many things wrong so many times that, if you're paying attention, you end up being considered an expert.

Uncounted hikes are behind me now. I've been out there a lot—out in the Rockies, the Cascades, the Appalachians, the Alaska Range; out in the canyons of Utah and Arizona; out on the altiplano of South America; out-back in Australia; out of my mind (almost) in the jungly forests of southern India. Hiking becomes an addiction. As with coffee, if you go too long without it, you get a headache.

Perhaps you don't need convincing. Perhaps you are an avid trail walker already or determined to become one. Bravo! Allow me to confirm the wisdom of your choice. If you are a wannabe or a novice hiker/backpacker, you will reap a bountiful harvest from the information herein. Those of you whom I will call "intermediates" will assur-

edly pick out many nuggets of usable information. If you think you know it all already, you are mistaken. There's at least one piece of info in here you've never read or heard before.

Hiking to some degree and backpacking to a major degree are gear-intensive undertakings. You need to know what to take and how to use it in order to travel safely and happily. Quite a bit of this book covers gear and clothing—what to choose and how to use it best or wear it best. (How magnificent are today's backpacks, able to fit your torso perfectly, with padded shoulder straps and thickly padded hip belts.)

In addition to gear, there's a chapter on food choices, including a few recipes I have enjoyed.

If you keep reading, you'll find thoughts on how to get all that stuff into your pack in a way that eases the workload, changes that you can make in how you walk to ease the workload (and hike safely), and how to get to where you want to go without getting lost.

After safety, it is increasingly most important to wild lands for you to travel and camp in ways that leave as little trace of your passing as possible, and you'll read about that—as well as about how to deal with the weather, and wild animals and plants, and how to manage some of the most common emergencies. There's information on how to care for your gear so it will last longer and how to get physically fit for the trail so you will last longer. There's even a resource directory leading you to more info, outside this book, and helping you put it all together.

While reminding myself of what's in this book, I thought of a hyphenated word: "self-reliance." As you master the art and science of the trail, you will become more and more self-reliant. Masters of the trail are, among other skills, home builders, navigators, nutritionists, cooks, hygienists, zoologists, botanists, doctors, nurses—and philosophers. Come to think of it, the feeling of self-reliance had a lot to do with my many return trips to the world of the backpack. In our culture of specialists, of which there are an ever-growing number, it is mighty refreshing to walk out where you're ready, willing, and able to deal with just about anything.

One more thing: With numerous choices in books on hiking and backpacking, why should you choose this one? The totally unique approach in what you hold is the dual and interwoven efforts of writer and photographer. Everyone has heard that "a picture is worth a thousand words." That's not always true. A bad photo might be worth only a few words, but a great photo cannot be traded for any amount of verbiage. The words in here are hard and fast, with little or no fluff—just the basic information laid out for quick access. And the photographs are great.

If you have any interest at all in going out there, please go. There is so little to lose and so very much to gain.

PACKS

Day hike or overnight, packs need to fit right and hold what you need

An ideal pack for your day hike or backpacking trip will hold what you need without excess space. Too little capacity, and you might leave something essential behind. Too much capacity, and you may overload your back or end up unstable from the gear shifting around inside the underloaded space. If you intend to enjoy trips of varying lengths, you are wise to own more than one pack.

A pack's capacity to hold gear and clothing is measured in cubic inches. Packs range from small hip models, no more than a few hundred cubic inches designed to hold a water bottle, a snack, and a light jacket, to expedition-weight monsters with 6,000 cubic inches of space inside.

Inexpensive packs may be no more than a bag evenly weighted across both shoulders. More expensive models

Fanny Pack

- Day hikers often prefer the less cumbersome weight of a fanny pack (a hip pack).

- All the weight of a fanny pack rides on your hips, and remember, as with standard backpacks, a fanny pack needs to fit you.

- The capacity is typically 1,000 cubic inches or less, although fanny packs are available with surprisingly large capacities. Too much weight may cause lower-back pain.

- A water bottle pocket provides quick access to all-important fluids.

Day Pack

- The capacity of a day pack will usually be less than 2,000 cubic inches, not enough space to load for an overnight trip.

- Choose a model with padded shoulder straps and a padded hip belt.

- Day packs seldom have frames. They should hug your back and not stick out too far from your back when loaded—attributes that keep you more stable as you hike.

- Most day packs are top-loading models with few extras available.

offer extras that may include exterior water bottle pockets, exterior pockets for keeping small items handy for quick access, and an array of stabilizing straps to help secure and balance the load. Budget considerations are often the limiting factor.

Packs also differ in the way in which they are loaded. Top-loading models are easier to stuff, but it's harder to get at the contents. Panel-loading packs have long, vertical zippers providing easy access to the contents. Some packs offer a combination of both designs. The choice is yours.

MAKE IT EASY

The fit of a pack is critical. If your shoulders and neck end up hurting, and the weight is not immense, your pack probably fails to fit properly. Try on as many packs as necessary to find the right fit. Better yet, pick a pack with assistance from an outdoor specialist.

External-Frame Pack

- External-frame packs are far less popular than internal-frame packs, but they do offer advantages over internal frames.

- Air circulates between the frame and your back, a fact that makes these packs especially appealing to those who perspire heavily.

- With a higher center of gravity, you can walk more upright, and it is easier to carry the weight on your hips.

- Many side pockets are the norm on external-frame packs, and they typically cost less than internal-frame packs.

Internal-Frame Pack

- Internal-frame packs appeared on the backpacking scene about twenty years after external frames.

- They hug your back, and you carry the weight lower and closer to your back.

- They allow you to hike with more stability on steep terrain and when you scramble over boulders or obstacles.

- As with an external-frame pack, an internal-frame pack's capacity runs from around 2,500 cubic inches and up. For weekend trips, a capacity of 3,500 cubic inches should be enough.

TENTS
More than just shelter, a tent is your home on the trail

First and foremost, tents are shelters, and the role of shelters is to provide protection: from rain, from wind, from cold, and from insects and other biters. But a shelter on the trail is also your home, at least for a few days every year.

It needs to be large enough to give adequate space for the correct number of people—that number being up to you—and you may want it large enough to provide space for your gear. Tents with large vestibules may have adequate gear space under the vestibules. In any case, the manufacturer will provide information about a tent's size in relation to how many people will fit comfortably inside and whether or not the tent's space will hold gear in addition to people. Sales personnel are often able to give you additional information, sometimes based on experience.

Tarp

- If it's not too cold, windy, or buggy, consider a tarp instead of a tent.

- Most tarps are lighter in weight and cost less than most tents.

- A tarp can be tied between trees or set with the ends held up by poles such as trekking poles.

- A tarp can be set up in many different types of terrain, serving as a shelter or an extra roof over a kitchen or communal area of camp.

A-Frame Tent

- An A-frame is the simplest and oldest design in tent styles.

- Steep walls shed water well, but, unless pitched very taut, those same walls rattle more under high winds than those of other designs.

- The steep walls cause some loss of floor space where the walls meet the floor.

- The easiest of tent styles to pitch, some A-frames are freestanding and some are not.

Tents are available in numerous styles from little more than a thin nylon roof and walls to luxurious models with an array of extras such as mosquito netting on doors, windows with mosquito netting, two-way zippers on door and windows, interior storage pockets, and interior loops for hanging gear. Generally speaking, the more extras, the more the tent will both cost and weigh.

But tent weight is also a result of the material used in manufacturing and the number of tent poles and stakes. If your plans include only summer trips, you will usually be well protected in a light tent with a few poles and stakes. To extend your hikes into spring and fall, a three-season tent will be required—with more weight due to the stronger nylon and a greater number of poles and stakes for more stability in heavier winds and rains and perhaps a little snow. Only the winter backpacker needs a winter-weight tent.

Freestanding Dome Tent

- A dome tent is the most popular style.

- Dome tents are available in numerous shapes—roundish, sort of a square or rectangle, even geodesic—but they all look something vaguely like an igloo.

- The rounded shape of the walls provides greater access to floor space than in A-frame tents.

- This one is freestanding, holding its shape without the use of tent stakes or guy lines.

Non-Freestanding Dome Tent

- The freestanding characteristic of tents is created by poles that crisscross. This tent is not freestanding.

- It is more difficult to pitch than a freestanding dome or an A-frame.

- Once it is pitched, there is good access to floor space, and the rounded walls shed wind well.

- As with other styles, a vestibule provides a useful covered area outside the main tent compartment and increased protection from rain.

SLEEPING BAGS
Sleeping bags need to keep you not only adequately warm but also comfortable

As with packs and tents, only more so, sleeping bags come in a great variety of shapes and sizes, weights and colors. Whatever the end result of your choice, the goal in all bag-choosing is the same: a good night's sleep.

The temperature rating of a bag gives you an idea of how cold the night can get while you sleep warm. A rating of 20 degrees F means you should be warm at that temperature, but no absolute standard for rating exists. However, most bags rated around 20 degrees F will provide comfort for spring, summer, and fall. Ratings above 32 degrees F may not provide enough insulation for most campers except on balmy summer nights.

Rectangular Bag

- Rectangular sleeping bags are squared at all four corners, which typically creates plenty of room inside.

- They cannot be closed at the head, so they don't hold in body heat as well as bags that do close at the head.

- Expect to pay less for rectangular bags, but also expect them to weigh more and compress less than mummy-shaped bags.

- On overnight summer trips, you may be well pleased with a rectangular bag.

Semi-Rectangular Bag

- Semi-rectangular sleeping bags are hybrids, part rectangular bag and part mummy bag.

- Some close snugly at the head to hold in body heat, and some do not.

- They usually cost more than rectangular bags but less than mummy bags, and they also fall in between as far as weight and compressibility go.

- For late spring and early fall trips, a semi-rectangular bag will probably keep you warm enough.

Bags are made with an outer shell and an inner liner. Quality shells and liners protect you against wind and some water, and should "breathe," allowing your body moisture to escape. Examples of shells include ripstop nylon (slightly water-resistant) and Gore-Tex (highly water-resistant)—and both breathe. Nylon taffeta is often found as a liner.

Between the shell and liner lies the insulation, synthetic, or down. Synthetics are easier to keep clean and dry and cost less, but they are heavier than down and don't compress as small. Today synthetic insulation is the most popular choice.

YELLOW LIGHT

You can sleep lousy in an expensive bag that doesn't fit your body. Before buying, get in, zip it up, roll around—and be sure there is enough room inside. But not too much room. Extra space inside your bag has to be heated by your body on a chilly night.

Mummy Bag

- Mummy-shaped sleeping bags are the most popular style.

- These sleeping bags are narrow at the feet, wide at the shoulder, and close snugly around your head via a hood for maximum body heat retention.

- Most people find there is less room inside for tossing and turning—but these bags also weigh less and compress more than other styles.

- The cost of construction is more, so you also pay more.

Zip-Together Bags

- Couples sometime prefer sleeping bags that zip together.

- They can be used separately if you wish.

- The space inside zip-together bags is greater than the space inside both bags when they are used separately—lots of room inside, but you can't close the head on a cold night.

- They are sometimes chosen by parents with a small child who can sleep between the parents.

SLEEPING PADS
The best sleeping pad often offers a better sleep than the best bag

Lay the most expensive and comfortable sleeping bag in the world on top of a thin and otherwise inadequate sleeping pad, and what have you got? You've got poor rest at night. Too thin, and the hard irregularities of the ground can—and will—bore into you, chasing away sleep. On a chilly night, you lose the most heat by far where your bag's insulation is compressed underneath your body. A pad needs to insulate you adequately from the cold ground. Although thickness can be an indicator of how much insulation is beneath you, some thin materials hold in body heat surprisingly well.

In addition to varying thicknesses, sleeping pads come in differing lengths and widths. Although most people prefer a pad that matches their full body length, some hikers opt for a three-quarter-length pad in order to save weight. A three-

Open-Cell Foam Pad

- Open-cell foam is less dense than closed-cell foam, so this sleeping pad protects you less well from sticks, rocks, and irregularities in the ground—and it rips without much effort.

- It soaks up water like a sponge, so open-cell foam requires care to keep it dry.

- These pads compress less than most sleeping pads, which means you have more bulk to carry.

- Open-cell foam pads are the least expensive of all sleeping pads.

Closed-Cell Foam Pad

- The density of closed-cell foam creates a very durable, semi-rigid sleeping pad that protects you well from the ground—but not as well as a self-inflating pad.

- It will not absorb moisture, and it does a good job of preventing body heat loss into the ground.

- These pads can be rolled up tight for easy packing.

- They cost more than open-cell foam pads but less than self-inflating pads.

quarter-length pad, however, may be too short on some of the cold nights of spring and fall. You may find you sleep better on a wider pad, but remember, more width—as with additional length and thickness—means more weight on your back. But a little more weight is a good choice when it means sleeping well.

And another tip: Some pads have a nonslip surface. The ones that do not are the ones you often slide off during the night when you roll over in your sleeping bag.

ZOOM

Sleeping pads that inflate are virtually useless if you spring a leak in one. Flat, they provide neither padding nor insulation. Many inflatable pads come with a repair kit—which works only if you carry it. You may also purchase repair kits separately from pads.

Air Mattress

- Air mattresses are available in sizes suitable for backpacking.

- They are usually blown up via lung power, but a pump can be carried by those who don't mind the weight and bulk.

- There are two basic styles: one that holds air in a single chamber, one that holds air in compartments running the length of the pad. You won't know which you prefer until you try both.

- Price varies depending on the brand, from expensive to affordable.

Self-Inflating Pad

- Self-inflating pads are the most popular, even though they are also the most expensive.

- When the valve is opened, air rushes in until the pad is filled. Many people like to blow in an additional lungful of air to firm up the pad.

- For comfort, most people agree a self-inflating pad is the best.

- As with air mattresses, these pads can rupture, so a repair kit is advised.

MORE ESSENTIAL GEAR
Many small items are essential for a safe and successful hike

When the word "essential" appears with the word "gear," more experienced hikers and backpackers are divided: What is essential to one, in other words, might not be essential to another. Back in the 1930s, a list of Ten Essentials was generated, a breakdown of gear that outdoor experts agreed should always be with you.

That list has been altered over the years. One reason for this is changes in the environment: It used to be okay to drop and drink from any stream, but now a means to disinfect water is considered essential. Another reason is technological advances in gear and the changes in attitude that have followed: Do you need a compass if you have a GPS unit? Opin-

First Aid Kit

- Your first aid kit should be adequate for the number of people and the number of days; kit makers often supply helpful numbers on the packaging.

- A kit should help you deal with the most common problems: blisters, wounds, sprains, stomachaches.

- Check your kit before each trip to be sure you have what you might need.

- First aid kits do *not* make a first aider. Remember, training in first aid is more important than the items in a kit.

Flashlights

- Every trip, day or overnight, should include a flashlight. You cannot be sure you won't need one.

- Today's flashlights do not have to be big to produce a big light—and a big light is most helpful.

- Test your flashlight before each trip, and pack an extra set of batteries.

- With a headlamp, your hands are free to set up or take down camp, to hold a book for reading, or to search through your pack for a missing item.

ions still vary, but what remains on every list represents gear providing safety and comfort that you should always have with you—or at least almost always.

No knowledgeable travelers heading deep into the wilderness would be caught without something resembling the Ten. And each individual in most groups should have the entire Ten Essentials (see page 99) if there is a chance, or a plan, that the group will be separated. However, a group of day hikers on a short and well-marked trail might choose to go without quite a few of the Ten. In between lies a group of backpackers whose members plan to stay close and function entirely as a unit, no one at any time setting off on his or her own. In such a case, several of the Ten could be shared by the group, maps and compass, for instance.

Some of the Ten Essentials are discussed in later chapters: extra clothing in Chapter 3, water disinfection in Chapter 4, extra food in Chapter 5, and map and compass in Chapter 8.

Knife

- One of the essentials has always been a knife.

- The blade does not have to be big. A big blade, in fact, is not only heavy but also most often less useful than a small blade.

- Remember, a sharp blade is safer than a dull blade.

- More often than not, today's backpacker carries a multipurpose tool, available in numerous sizes with a wide variety of choices in tools.

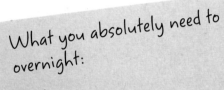

What you absolutely need to overnight:

- Pack
- Shelter
- Sleeping bag and pad
- Adequate clothing and footwear
- Food, stove, fuel, and kitchenware
- Matches and/or lighter
- Means to disinfect water
- Map and compass (or GPS)
- First aid kit, flashlight, and knife

SOME LUXURY GEAR
Little things can mean a lot in terms of comfort and enjoyment

To ensure proper communication here, "luxury" gear refers to things that you do not need but that would add comfort, increase ease, boost enjoyment, and otherwise make your trip more pleasant. Those plusses, of course, must be balanced against the fact that luxury gear adds weight and bulk to your pack—and takes away from your bank account.

As with "essential" gear, hikers and backpackers do not agree unanimously on what constitutes "luxury" gear. As one example, one or two trekking poles (or ski poles for those who already own them) are considered a luxury by some. For others, who find that the use of poles eases stress on knees and shoulders and helps them maintain balance on the trail,

Backpacking Chair

- Generally speaking, sitting in a backpacking chair is far more comfortable—and easier on your back—than sitting on a log, rock, or the ground.

- These chairs fold flat for ease of packing, and their weight is not alarmingly high.

- They can be flattened and placed under your sleeping pad for additional padding.

- As with most outdoor gear, you'll have choices in sizes, colors, and the level of luxury provided.

Camp Shoes

- A soft shoe for hanging out in camp is a big plus for tired feet.

- Many types of footwear qualify as camp shoes: sneakers, plastic slip-ons, flip-flops, even a thick pair of socks.

- Modern materials offer the opportunity to acquire camp shoes that weigh very little.

- Camp shoes are easier on the environment than trail shoes, causing less scarring of the ground and less compaction of the soil.

a trekking pole or two are essential. Gaiters, short coverings that enclose the lower legs and the tops of boots, keeping out sand, gravel, and rain, are another example of an item thought necessary by some and luxurious by others. If you hike with your children, you may decide a few games or toys are necessary for a successful trip, while other parents will choose to have their kids play with whatever nature provides. In rainy climes, some think a rain cover for a pack is an item that everyone should have. Other trailwise hikers think a pack made from water-resistant fabric provides ample protection from precipitation. And, as a final example, backpackers in rainy weather often carry a small sponge to wipe water out of tents—luxury or essential?

In the end, as you gain experience on the trail, you will get to decide what you consider essential to have along (see page 08), what you think important but not necessarily essential, and what you will add to your list of luxury items.

Lantern

- Small, lightweight backpacking lanterns can illuminate camp setup, meal prep, cleanup, a book for reading, or the inside of a tent for numerous activities.

- Most people prefer lanterns that can be hung from the limb of a tree or the inner peak of a tent.

- Lanterns may be battery-powered or candle-powered. If candle-powered, use only as directed by the manufacturer to ensure safety.

- Lanterns do not have a beam and should *not* be considered a substitute for a flashlight.

More luxury items:

- Trekking poles
- Camera and film
- Journal and pen
- Books to read, guidebooks
- Pack towel

STOVES

The heart of every backpacking kitchen is a reliable one-burner stove

Technological advances in backpacking gear have been most rapid and dramatic, in recent years, where stoves are concerned. Although all backpacking stoves have their strong points and weak points, the market today offers products that are more efficient and reliable than ever before. Since you will ultimately choose a stove based partially on the type

of fuel the stove utilizes, it is important to read the next section on fuel before shopping.

Other than being sure the stove you choose will burn the fuel you prefer, here are some other considerations: 1) The weight will be carried on your back, so consider the ounces of difference between models. 2) Your stove will often sit on un-

Canister-Type Stove

- The fuel for this stove comes in a pressurized canister that is attached to the stove for cooking and usually removed and packed separately on the trail.

- This stove is the lightest, smallest, and easiest to use of all backpacking stoves.

- All you do is turn a valve, ignite the gas, and start dinner. And you control the flame from a simmer to a boil.

- It is typically difficult to know how much gas is left in a canister so carry a spare.

Stove with Integral Fuel Tank

- This type of stove uses liquid fuel, usually white gas.

- The tank that holds the fuel is an integral part of the stove, permanently attached.

- When the tank is empty, it must be refilled from a fuel bottle, a job made easier

if you have a small funnel or a fuel bottle with a pour spout.

- Before the stove will light, pressure must be pumped into the tank via an integral pump.

even surfaces, so choose one with supports wide enough to provide a stable base. If it tips over during meal preparation, you could be missing out on dinner. 3) Choose a stove that lights easily, or you will spend too much time fiddling with firing yours up. 4) If you plan to do more than just boil water, choose a model that allows you to simmer. 5) Some stoves come with windscreens, and some do not. If your stove has no windscreen, buy one. Eventually you will be glad you did. 6) One stove will usually handle the needs of three to four people. More people mean another stove.

········· GREEN ● LIGHT ·········

Even the most expensive and durable stoves sometimes clog up or break down. Choose a stove that repairs easily on the trail, one that includes instructions on how to perform repairs. And carry the appropriate repair kit. If your stove does not come with a repair kit, choose a model for which a kit is available.

Stove with Separate Fuel Tank

- This stove uses liquid fuel, usually white gas. These stoves are more complex to use than other stoves.

- The tank that holds the fuel is separate from the stove, connected during cooking via a small tube.

- The tank is a fuel bottle. When it is empty, it is simply exchanged for a full bottle or refilled.

- Before the stove will light, pressure must be pumped into the tank via an integral pump.

Stove with Pot Attached

- Innovations in cooking systems allow you to have many more choices than ever before, including, as an example, this stove.

- This is a canister-type stove with a pot that attaches to the stove itself.

- The unique attachment point saves fuel by heating the pot much faster than a typical stove.

- If you wish, you can eat or drink from the pot, saving weight on a bowl and a cup.

FUEL

Without the proper fuel, a stove is just a useless hunk of metal

Stove fuels are far from created equal. Some burn hotter than others, and fuel that burns hotter boils water faster. Some burn cleaner than others, and clean-burning fuels clog your stove less often—and smell less offensive. Some fuels must be carried in canisters that attach directly to your stove, and some must be carried in fuel bottles and poured into the

tank of your stove. The plusses and minuses of fuels are explained below.

Whatever type of fuel you use, you will need to answer this question: How much fuel should I carry? Part of that answer depends on what type of cooking you plan to do. If boiling water will satisfy your culinary needs, you will use less

Kerosene

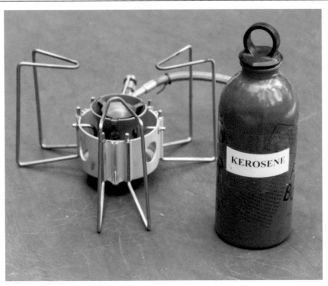

- Kerosene, as a backpacking stove fuel, is becoming less and less popular.

- Kerosene is the most inexpensive fuel, but it burns with less intensity than most fuels. It does not produce as much heat as you most often will want.

- Many people agree it has the least appealing smell of all fuels.

- Kerosene produces a greasy film that can coat everything in the campsite kitchen.

Alcohol

- Alcohol can be burned as fuel for cooking in the backcountry.

- Many forms of alcohol will work, but denatured alcohol is considered the best.

- Some backpacking stoves are designed to use alcohol, but this fuel is not burned

under pressure, so any container that won't ignite or melt, such as an aluminum can, could serve as a "stove."

- Alcohol burns with the least intensity of all fuels, but it burns very cleanly.

fuel than if fresh-baked, stove-top biscuits are on the menu. The ambient air temperature will also partly determine how much fuel you need—you'll use more when it's colder. Generally speaking, however, one person will use about 1/6 quart of fuel per day on a summer trip. On a spring or fall trip, with colder temperatures, one person will use about 1/4 quart of fuel per day. If the temperature may drop really low, such as on winter trips or trips to high altitudes (where thin air reduces stove efficiency), better carry 1/2 quart per person per day to be safe.

RED ● LIGHT

Spilled fuel can ruin more than the opportunity to enjoy a hot meal. Fuel can destroy food and damage gear and clothing. If you carry fuel in bottles, the bottles must be manufactured for fuel storage. Be sure the rubber rings that seal the cap on the bottle are intact, and be sure to fully tighten the caps before packing the bottles in your pack.

Butane

- Canisters (or cartridges) of fuel are filled, most often, with butane or a blend of butane and propane. Some canisters contain only propane.

- This fuel is packed under high pressure. It ignites easily and quickly without pumping or priming, and it burns cleanly.

- It produces higher heat than kerosene or alcohol.

- On very cold days, this fuel may refuse to release from the canister.

White Gas

- White gas is the most popular backpacking stove fuel.

- It must be carried in a separate fuel bottle from which the tank of a white-gas stove is filled. The fuel in the tank must be pressurized via pumping, and then the stove must be primed (heated) to get the fuel to rise to the burner.

- This fuel burns the hottest of all fuels. It burns cleanly and with very little odor.

- It is highly flammable.

COOKWARE
The right pot or pan makes cooking easier and often more successful

With pots and pans, your gear decisions will include how many and how large. The number will depend on the number of backpackers in your group and the complexity of the meals you plan. If your food plan calls only for hot water for drinks and the rehydration of freeze-dried fare, you will most likely need only one pot per cook group of three to four peo-ple. If you anticipate some real cooking, from scratch or nearly so, you will want at least two pots: one for cooking and one for mixing ingredients.

Pots are usually measured in liters. A one-liter pot will hold slightly less than a quart. With a one-liter pot, you can boil a few cups of water for hot chocolate or two small servings

Stainless Steel

- Stainless steel pots are extremely durable, standing up well to the abuse of backcountry travel.

- New stainless steel is light in weight compared with older products, but it still weighs more than other materials used in cookware.

- Heat from the stove spreads evenly over the bottom of stainless steel pots.

- With a nonstick surface, stainless steel cleanup is a snap.

- To save fuel, heat with a lid on your pots, or use a frying pan as a pot lid.

Aluminum

- Lighter and less durable than stainless steel pots, aluminum pots are also quite a bit less expensive.

- Heat from the stove spreads quickly but not always evenly over the bottom of aluminum pots.

- The whole pot gets hot, so lift it off the stove with pot grips, small pliers, or a folded bandanna.

- When you carry more than one pot, be sure the two (or three) pots nest together to save space in your pack.

of pasta—just right for two people. A 1.5-liter pot is large enough to hold one-pot meals for an average couple or for side dishes in a bigger party. Two-liter pots have enough room for water to make hot chocolate for six or one dinner entree for three to four hikers.

A frying pan adds the possibility of more interesting cooking, including stove-top baking. A 10-inch-diameter pan will do in most cases, but a smaller one will suffice for two people who envision small meals. A pan with a snug-fitting lid allows baking.

MAKE IT EASY

Backpacking cookware is available with nonstick surfaces, and you will find cooking easier and cleanup much easier with nonstick cookware. Do not, however, use a knife to cut food on a nonstick surface, an act that cuts the surface, reducing its effectiveness.

Titanium

- Titanium is the newest material used in the evolution of cookware.

- It is unbelievably light in weight and almost as unbelievably high in price.

- The transfer of heat from the stove across the bottom

is so fast you might burn dinner if you fail to pay close attention.

- Large titanium pots are difficult to find. The high cost of even small pots has made large pots low on marketability.

Basic Backpacking Cookware

- Most backpacking groups prefer to carry at least two pots for every three to four people.

- These pots are often a 1.5-liter pot and a 1-liter pot.

- A small frying pan offers the possibility of more interesting meals. The handle

should be removable, or it should fold into the pan for easier packing.

- You will want lids for the pots, but the pan can serve as a lid as well.

MORE KITCHEN GEAR
You need a few small kitchen items, and you may want several others

Backpackers eventually generate personal lists of small kitchen items they want to have along on trips. Some of these items almost always show up, a cup being one example. But this list changes depending on what the menu

Lexan is a brand of polycarbonate plastic, light in weight, virtually indestructible.

looks like: You do not need a spatula if you do not plan to flip falafel patties.

Once you have decided what you want to bring (see options below), there are ways to save money with these items. Insulated mugs are preferred by many because most people enjoy keeping their hot drink hot longer, but any old plastic cup will do. Consider carrying a margarine tub instead of a

Personal Kitchen Gear

- Many backpackers want an insulated mug with a tight-fitting lid. How big a mug is up to the individual.

- Everyone will want a small bowl and a strong plastic spoon. Some people like to have a fork, and some don't.

- A pocketknife, at least a small one, should be in the pack (or pocket) of all hikers.

- Most backpackers carry at least two water bottles. You do not want to be without water at any time.

Spatula

- If you choose to pack a frying pan, you'll want a lightweight plastic spatula.

- Plastic will not scratch the nonstick coating on your cookware.

- A spatula with a short handle is all you will need,

and less handle means a bit less weight.

- You can use your spatula to stir and serve from pots of food so you won't need a large spoon.

backpacking bowl. If you bring the lid for the tub, you can keep forest debris out of the oatmeal while it thickens in your bowl. Lexan utensils are nice, but you could get by with a cheap plastic spoon. (Cheap plastic does, however, break easily.) Most seasoned backpackers agree that plates are unnecessary, but if you want one, cheap plastic again saves money. At cleanup time, you can use natural "scrubbers" such as sand or pine needles, but you might appreciate a small, lightweight scrubbing pad.

MAKE IT EASY

Choose a one-liter water bottle with a wide mouth. It is easier to fill, and a wide mouth makes adding drink mixes easier. Choose a water bottle with graduated measurement lines on the side. You can use it instead of carrying a measuring cup and take some guesswork out of dinner.

Water Bags

- Many backpackers like to have one or two lightweight, collapsible water bags or water jugs.

- These containers typically hold one to two gallons.

- With a full water bag you don't have to hike back and forth to your water source during meal preparation and cleanup.

- You can add water disinfection tablets to a gallon or more of water and refill a group's collective water bottles.

Other kitchen gear to consider:

Coffee pot, personal French press, or drip cup with paper filters

Large plastic or wooden spoon

Small can opener

Collapsible grill to cook over coals

Screw-top containers for food

- "Luxury" items in the camp kitchen are carried entirely as a result of personal preference.

- They result partially from the weight you are willing to pack.

- They result partially from what you decide to eat and drink.

- They result from how much cooking you plan to do.

CLASSIC MESS KIT

Basic necessities of mealtime can be met with a very simple kit

KNACK HIKING & BACKPACKING

The word "mess" in reference to food has been with us for centuries, and it's often associated with military personnel, people who still take their meals in mess halls. The military invented, and used for many years, the mess kit. You'll still see mess kits labeled as such in Army-Navy surplus stores, outdoor specialty stores and catalogs, and a simple mess kit, with a stove and a source of water, can meet all your needs at mealtime in camp. Just ask any Boy Scout. And the cost can be surprisingly low.

Traditionally made of aluminum and light in weight, mess kits are now available in heavier material, such as stainless steel, and lighter (more expensive) material, such as titanium.

Mess Kit Frying Pan

- A small frying pan with a folding handle is the heart of the classic mess kit.

- The handle folds to hold a second pan, more like a plate, in place. With the two pans locked together, the space inside holds a cup and utensils.

- Food can be cooked or quickly warmed in the frying pan and then eaten out of the frying pan.

- While the meal is being eaten the second pan/plate can be used to serve a second person.

Mess Kit Pot

- If a closed mess kit has room for a small pot inside, you will probably find one there.

- This small pot can be used to heat water for a hot drink while the meal is being eaten.

- It can be used to mix ingredients for a more complex meal or to cook a side dish.

- It can be used to boil water for kitchen cleanup.

A classic mess kit is also characteristically designed for compactness, the items nesting snugly together so they take up little room in your pack.

A small fry pan is almost always included. A concept important in the original mess kit design was "heat it quick, eat it quick, and get moving." A fry pan served that purpose. The fry pan may or may not serve a second function as a lid for a small pot. The pan's handle rotates or completely detaches, and both methods allow the handle to be turned so it can lock the pan to the top rim of the pot. And into the pot fit a cup and perhaps a second, even smaller pot. There may be space inside the pot for camping utensils: knife, fork, and spoon.

The classic mess kit, arriving on the backpacking scene after World War II, serves one hiker. But you can find kits enlarged for public consumption, in numerous shapes and sizes, and able to meet the needs of two, four, and even eight backpackers. Larger kits may include light, plastic plates.

Mess Kit Cup

- Most mess kits today include one or two small, lightweight plastic cups.

- These cups nest inside each other and fit inside the small pot that fits inside the mess kit.

- Many of these cups have graduated markings so they can be used as measuring cups as well as drinking cups.

- Small indeed, most of these cups hold little more than one measured "cup."

Mess Kit Utensils

- Some mess kits include a set of utensils: spoon, fork, and knife—often made of aluminum.

- If the utensils are attached to each other via a ring, they should separate easily.

- This set of utensils will work for two hikers: one eating with the spoon, one eating with the fork.

- With all mess kits, you are free to add to it or take away from it as you wish.

QUALITY OF LIFE ESSENTIALS

Quality gear, big and small, kept in good condition enriches your quality of life

Everything you pack and carry on your back will either add to or detract from the quality of your life on the trail. Gear detracts from your quality of life when you either carry something manufactured or designed poorly, and it fails to do the job you need it to do, or you just plain forgot something important.

Basically, you want to hike comfortably, sleep comfortably, and eat well. With that in mind, many backpackers believe the three most important pieces of gear are your footwear, your tent, and your stove. If one of these three goes bad, your trip will probably go bad. (Footwear is discussed on page 24.) You also need to stay warm and dry, a matter of clothing and

Toiletries

- In the toiletries department, individualism reigns, but most backpackers want a toothbrush and a small container of toothpaste.

- Choices in hair care vary from nothing to comb, brush, and a small bottle of shampoo.

- Some people carry soap for body washing, some carry a few "baby wipes," and some are satisfied to go unwashed.

- A small bottle of moisturizing lotion is often much appreciated.

Bathroom Supplies

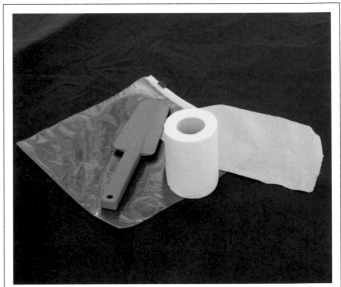

- Although some hikers do without, most pack along toilet paper. You don't often need the whole roll, so you can pull off what you think you'll use and carry it in a plastic bag.

- You may want to pack small plastic bags with the toilet

- paper if you're packing out your used paper.

- You will want a small trowel to dig holes for fecal matter.

- All can be packed together if you obey the sensible rule of never letting the trowel touch feces.

knowledge, and these topics are discussed in later chapters.

Where quality is concerned, there are significant advantages to buying all your stuff in person rather than ordering online or via mail order catalogs. In a store, you can see, handle, try out, and compare different models, shapes, and sizes. More importantly, good stores give you access to trained staff who will give you sound advice based, in the best cases, on personal experience and as reported to them by others. And if you don't like something, you can take it back and talk to a person rather than a disembodied voice on the phone. As a bonus, outdoor stores almost always give you not only a source of gear but also a source of information about trails, weather, and specifically useful ideas related to hiking and backpacking.

As you generate your own checklist of gear and clothing—something you definitely want to do—the possibility of leaving something behind grows slim. Below are a few more thoughts on things you will need or want on the trail to boost your quality of life.

Repair Kit

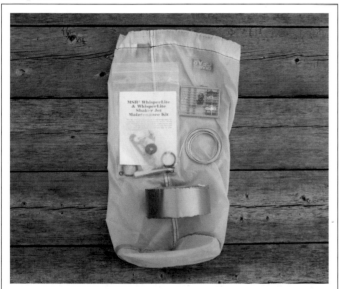

- An amazing amount of repair work can be done with a few yards of duct tape and a few yards of parachute cord.

- A short piece of sturdy wire will hold broken joints together, such as where packs join frames.

- A small sewing kit (a needle and some thread) allows you to close tears in clothing and some gear.

- Pack a repair kit for your specific brand of stove (see page 000).

Miscellaneous gear you might want:

- Binoculars

- Thermometer

- Fishing gear (and license)

- Miniature games (chess, checkers)

- Playing cards

BOOTS AND SOCKS
Proper footwear is the foundation of clothing for the trail

There are choices in types of footwear for the trail (see below), but the single most important factor is the fit. Try on boots wearing the socks you intend to hike in. In boots that fit, your heel will have very little space for side-to-side movement and a minimum of up-and-down movement. (However, you can anticipate a small bit of up-and-down shifting of the heel in new boots.) Your toes need plenty of room to wiggle around freely.

No matter how well boots fit, you'll still need some break-in time, time for footwear to take on your personal flex patterns. For the first week wear the boots around the house or on short evening walks. By the end of the week, you should

Lightweight Hiking Footwear

- These lightweight hiking shoes may look like they are designed for sports other than hiking.

- The upper part of the shoe is made of fabric, and the soles are highly flexible.

- They are made for day and overnight hikes over easy to moderate terrain with the hiker carrying a light load in his or her pack.

- Hikers determined to go light can be found wearing lightweight hiking shoes on trips the shoes really are not designed for.

Midweight Hiking Footwear

- These midweight hiking shoes appear similar to lightweight shoes, but the overall construction is heavier.

- The upper part of the shoe is fabric, the soles thicker and less flexible than those of lightweight hikers.

- They are made for weekend hikes over moderate terrain with the hiker carrying a moderate load in his or her pack.

- They provide enough support for hikes a bit longer than weekends when the hiker is strong—and hikes carefully.

24

be able to wear the boots all day, but keep wearing them around town for a second week before hitting the trail.

Like boots, socks also need to fit. Too tight is uncomfortable, and too big is not only uncomfortable but also a source of blisters. For comfort and protection, wear two pairs—light-weight liner socks of wool or synthetic to wick moisture away from your feet and to slide like a lubricating layer against the outer sock, helping prevent blisters. The heavier outer pair of wool or synthetic is for insulation and comfort.

ZOOM

Painful feet are the number one problem for walkers. Choose your trail footwear with the help of a professional to be sure 1) it is adequate for your type of trail, and 2) it fits properly.

Heavyweight Hiking Footwear

- These heavyweight boots have strong rigid material in the upper shoe, often leather, and soles of rugged material that flexes only a little.

- The sole often contains a shank, a piece of slightly flexible or nonflexible material that runs from two-thirds to the full length of the sole.

- They provide excellent support for long hikes over rough terrain.

- They require quite a bit of break-in time and are never quite as comfortable, to most people, as a lighter shoe.

Socks

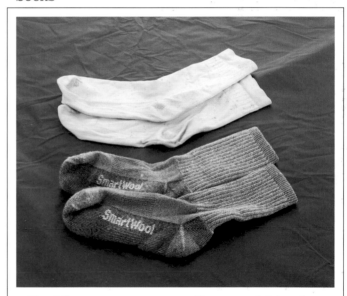

- Most hikers are more comfortable and almost always develop fewer blisters with two pairs of socks.

- The inner pair is lightweight, made from light wool or a synthetic material or a blend of the two. These materials wick moisture away from the foot.

- The outer pair is heavier and again wool, synthetic, or a blend. This pair of socks provides insulation and comfort.

- The two pairs move against each other instead of rubbing against the foot of the hiker.

INNER LAYERS

Next to your skin, go for comfort and wick away moisture

A time-honored guideline for clothing yourself for the outdoors says you should "dress like an onion," wearing several lighter layers of clothing instead of bulky garments. Layers allow you to peel off and put back on clothing in order to control your body heat, and therefore your sweating, so you remain not only more comfortable but also, more importantly, less wet.

The choice of an inner layer, the one next to your skin, may not be critical in hot, dry climates. But when the temperature falls, the best undergarments are made of a synthetic material or a light synthetic/wool blend, both of which wick moisture away from skin and into outer layers. In almost all environments, these undergarments should be long-sleeved on top and long-legged on the bottom, providing maximum pro-

Cotton Inner Layers

- Cotton feels very comfortable against your skin, but cotton is an excellent conductor of heat and a greedy absorber of water.

- It pulls your body heat away with amazing quickness on a cold day, which could be fatally dangerous.

- On a hot day, it holds body moisture near your skin, encouraging evaporation and keeping you cooler.

- Cotton has its place in an outdoor wardrobe but needs to be worn thoughtfully.

Wool Inner Layers

- All wool used to feel scratchy, but some newer wool garments are made in ways that leave them easy on your skin.

- Wool is a poor conductor, so it does a good job of holding in body heat.

- Wool holds onto a lot of moisture, but it holds in your body heat even when wet.

- Wool clothing takes a long time to dry.

tection. Although not critical, the addition of a collar on the top increases your protection a bit more. If the collar opens with a zipper, you can close it for added warmth or open it to increase ventilation and decrease sweating. And go for soft. You don't want a scratchy undergarment lying beneath what could be a great wardrobe.

Cotton skivvies beneath synthetic long underwear defeat the purpose of the synthetic.

Synthetic Inner Layers

- Synthetic garments are made from plastic spun into fibers and then woven into cloth.

- Synthetic fibers are an even poorer heat conductor than wool, so they hold the most body heat of any material.

- Synthetics absorb no moisture. Wetness moves along the fibers away from your body, a process known as "wicking."

- Synthetic garments dry quickly, even while you're still wearing them.

············· RED ● LIGHT ··············

Cotton is a great conductor of heat, so it does a poor job of keeping you warm. Cotton absorbs water, keeping it near your skin and sucking your heat from your body. Wet cotton, goes the old saying, kills. Save cotton for daytime in a desert.

Body heat is lost via:

- Radiation—infrared heat is lost persistently from warm skin, but clothing reduces the loss.

- Conduction—heat moves from a warm skin into any colder surface, but insulating clothing stops the loss.

- Convection—air carries heat away, and the faster the air moves, the faster heat is lost, but windproof clothing stops the loss.

- Evaporation—heat is lost via the vaporization of moisture on skin, and clothing that encourages dry skin slows the loss.

CLOTHING

27

MIDDLE LAYERS

Clothing between the inner layer and the outer layer provides insulation

On your upper body, vests, sweaters, and jackets are mid-layer wear, and on your lower body, pants. Remembering the guideline of "dress like an onion," the best middle layers—one based on the temperature—are made of material providing the most insulation with the least weight while, like inner layers, continuing to wick moisture away from your skin.

Synthetics, your best choice in mid-layers, are petroleum products, made from plastic spun into thread, which is then woven into clothing. Synthetics conduct heat poorly, keeping your body heat near your body, a great idea when it's cold outside. Synthetic fibers hold on to water weakly, absorbing almost none of it, and actually moving moisture

Vest

- A vest covers most of the core of your body but leaves your arms free.

- When you need only a little clothing as a middle layer, a vest is an excellent choice.

- Some vests are made of a windproof material allowing them to hold in body heat even better than vests of a nonwindproof material.

- Most hikers prefer a vest with pockets so small items—snack, knife, bandanna—can be kept handy.

Fleece Jacket with Full Zipper

- Jackets and sweaters cover most of the core of your body as well as your arms.

- This jacket has a full zipper, allowing you to choose a little bit of ventilation or a lot of ventilation.

- Some jackets have zippers in the armpits, permitting increased ventilation of those areas of your body.

- Some hikers prefer jackets that reach well below the waist, adding protective covering to the entire core of the body.

away from skin while being worn, a process mentioned earlier and known as "wicking"—so synthetics work best to keep you dry. Synthetics even when damp will continue to hold in your body heat. And synthetics are lighter in weight than wool.

Wool, the other material you may consider for mid-layer garments, is also a poor conductor of heat, but it will not keep you quite as warm as a synthetic. Wool fibers hold on to moisture more aggressively than synthetics, but they also hold in your body heat even when they are wet. And because wool fibers can hold a lot of water, wool garments can gain a lot of weight in rain, making them less comfortable.

Both synthetic and wool clothing, once wet, will dry as you wear it, but synthetics dry much quicker.

Cotton clothing may be chosen as middle layers in hot climates. Cotton aggressively holds on to moisture, increasing the rate of evaporative heat loss, something you might enjoy in the Mojave Desert. When you choose cotton, carry non-cotton layers to change into when the temperature falls.

Pullover Fleece Sweater

- This fleece sweater (and other mid-layer garments) pulls over instead of zipping up.

- No zipper means it will hold in body heat a bit better because none can leak out around the zipper—but this garment cannot be ventilated.

- This hiker is wearing lightweight fleece pants to reduce heat loss from the legs.

- Heat lost from your legs may be substantial on cold days.

Heavyweight Fleece Jacket

- This heavyweight fleece jacket will hold in a great deal of body heat, but it can also be ventilated via the full zipper.

- Some hikers prefer jackets with hoods in order to have handy a quick covering for the head on cold days.

- These pants are also heavyweight fleece.

- Many prefer fleece pants with half or full side zippers that allow ventilation.

OUTER LAYERS
Choose correctly to keep out rain, wind, and snow

Outer layers, sometimes called "shells," are not always worn. You carry them for the possibility of wind, rain, or snow and for an additional layer when the temperature drops.

For wet conditions, you need upper and lower garments—parka and rain pants—designed to keep you dry. Synthetic shells are often advertised as being waterproof and breathable at the same time. How well they work varies, depending on the ambient air temperature and moisture. You could be comfortable on a day when it is cold and dry outside, or you may find yourself wet with sweat inside one of these shells when a warm rain falls.

Coated nylon shells are 100 percent waterproof, and they do not breathe. They allow no water to get in and no sweat to get out. You will not get wet from the rain, but you may

Wind Shell

- Wind can blow body heat away with astounding speed, even on a warm day.

- An outer layer of a light-weight wind shirt prevents the loss of body heat via convection.

- In addition to being wind-proof, this wind shirt is extremely thin and stuffs into a very small space in your pack or even your pocket.

- These hiking pants are woven tightly enough to prevent most heat loss from wind.

Light Rain Shell

- The combination of wet and windy sucks heat out of your body more quickly than any other environmental conditions.

- This anorak (a waterproof pullover jacket) protects against rain and wind. It also adds a layer of insula-tion. A hood adds head protection.

- It does not have a full zip-per and therefore cannot be ventilated as much as many hikers prefer.

- These lightweight rain pants also repel water and wind.

become a sweathouse inside your coated rainwear. In an environment known for heavy rains, though, choose coated nylon rainwear.

For the upper half of your body, a parka with a roomy hood is the best choice. For the bottom half of your body, the choice is most often rain pants. Full-leg zippers on the sides of pants provide for ease of putting on and taking off and allow better ventilation. Half-leg zippers are almost as easy to use.

Ponchos are essentially small, waterproof tarps with a hooded hole in the middle for your head. Although ponchos can be spread out over your pack while you're hiking in rain, they simply don't work as well as a parka and pants.

If your hike will take you into very cold temperatures, choose an insulated parka, one filled with down or a synthetic fill, and consider a pair of insulated outer pants.

Heavy Rain Shell

- Despite the thickness of this hooded rain parka, it "breathes," allowing body moisture to pass through but keeping rain and snow out.

- The large hood shelters the head and face from a downpour.

- Large pockets provide carrying space for items that might be needed quickly: gloves, stocking cap, snacks, water bottle.

- If the rain pants have a partial or full zipper, they can be put on without taking hiking boots off.

Cold Weather Shell

- This down-filled parka will repel some wind and some moisture, but its main function is to serve as an outer layer of insulation when the weather is very cold.

- It holds in too much body heat to be a practical layer when you're moving on

the trail unless the cold is extreme.

- Winter campers find this type of parka an excellent choice for hanging out in camp.

- These pants are also down-filled.

31

HEAD AND HANDS

The right hat and gloves can often be of critical importance

Your brain, usually functioning at ease inside your head, demands its temperature be maintained—or it will make your whole body unhappy. In heat, you need a hat with a brim to keep your head cooler and your face shaded from the sun. In intense sunlight, it's best if the brim extends all the way around your head, although you can make do by tucking a bandanna under a baseball cap and letting it fall down to cover your ears and neck.

When it's cold, even when it might get cold, you'll want a stocking cap, one large enough to pull down over your ears. With the hood of your parka up over your head, you should be warm enough. You may also choose a fleece-lined cap

Stocking Cap

- Your head accounts for approximately 10 percent of the surface of your body, which is a lot of area to lose heat from.

- The contents of almost every pack should include at least a lightweight stocking cap. You never know for sure when the temperature will drop.

- A stocking cap should be comfortable, not scratchy.

- It should be long enough to cover your ears.

Cap with Ear Flaps

- Some hikers are more comfortable in a cap with ear flaps that can be rolled or tied up and out of the way when not needed.

- This cap insulates the head with soft fleece and offers better shade for the face and eyes than a stocking cap.

- In addition to insulating the head, it repels wind and precipitation.

- This cap is typically a bit heavier, bulkier, and more expensive than a simple stocking cap.

with earflaps that can be turned up if you don't need them. In extremes of cold, go for a balaclava, a head covering that insulates your entire head, including your face.

The smaller the body part, the more difficult it is to keep warm. A pair of lightweight gloves is advisable, even on summer trips. If you anticipate chillier days, you can pack light overmitts that are worn over your gloves. If the weather may get quite cold, go with mittens. Your fingers stay warmer together than spread out, each in its own finger of a glove.

ZOOM

You may have heard the old adage: If your feet are cold, put on a hat. There is an element of truth here. When your critical body parts—such as your head—are adequately protected, more warming blood will flow to less critical body parts—such as your feet.

CLOTHING

Balaclava

- A balaclava provides a step beyond stocking caps and caps with ear flaps as protection for the head.

- A balaclava covers the entire head, including the face, leaving only the eyes exposed.

- It provides a layer of insulation for the entire neck.

- When the whole balaclava is not needed, it can be rolled up and worn like a simple stocking cap.

Gloves and Mittens

- Many backpackers choose to carry at least a light pair of gloves at all times.

- Mittens are more protective than gloves because the fingers can "snuggle" together, sharing warmth in a unified space.

- As with gloves, mittens come in different weights and thicknesses.

- As an additional layer for the hands when the cold may be extreme, carry a pair of overmitts (a light shell or outer layer for the hands).

DRESSING FOR THE CLIMATE

Your final choice of wardrobe will depend largely on where and when you're going

Desert nights, after a blistering hot day, can grow alarmingly cold. You can sweat in stunning midday heat on a high mountain snowfield, then arise the next morning to find the water in your bottle has turned to ice. How do you know what to carry for clothing? You will never fail to pack the right wardrobe by following this simple guideline: Prepare for the worst conditions ever known for your area of travel at the time of year you're going. And you'll know by gathering information before you ever dig the pack out of storage. If it froze once, ten years ago in July, it might freeze again the July you hike there. Pack right. Better safe, and comfortable, than sorry, and miserable.

Woodland Clothing

- Woodlands (or forests) are almost as diverse as America itself. They could be hot or cold, wet or dry, tall or short, dense or thin, flat or steep.

- Gather information about the specific woodland you'll be visiting, and prepare accordingly.

- In general, woodland hikes require the most basic gear and clothing.

- A true woodland tends to have a relatively constant temperature range throughout the day.

Mountain Clothing

- Mountain weather, where you may be hiking above the clouds, is famous for rapid changes. You can often watch, or even feel, it change.

- You may be comfortable in shorts and a T-shirt at noon but require long underwear and long pants at night.

- Raingear, stocking cap, and gloves or mittens should always be in your pack.

- There is probably no environment where you'll put on and take off layers of clothing more often.

That said, you will sometimes be hiking in loose-fitting nylon shorts and a light shirt at noon and huddled by a campfire in fleece sweater and pants that evening. And that's okay; it's a part of the outdoor experience.

A few more suggestions: Lightweight, long underwear, top and bottom, is almost always recommended, no matter the anticipated climate. Such garments pack small, are available as an extra layer of insulation, and can be put on under any other garments. And they serve well as pajamas.

When hot days are the rule rather than the exception, wear loose-fitting clothing that allows air to circulate better near your skin, evaporating your body moisture and keeping you cooler. But choose tightly woven fabrics. Ultraviolet light from the sun can, and will, penetrate loosely woven fabrics.

Remember that mid-layers and outer layers will need to fit over layers of clothing worn closer to your skin. For that reason, purchase these layers a bit larger than you would otherwise. Better yet, try all the layers on together before you buy.

Desert Clothing

- Most deserts are hot during the day and chilly at night, sometimes even in midsummer.

- In the heat, you need loose clothing of natural fibers that allows air to circulate near your skin and moisture to evaporate from your skin.

- Your head, face, and neck need to be well-shaded by your hat.

- With plenty of sharp plants and rocks expected, your footwear should be sturdy and ready for abuse.

Beach Clothing

- All beaches are not created the same: Environments differ greatly depending on where the beach is.

- With any beach, be prepared for rain and wind.

- Keep in mind there's a good chance your feet will get wet, and your choice of footwear should reflect this fact.

- You may also find your feet on changing terrain: sand, pebbles, rocks, mud, and driftwood. You will need sturdy footwear.

DRINKING RIGHT

It's not just how much but also when you drink water

The need to drink enough water is well known, but less known is the fact that you can use the water you drink at a faster rate than you feel the need for replenishment. Individuals differ a bit, but thirst is not always an indicator of the need to drink, especially during exercise on the trail. To be safe, drink before you get thirsty, and if you become thirsty, drink until after your thirst is quenched. Remember that dehydration can be cumulative, carrying over from previous days. Rest and plenty of fluids are the treatment for dehydration.

You should be drinking water on a disciplined schedule when you are traveling hard outdoors. Because the human body can absorb only so much water at one time, the rate of ingestion should be matched, as closely as possible, to the rate of absorption. Most people fall into a rate-of-absorption

Sweat

- On a normal day, the average person loses three to six liters of water from his or her body.

- On an average day, one to two of these liters of water lost leave the body via sweat.

- On the trail, exercising hard with a backpack on your shoulders, you can lose one to two liters of water in sweat in an hour!

- The other sources of lost water are urination, defecation, and respiration.

Four One-Liter Bottles of Water

- Some of the water lost from your body is replaced by the food you eat, especially if the food is "wet" (has a high water content).

- For maximum health and performance, you should be drinking about four one-liter bottles of water each day on the trail.

- You will probably need more if you have been sweating profusely.

- Drink enough to keep your urine clear or at least a very light yellow in color.

range of 250–300 milliliters per quarter hour. That means that drinking at least one-quarter liter of water every fifteen to twenty minutes during periods of strenuous exercise should meet most of the body's needs. You might need less, or you might need more. Almost everyone needs more when hiking in a hot, dry region. The most important factor in hydration may be self-monitoring: Do you feel okay? Are you thirsty? Is your urine relatively clear?

•••••••••••••• RED ● LIGHT ••••••••••••

The mild signs of dehydration are subtle: dark yellow urine, a loss of energy, perhaps thirst. Moderate signs include a very dark urine, substantial loss of energy, a rapid pulse, and thirst. Severe dehydration is difficult to treat. Signs include intense thirst, drowsiness, lethargy, disorientation, irritability—then shock.

Drink at a Disciplined Rate

- Because you don't always feel thirst as soon as your body needs water, drinking should be an act of discipline.

- Start the day hydrated: Drink at least a half-liter of water before heading out on the trail in the morning.

- On the trail, while you are hiking, drink about one-fourth liter of water approximately every fifteen–twenty minutes.

- If you feel thirsty, take a break and drink until the thirst goes away.

When you are dehydrated:

- Your urine gets darker in color.
- You get a headache.
- Your endurance diminishes.
- You get irritable.
- Your heart speeds up.
- You may collapse.

WATER

CARRYING WATER

You must carry some water, so carry it near at hand in an appropriate container

The short version of this section is this: You do not want to carry more water than you have to. But carry it you must—along the trail between water sources, from a water source to camp, and, from time to time, from a water source to a spot where you can bathe.

One liter of water, the amount in a standard backpacking water bottle, is approximately 2.2 pounds. A quart is a little less than a liter, so the weight is slightly less, and the weight of a U.S. gallon (four quarts) is about 8.3 pounds. With all the gear and clothing on your back, every additional pound, sometimes every ounce, that you can lose is a plus.

Keep Water Handy

- A one-liter water bottle is, by far, the most common water-carrying container for hikers.

- Full of water, one of these bottles weighs approximately 2.2 pounds. Two full bottles, almost 4.5 pounds, is about the most any hiker wants to carry.

- This bottle rides in a side pocket of a pack that is designed for the bottle.

- Keeping water handy will encourage you to drink enough.

Hydration Bladder

- This hiker is drinking from a hydration bladder, a product that keeps water very handy—so handy he does not have to stop walking in order to drink.

- Available in different sizes (and shapes), bladders hold up to about three liters of water.

- Because these bladders ride on your shoulders, many day hikers use one in combination with a fanny pack.

- Some bladders come in a small pack that allows you to carry a few small items, such as snacks.

The amount of water you need to pack on your back will be determined, at least in part, by how far you have to travel between sources of water. A map can be very helpful in making that determination, the blue of lakes, rivers, and streams being clearly marked. Although it's best to drink at a disciplined rate (see page 36), starting out in the morning well-hydrated can reduce the amount of water you need between water sources. But because your body needs about a liter per hour during periods of exercise, try to pack accordingly.

(see page 36)

MAKE IT EASY

A water bottle buried in a backpack can make drinking a bothersome chore. The market is swamped with accessories that allow you to keep a water bottle handy: clips to attach bottles to the outside of packs, straps that hold a bottle near at hand, and bottle pockets that can be attached to packs.

Bladder as Part of a Pack

- This hiker is drinking from a hydration bladder carried as a part of his backpack.

- Water from a natural source should still be disinfected prior to drinking. It can be disinfected prior to putting it into the bladder or disinfected chemically in the bladder.

- A filter is available that inserts between the water bag and the mouthpiece of some bladders. The filter disinfects the water you suck from the bag.

- Hydration packs cost quite a bit more than a couple of water bottles.

Improvised Canteen

- Without an outside pack pocket for a water bottle or a bladder, you can improvise this simple canteen, a water container with a strap.

- It is a loop of tubular nylon webbing attached to a one-liter water bottle with several wraps of duct tape.

- The strap allows you to clip your water bottle handily to your pack.

- The duct tape can be reclaimed if you need to do some field repairs.

WATER

SOURCES OF WATER
You should always know where water is in relation to where you are

It is by far best, and about this there is no doubt, to know where you are on the trail in relation to water sources at all times. Your maps should be as up to date as possible, and, as mentioned earlier in this book, they should clearly indicate water. Despite your map, however, seasonal fluctuations in water levels can cause the blue line on the map to be a dry wash when you arrive. Add to your map, then, information from knowledgeable people about the dependability of water sources before hitting the trail.

If you don't find water where you thought you would, keep in mind these several suggestions: Because water seeks the lowest level, follow dry streambeds or ravines downhill. Animal tracks and game trails often lead to water sources, so you can follow those downhill as well. Birds often circle water

Water from a Lake

- Lakes and rivers marked on maps are almost always dependable sources of water on the trail.

- You can usually find water in small streams marked on maps as a thick blue line.

- If the blue line is thin, it means the water runs sea-

sonally and may not be running when you get there.

- It is safest to check with local land managers before a trip to see if streams are actually running.

Water from a River

- Moving water, surging through narrows or tumbling over rocks, often looks clear and clean—but this is not the best water to gather.

- Water from deep, still pools will have fewer germs in it because the germs settle toward the bottom.

- Even though you will be disinfecting the water, the fewer germs in the water at the start, the better.

- Reach as far as you can safely reach from shore to gather water.

early in the morning and late in the evening prior to landing to drink. If you come across an old campsite, check nearby for water. There may be an old trail visible where previous campers walked to a water source. You can sometimes find springs and seeps of water emerging near the foot of cliffs or boulder fields. In arid country, keep an eye peeled for green vegetation that may be growing near water. In canyon country, such as you find in southern Utah, look for water sources up side canyons in places where shade lingers the longest. Long after a rain in canyon country, water can be found in depressions in the sandstone, and sometimes these depressions are large enough, and hold water long enough, to be marked on maps. And, finally, snow and ice can be melted for water, and ice will give you the most water for the least amount of fuel burned.

Water from Snow

- On a winter day, snow can be an excellent source of water.

- Fresh snow usually has few or even no germs.

- You can often find snow in high country even in the middle of summer. Look in shadowy ravines and on slopes that face north.

- To melt snow for water, start with a little water in the bottom of the pot to prevent scorching the water. Scorching gives the water poor taste.

Water from Rain

- On some of your trips, rain may be a source of useful water.

- You can collect it in pots and pans, and you will collect rain fastest where it runs off in rivulets from something such as your tent or natural channels in rocks.

- Look for places where rain collects naturally in depressions in the ground and rocks.

- It is safest to assume that rainwater needs to be disinfected prior to drinking.

FOUR WAYS TO DISINFECT WATER

No source of water in the backcountry should be considered safe prior to disinfection

Despite the fact that wilderness water sources often look ready to drink, they typically are not. The water might be, occasionally, safe to consume, but the risk if you're wrong can be gut-wrenching misery from waterborne germs. The answer is simple: Disinfect all your water before you drink it.

There are four easy and acceptably safe ways to disinfect

water. One is by raising the temperature of the water to the boiling point. Extended boiling does no harm, but the time it takes to raise the temperature to the boiling point also works to kill germs, so by the time water boils, it is safe. A second method involves the adding of chemicals that kill germs. The best-known, proven, and readily available are iodine, chlorine, and chlorine dioxide.

Boiling Water

- When water reaches a rolling boil, you can be sure it is safe to drink, even at higher altitudes.

- Water used in cooking does not have to be disinfected first. The heat of cooking will disinfect it.

- Cover the pot of water with a lid to reach the boiling point more quickly.

- If you plan on boiling as your means of disinfection, plan on carrying extra fuel for your stove.

Chemical Disinfection

- Iodine and chlorine kill most of the germs in water that will make you sick. Some germs are resistant to these chemicals.

- Chlorine dioxide will kill all germs in water.

- Read and follow the directions on the label of disin-

fecting chemicals carefully to be sure what you want to happen is going to happen.

- If you add anything to improve the flavor of chemically disinfected water, you must add it *after* the chemicals have done their job.

Filters don't all work the same, although some are highly effective. Some, for instance, filter out only protozoa while others eliminate protozoa and bacteria. None filters out viruses, but some do a pretty good job of killing viruses via an iodine resin on the matrix of the filter. Once again, read the filter label carefully.

Only recently have lightweight, portable devices that utilize ultraviolet light for disinfection been available. You can safely add those devices to your choices when you make your final decision.

················ RED ● LIGHT ··············

Cryptosporidium is a protozoa, a parasite commonly found living in water. It can live in your gut, causing tummy cramps and explosive diarrhea. Heat and filters can rid your water of this germ, but chemicals for camp disinfection of water fail to kill it, except for chlorine dioxide.

Water Filter

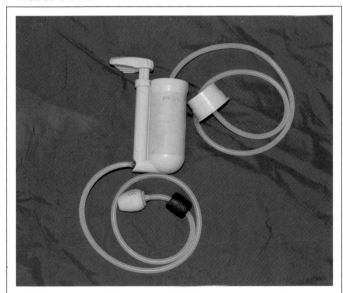

- Many types of water filters are available for hikers and backpackers. They do not all work the same.

- Before buying a filter, read the packaging carefully and understand what that particular filter will do and how it should be used.

- A big advantage of a high-quality filter is that your water is ready to drink immediately.

- Some hikers prefer to use a filter for the "big" germs and then add a chemical for the "small" germs.

UV Light Disinfection

- Ultraviolet light has long been known as a means to disinfect water. Water that sits in direct sunlight long enough will be disinfected.

- Only fairly recently have devices that emit UV light been available for field water disinfection.

- These devices are the fastest method of water disinfection, but they don't work well in all water—so read the directions.

- They are battery powered. Carrying extra batteries for the device is advised.

WATER

WATER DISINFECTION TIPS

Several techniques will help you in achieving your goal of safe drinking water

Natural water sources not only are potential homes for disease-causing germs such as protozoa, bacteria, and viruses, but also they may house dirt and debris that make drinking less than pleasant and increase the difficulty of disinfection.

If you use a filter, dirt and sand can clog it. One answer is to use a prefilter on the end of the intake hose, the part of the hose that goes into the water source. A quality prefilter will keep out most of the stuff that causes clogs.

Or you can pour water from the source through a strainer such as a T-shirt or bandanna. After passing through the strainer, the water is, of course, still contaminated, so the use of one of the methods of disinfection is still required.

KNACK HIKING & BACKPACKING

Prefilter

- To reduce the amount of debris your water filter has to deal with, it is advisable to have a prefilter for your water filter.

- The prefilter attaches to the end of the intake hose, the part that goes into the water source.

- It prevents large particles such as bits of leaves and grass, even large particles of sand, from getting into and clogging your filter.

- Your filter will work better and last longer with a prefilter.

Straining Water

- The less foreign matter is in the water prior to any means of disinfection, the better the disinfection method will work.

- Obvious debris, and some not-so-obvious debris, can be removed with a simple strainer.

- You can use a clean bandanna as a strainer. Pour water from the source through the bandanna into your water bottle or pot.

- Remember: No matter how well the strainer works, the water still needs to be disinfected.

If you have a large pot, bucket, or collapsible water jug, you may also allow water to sit long enough for the dirt and debris to settle to the bottom. Clear water can then be filtered out or scooped out for boiling or the adding of chemicals.

Some chemical disinfectants, chlorine dioxide being an exception, impart a distinctive taste to the water that most people find unpleasant. Potable Aqua Iodine Tablets, a popular brand, is available with a small bottle of a taste-removing ingredient. Or you can simply add some flavorful, instant-drink mix crystals or powders to the water. In both cases, however, it is of critical importance to add the drink mix after the chemical has had enough time to do its job. The label of the chemical disinfectant will tell you how much time that is, usually somewhere between thirty minutes and four hours.

Letting Water Settle

- Murky water, full of sediment, does not disinfect well.

- This type of water can be collected in a large container and allowed to sit long enough for the sediment to settle to the bottom via gravity.

- The time required for settling depends on the type and amount of sediment.

- After settling has occurred, water can be filtered from the large container or drawn off for another means of disinfection.

Adding a Drink Mix

- Flavorings of any kind—coffee, for instance—can be safely added to water you intend to boil prior to boiling.

- Other means of disinfection are hindered and possibly negated if you add flavorings prior to completion of the disinfection process.

- Chemicals, as one example, attack everything in water, including the sugar in drink mixes.

- If you want flavored water, patiently wait until the disinfection process is complete—and then add the flavoring.

BEYOND WATER
For health on the trail, you don't have to drink only plain water

The importance of drinking enough water is inarguable, although arguments over how much is enough are interminable. One fact you can count on is this: When your body needs water, it will absorb it from anything you consume that contains water. And here are interesting things about that fact:

Some experts say that cold fluids, fluids at a temperature in the 40s F, are emptied from the stomach at a higher rate than fluids at other temperatures and are therefore absorbed faster. The data remain inconclusive, and the most important impact of fluid temperature may be palatability—when you're thirsty, cool fluids usually go down easier.

Most people obtain ample salt with a balanced diet. Salty snacks when exercising hard are probably of benefit. There may be small advantages to having a tiny bit of salt—a

Energy Drinks

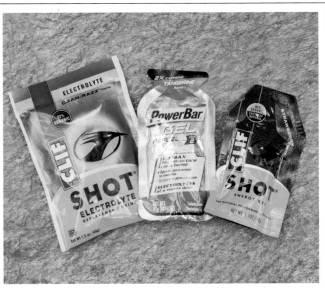

- Energy drinks are mostly water, and your body will certainly use the water. Drinks are also food—carbohydrates to be more precise.

- These drinks typically contain 4–8 percent carbohydrates, providing energy. If the taste is too strong, watering these down is fine.

- If you hike at a sustained pace for more than an hour, you may benefit from energy drinks.

- You may also use them simply because you like the taste better than that of plain water.

Coffee

- High concentrations of caffeine in coffee can dehydrate you instead of hydrate you because it stimulates urination.

- The amount of caffeine in coffee varies quite a bit depending on the type of coffee and the way you make it.

- Instant coffee contains little caffeine compared with a mug of French-pressed coffee.

- If you consume the recommended amount of water daily, there is little risk of dehydration from coffee while hiking.

"pinch"—in a liter of fluid when you're active. For one thing, salt helps you retain water during exercise, and, for another, salt stimulates the need to drink. Too much salt, of course, would be counterproductive, causing you to need more water than normal.

During exercise lasting less than one hour, there is little evidence of physiological or physical performance differences between consuming a carbohydrate-electrolyte drink and plain water. Participants in longer hikes may consider solutions containing 4 to 8 percent carbohydrates. The carbohy-drates can be sugars (e.g., glucose or sucrose) or starch (e.g., maltodextrin). For most hikers the primary value in these sports drinks is probably taste. Most sports drinks have acceptable concentrations of sugar, but on an individual basis people may like to dilute the drink, certainly an acceptable act. Sports drinks alone may not provide enough sodium.

And, finally, drinks with caffeine—coffee, tea, and hot chocolate—have a reputation for increasing the risk of dehydration, causing you to urinate excessively. The amount consumed by most hikers is rarely a problem.

WATER

Tea

- Noncaffeinated (herbal) teas provide water, some nutrients, and a chance to relax while sipping.

- Green and black teas give you some caffeine and some health benefits. A strong cup of tea has about one-sixth the caffeine of a strong cup of coffee, on average.

- Sugar or honey added to tea (or coffee) gives you a little energy boost.

- Teas are an excellent backcountry drink, hot or cold, that can be consumed without fear of dehydration.

Hot Chocolate

- Hot chocolates of all kinds do not contain much caffeine, certainly not enough to be concerned about on the trail.

- Regular hot chocolates contain enough sugar to give you an energy boost.

- If you don't want the boost, choose artificially sweetened hot chocolates.

- There are health benefits from dark chocolate drinks that should not be overlooked. The benefits are not fully understood, but hot chocolate is another excellent camp drink.

BREAKFAST

On the trail, as with off, it's the most important meal of the day

Regardless of what you eat on the trail, you must plan to eat. Food is your fuel, your go-power, and a deficiency of it brings on early fatigue, a decline in sharp thinking, and an overall shortage of fun. Pay attention to details. Pack a little more than you think you'll eat. With experience, you'll know better how much to bring, but you don't want to run short. It all starts with breakfast.

No matter what you pack, personal preferences in food should reign supreme. You don't want to carry what you don't like to eat.

That said, a few suggestions are in order: Breakfast foods should be easy to prepare. You usually don't want to linger while the trail beckons. Breakfast should be heavy in carbohydrates, foods that your body can use right away. Simple car-

Some suggested breakfast foods:

- Hash browns with cheese
- Instant potato pearls with margarine and cheese
- Couscous with brown sugar
- Egg Beaters
- Quesadillas

Bagels

- Bagels are an excellent and versatile breakfast food that will stay good for days in your pack.

- Add peanut butter, jelly, cheese spreads, honey, or another delectable topping.

- Butter a half and fry it face down. Flip it over and add a slice of cheese. Cover the pan while the cheese melts.

- After the cheese melts, if you wish, add a slice of fresh onion or sprinkle on bacon bits.

bohydrates (sugar, honey) get into the bloodstream quickly, providing a boost almost immediately. They're great as a part of breakfast, but they burn up fast. Complex carbohydrates (whole grains, whole-grain products such as cereals and breads, fruits) provide energy for the long haul. Water, at least a half-liter, needs to be a part of every breakfast, replenishing the fluid you lost while sleeping. Without adequate water, you can't process the food you eat to maximum benefit.

ZOOM

Backpackers, as a rule of thumb, should eat somewhere between 1.5 and 2.5 pounds of food per day on the trail. Calorie-wise, you should aim for somewhere between 2,500 and 5,000 per day. On strenuous and/or cold-weather trips, you want to shoot for the high end of this calorie range.

Cereal

- Hot cereals are a warm, tasty, and nutritious way to start a day on the trail.

- Add butter, powdered milk, brown sugar, nuts, raisins, or other dried fruit, and/or chocolate chips to oatmeal.

- Many grains are available in packages that rehydrate instantly—including grits with cheese already added.

- Cold cereals are, of course, less bother, and a wide variety of granolas that pack and keep extremely well is available.

Pancakes

- Pancakes are filling and provide power for the trail. Just-add-water mixes are simple to prepare, but they require a bit more cleanup.

- Foods you can add to pancake mix are virtually limitless—granola, nuts, dried fruit, and seeds, to name a few.

- Wild berries, when available, make pancakes a special treat.

- Leftover pancakes can be saved for lunch on the trail and eaten plain or with summer sausage, peanut butter, or cheese.

FOOD

DINNER
With a little forethought, it's more than just another meal

Dinnertime can be much more than downing a bowl of food. This is a time for relaxing, going over the past day and the next day with friends, and generally just enjoying the outdoors. Sure, you can get by nutritionally with a quick and simple freeze-dried meal. Many hikers do. But you can also be creative. You are limited only by your willingness to pack the extra pounds, but delicious grub, spread around a group, does not have to weigh a ton.

Sip a hot drink while the pasta boils. Chop up fresh green onions to add to the simmering sauce. Slice up the apple, and pass it around. Set the fresh bread, foil-wrapped, to warm near the fire. After the hot drink, fill the mugs with red wine.

Some suggested dinners:

- Falafel with cheese
- Instant potatoes with butter and bacon bits
- Instant potatoes with cheese and mustard
- Couscous with seeds and cheese
- Quick-cook lentils
- Bagel sandwiches

Rice

- Quick-cooking rice requires little fuel and time, and the results provide a basis for numerous meals.

- Buttered rice, with a few nuts or seeds added, is wholesomely nutritious.

- In oil or margarine, you can fry rice to a golden brown and top it with cheese and spices such as garlic or curry. Try adding some fresh onion and a green pepper.

- Add a dash of soy sauce, raisins, and a packet of sweet-and-sour mix to rice for an Asian flavor.

An emphasis on carbohydrates should continue at dinner, but it's also time for some fats (see page 54) and proteins, the building blocks your body needs to restore the tissues depleted by a day of exercise. Sources of protein on the trail can include meat, powdered milk, powdered eggs, nuts, seeds, legumes, and whole grains. You can add some of them to dishes for a flavor boost.

Why waste water you drain for pasta? Use it for hot drinks.

MAKE IT EASY

Put all the ingredients for a one-pot meal, including spices, into a plastic bag. You may need a smaller bag (the grated cheese and nuts) within a larger bag (that holds the rice). But at mealtime everything you need foodwise is ready to go.

Pasta

- Pasta is easy to cook and satisfies almost any hunger.

- For mac and cheese, a backpacking standard, carry a package with all you need included. Throw in sunflower seeds for a nutrition and taste bonus.

- An excellent dish is made by adding a packet of chicken broth, dried tomatoes, garlic, and smoked salmon to pasta. Butter and Parmesan cheese make it even better.

- Try preparing spaghetti with a dash of oil, Parmesan cheese, garlic, and basil.

Tortillas

- A quesadilla is cheese melted in a tortilla. Add a splash of salsa for a huge taste boost.

- Warm a tortilla and roll it up around summer sausage and cheese. Add a dash of hot sauce if you like it.

- Roll a warm tortilla around instant black beans, after you rehydrate them, with cheese and salsa.

- Roll a warm tortilla around Egg Beaters and summer sausage with a few chopped onions and/or green pepper.

FOOD

51

FOUR GREAT TRAIL FOODS
Between breakfast and dinner lies the trail and the food it invites

Experienced hikers are sometimes heard saying "lunch" starts right after breakfast and ends just before dinner. The idea behind this is simple: With the trail rising ever to meet you, or rising ahead of you, you don't want your energy to lag for lack of fuel. You can, and should, take rest breaks, and one of those might be designated as lunch time, but eating on the trail is more often a quick snack until the next rest break.

Great trail foods have several common characteristics. They are high in quick energy and high in sustained energy. They require little or no preparation on the trail. And some of them are readily accessible at all times.

Supermarket shelves are laden with foods appropriate for the trail—energy bars, granola bars, dried fruits, candy, yogurt-covered pretzels, nuts, chocolate chips, butterscotch chips,

GORP

- *GORP* stands for "good old raisins and peanuts," but nobody stops there.

- Candy—chocolate chips, M&Ms, butterscotch chips—is a popular addition to basic GORP.

- You're not limited to peanuts. Try almonds, cashews, hazelnuts, Brazil nuts, walnuts, and honey-coated peanuts.

- You're not limited to raisins, either. Try dried cranberries, apricots, apples, banana chips, and pineapple. If the chunks of fruit are too large, cut them up before adding them.

Crackers

- Crackers often offer a surprisingly large amount of calories in addition to great taste.

- Wheat Thins, Wheatsworth, Pilot Bread, and Pilot Crackers hold up well in your pack (they don't turn into crumbs as easily as other crackers).

- You can always pack your favorite cracker in a crush-proof, lightweight container.

- They are great with cheese, peanut butter, cheese spreads, tahini, summer sausage, or hummus.

crackers, jerky, peanut butter. Or you can buy a bag of trail mix with the decisions made for you by the manufacturer.

Some hikers delight in making their own trail bars, such as by melting chocolate, mixing it with granola and raisins, chilling it, and cutting it into snack-sized pieces.

A quick trailside "sandwich" works well, too. Carry durable bread, such as pita, and smear it with peanut butter or a cheese spread, or lay on a slab of summer sausage.

Another aspect of trail food common among hikers is the fact that people tend to carry more than they can eat. It won't spoil, but it is heavy. As a rule of thumb, most folks can handle about a half pound of trail food during an eight-hour day of hiking.

Keep high-energy foods easily accessible.

Energy Bars

- Store shelves sag under the weight of the vast variety of energy bars. They can provide a boost and serve as a part of lunch.

- The bulk of good energy bars should be complex carbohydrates (such as rice, oats, maltodextrin) and not simple sugars.

- A good energy bar should be no more than approximately 25 percent fat.

- You need to be well hydrated when you eat an energy bar for it to work its best.

Pita Bread

- Pita bread (sometimes called "pocket bread") is a nutritious food that holds up well on the trail.

- When you cut it in half, the two halves separate to form a pocket into which you can stuff anything you're willing to eat.

- You don't have to cut it. You can add spreads, such as peanut butter, on top.

- Cut in half, the two halves can be the sides of a sandwich of peanut butter and jelly, summer sausage and cheese, or hummus and fresh vegetables.

FOOD

HIGH-FAT FOOD
The right fats in the right amount are necessary for healthy hiking

Fats, more than any other foods, are misunderstood by many people. Fat is necessary for a healthy life. Your body, in fact, will manufacture fat from carbohydrates and proteins if you run short. Your body worries about running out of fat so much that it'll store unbelievable quantities against a fatless day. But you will hike better if you include some fat in your diet on the trail.

Fats, like carbohydrates, provide energy. But they break down very slowly in the digestive process, so more time is required if energy is your goal. A little fat during the day is fine, but, because high-fat foods burn slowly, they work best for hikers near the end of the day, when the heat they produce will keep you warm through the night and build up your energy reserves for the next day of hiking.

Cheese

- Hard cheeses—cheddar, Swiss, jack, Parmesan— keep better without refrigeration than soft cheeses.

- Soft cheeses may be carried a couple of days, especially if the temperature is cool. Special containers are not required.

- Consider buying and packing your cheese grated (or grate it yourself) if your intent is to use it in dishes that require the cheese to melt.

- If you're going to put the cheese on crackers, save time by slicing it before your trip.

Butter

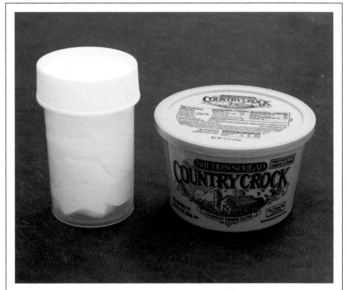

- Butter is an excellent food, made without chemicals, that provides nutrients as well as a dose of fat.

- Butter adds great flavor to just about everything.

- It will last for days in your pack, despite the fact that it becomes watery at high temperatures. It will not grow bacteria. It will, however, over time lose its peak flavor and eventually turn rancid.

- If you fry with butter, remember it burns easily.

Sources of fat for the hiker include meats, cheeses, oils, butter, margarine, and nuts. Meats don't keep well unless they're dried (like jerky) or laced with preservatives (like many meat sticks). But there are ways to work with them (see below). Hard cheeses keep better than soft cheeses, so go with cheddar, Swiss, jack, or Parmesan. And some American cheese products require no refrigeration.

MAKE IT EASY

If you want fresh meat—steak, chicken, pork chop— for the first night's dinner, freeze it solid at home. When you're ready for dinner, it will be ready to cook. Or cook the meat at home, seasoned appropriately, freeze it, and warm it up for dinner.

Meat

- Meat that has been frozen solid will thaw slowly deep in your pack, ready to be cooked the first night on the trail.

- You can cook meat at home, freeze it solid, and pack it in for the first day when you'll warm it on the stove. It tends, however, to lose some of its flavor.

- By packing a bit of extra weight, you can have meat from cans. The pop-top cans require no can-opener.

- Dried meats—jerky, pepperoni, summer sausage—please numerous hikers.

Oil

- Cooking oils will last for a very long time unrefrigerated. The cooler and drier they stay, the longer they last. But for weight purposes, carry only what you'll need.

- Avoid flavored oils. They may grow harmful bacteria in your pack.

- Canola oil, sunflower oil, and soy oil are three that will bear up under the high heat of frying.

- Similar to butter, oils can add flavor—and fat—to many foods, but don't overdo it.

FOOD

DESSERTS
Just like at home, a good meal ends best with something sweet

There are three kinds of desserts: spontaneous, planned, and created. Spontaneous desserts are discovered while unpacking your pack—candy or GORP (good old raisins and peanuts). Planned desserts are packaged and waiting for after-dinner—cookies, s'mores, instant pudding. Created desserts, the best by far, are generated with forethought and field preparation. And most important, none of the three ever fails to please.

Check out your supermarket. Incredible desserts—cheesecakes, no-bake pies—are available that require little more than whipping up the ingredients and, the hard part, waiting while they firm up.

Check out backpacking cookbooks. Recipes for mouth-watering no-bake desserts abound. Here's a sample: Mix 1 cup of oatmeal with 6 tablespoons of margarine, 6 table-

Some suggested desserts:

- Peanut butter, chocolate chips, and raisins rolled in warm tortilla

- Cheesecake from a commercial package

- Instant rice mixed with brown sugar, powdered milk, and raisins

- Your favorite candy bar

- Granola bars

Cookies

- Fig bars and soft-baked cookies hold up better in your pack. Even smushed they are easy to eat, though a bit messy.

- You can always pack cookies that crumble in a lightweight, sturdy plastic container.

- Or let them crumble. You can mix them with melted butter and peanut butter and then let the mixture chill in a frying pan.

- Use large cookies instead of graham crackers to make s'mores.

spoons of brown sugar, 3 tablespoons of cocoa mix, a half teaspoon of vanilla, and a half tablespoon of water. Form into little balls and eat, or wait for some firming up and eat.

Or, in the absence of planning, use your imagination. For instance, smear butter on a tortilla and warm it in a frying pan until the butter softens, and then sprinkle on lots of sugar, brown or white, and maybe some raisins. Roll it up and enjoy.

Cookie or cracker crumbs, the result of slamming around in your pack for days, can be mixed with melted margarine and sugar and pressed into a pan. After you mix a pudding, and before it chills, pour the pudding onto the crumbs. When it all chills, you'll have a delicious pie for dessert.

Add leftover rice, unflavored, to pudding.

Pudding

Brownies

- Instant pudding—chocolate, tapioca, banana, coconut—with no cooking required (just add cold water), makes an excellent camp dessert.

- Add some powdered milk to make it even better and/ or a packet of hot chocolate to make it more chocolatey.

- Throw in a handful of GORP, granola, a crumbled granola bar, or the Oreos that turned to black dust in your pack.

- In their season, add wild berries harvested near your campsite.

- You can bake amazing desserts, such as fresh brownies, using a convection dome (the Outback Oven is pictured) on your backpacking stove.

- Flip-baking makes a denser version of your favorite baked dessert. Oil a frying pan, add the complete mix you bought at the store, cook over low heat.

- As the name implies, you have to flip the dessert over when it's half cooked, like making pancakes.

- Or you can bake at home and pack the dessert along.

FOOD

GOURMET CAMP FOOD
The difference between a camp cook and a gourmet cook is attitude

On opposite ends of the food spectrum are those people who think food is fuel and nothing more, and those who think of food as not only a meal but also as an experience. A gourmet might not be a great cook, as far as this section is concerned, but a gourmet chef cares about food. Because this is your vacation, consider adopting, if you haven't already, the attitude of the gourmet.

Treat yourself to something special at mealtime: the richest coffee, the darkest chocolate, smoked salmon, exotic cheese, and sun-dried tomatoes. Dally in camp over a breakfast of pancakes drenched in real butter and maple syrup or strawberry preserves. The shelves of your local market offer quick-cooking, flavorful dishes with couscous, bulgur, wheat pilaf, and spicy rice. As a change from instant mashed potatoes, go

Ramen Noodles and More

- Ramen noodles are quick and easy, but you don't have to stop there.

- Drain off the water first. Then add sunflower seeds and some fresh chopped onion. Sprinkle on black pepper, enough to meet your taste requirements.

- Or rehydrate a package of freeze-dried vegetables (peas and carrots work well). Add the veggies and top it all with Parmesan cheese.

- Or add a can of shrimp and a dash of oil, then garlic, oregano, and red pepper.

Fried Rice

- Add a pinch of salt to two cups of water, and bring it to boil.

- Toss in one cup of instant rice and a pat of butter. Do not stir the rice too much unless you like it starchy.

- When the rice is ready, heat oil in the fry pan, and fry the rice until it is golden brown.

- Spice it with garlic, salt, and pepper—or curry if you prefer it.

with potato pearls, herbal seasoning already added. Learn to stove-top bake (see the Resource Directory on page 231) and create desserts from brownies to cakes and fresh breads from biscuits to pizzas. Apples, carrots, onions, and garlic stand up well to the rigors of the trail. Avocados, summer squash, mushrooms, and bell peppers can last up to five days packed in a paper bag (they need air) in your pack. Slice fresh fruits and vegetables at dinnertime, not at home, to save flavor and nutrition. Purchase a lightweight flask from an outdoor

specialty shop or catalog, and enliven dinner with your favorite before- and/or after-dinner drink.

But don't just pack fine food. Pick several recipes, write them down, and put them into the food bag after shopping accordingly. Measure the ingredients at home, and carry only what you need. Besides saving weight, you'll shorten preparation time.

A spice kit can turn bland into bursting with flavor.

Bulgur

- Cook two cups of bulgur in four cups of water, and throw in a bouillon cube for more flavor.

- Add to the pot at the same time one tablespoon of dried onion and three pats of butter. You can also add a couple of tablespoons of dried mixed vegetables.

- When the bulgur is cooked, mix in grated cheese.

- You can eat it now, or fry it until light brown in an oiled frying pan.

Spice Kit

- Any meal can be improved if you pack a small spice kit.

- Salt and black pepper go well with just about anything. Pack cayenne pepper if you like it hot.

- Garlic powder and onion flakes are excellent additions to many foods, and curry powder adds much to rice dishes.

- Add oregano to pasta, basil to pasta or potatoes, and a little hot sauce to anything that tastes blah.

NO-COOK CAMPING

For those who hate cooking, or just don't want to cook, there are options

There are backpackers who hate to cook, or don't want to cook, or think they can't cook, but they still need to eat. Good news: You don't have to cook on the trail to eat, and sometimes eat well. No-cook campers fall into two general categories: those who backpack with someone who loves to cook and those who make a no-cook meal plan. Forget gour-

met meals maybe, but otherwise fear not. You can feast fine with nothing more on the stove than a pot of hot water, and often not even that.

Meals, Ready-To-Eat (MRE) mark the current apex of military fast food. In a full field package MRE you'll find entree, bread, dessert, snack, juice, coffee, gum, even a spoon and napkin,

MRE

- Meals, Ready-To-Eat (MRE), pioneered by demands of the military, are available for hikers who have no interest in cooking.

- You can even eat out of the package so you don't have to carry much kitchenware. Some of them provide

- a spoon as a part of the package.

- You can eat MREs cold and not even pack a stove.

- They are fairly heavy, and you end with quite a bit of trash to pack out.

Instant Food

- With a stove and pot to boil water in, you can have hot meals without cooking.

- Instant hot cereals for breakfast can be boosted with a pat of butter and the addition of nuts and raisins.

- A wide variety of instant soups can be a meal or an addition to another meal plan.

- Freeze-dried meals and snacks, of which there are many, sometimes require no more than hot water and a spoon.

all packaged in indestructible plastic bags. You might see similar products, at least the entrees, on supermarket shelves being sold as "retort" foods—foods that have been cooked and sealed in a flexible foil package that you just throw into hot water to reheat, sort of like a soft can. MREs show up semi-regularly in Army-Navy surplus stores and, sometimes, in outdoor specialty stores.

No fire, no stove, no mess, no bother, no hot food: the elements of cold camping. What you eat, three meals a day, are food products—from a bag, a can, a box—with no cooking.

You can also prepare some foods pretrip, simple foods that you can eat cold on the trail. A couple of already-baked potatoes can be cut open and filled with cheese, canned tuna, or whatever tickles your taste buds. Precooked rice can be carried in a plastic bag and, at mealtime, stuffed (without the plastic bag) into a green pepper or a pita pocket with some cheese on top. Only your imagination stands between you and a cold dinner.

Cold Camping

- Those rigorously committed to cooking nothing, to not even boiling water, can camp and eat cold.

- For protein, there are meat sticks, packages of jerky, summer sausages, and tuna (in cans or in soft bags).

- For fats, there are cheeses, peanut butter, and nuts.

- For carbohydrates, pack some dried fruit, candy bars, granola bars, crackers, and GORP. Pack drink mixes to add calories and flavor to cold water.

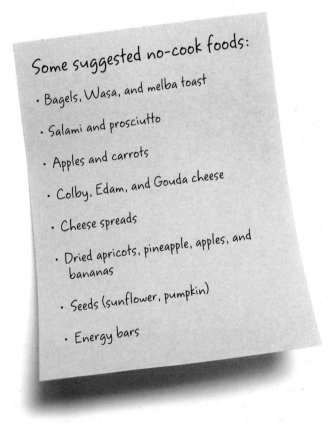

Some suggested no-cook foods:

- Bagels, Wasa, and melba toast

- Salami and prosciutto

- Apples and carrots

- Colby, Edam, and Gouda cheese

- Cheese spreads

- Dried apricots, pineapple, apples, and bananas

- Seeds (sunflower, pumpkin)

- Energy bars

EDIBLE WILD PLANTS

Many areas are a wild garden waiting to be harvested

To those who are trained and wary, edible wild plants offer an excellent source of food, often tasty. To those who experiment haphazardly, illness, even death, is possible.

For most novice wild-plant eaters, berries are a common starting point. Of all aggregate berries—such as raspberries, thimbleberries, blackberries—99 percent are safe and delicious. In fact, most berries that are black, blue, or purple are safe. About one-half of all red berries are safe. In almost all cases, white, yellow, and green berries should be avoided.

There are safe green plants that almost everyone can identify. All grasses, though often lacking in delectability, are safe to eat. You can add them to other dishes. But avoid grass if

Wild Berries

- Aggregate berries (each berry looks like a bunch of tiny berries), such as blackberries and thimbleberries, are rarely unsafe to eat.

- Almost all berries that are blue, black, or purple are safe to eat.

- About one-half of all red berries are dangerous to eat, so be sure you can positively identify a red berry before dining.

- Avoid berries that are white, yellow, or green. A few are safe, but most are not.

Wild Greens

- If you take the time to positively identify them, many wild greens are available to add flavor and nutrition to a meal.

- Carry a guidebook to edible plants.

- Some are edible raw—such as young dandelion leaves, watercress, and the stems of cattails—but all should be washed prior to eating.

- Some should not be eaten until they have been boiled—such as stinging nettle, chickweed, and lamb's quarters.

the seeds have turned black or purple. Cattails are safe to consume but best in spring and early summer when you can peel and eat the young shoots and the flower heads. Pine trees offer food in several ways. Pine needles are astringent but edible, and they can be boiled to make a tea. Under the scales of pinecones hide seeds that are good raw or cooked. For beach hikers, green seaweed is a tasty treat sought by many, best if plucked from a rock or found floating free.

•••••••••••••••• RED●LIGHT ••••••••••••••••

Be absolutely sure it's safe before eating a wild plant. Be especially wary of plants with one or more of six characteristics: looks like a mushroom, looks like a carrot, looks like a bean or pea, looks like an onion, the flowers are shaped like an umbrella, the leaves are shiny or hairy. If you're unsure, don't eat it.

Prickly Pear Cactus

- If you're up for the challenge, you can carefully peel and eat raw the fruit of the prickly pear cactus.

- Peel and cook the tender young pads of the prickly pear cactus.

- Barrel cacti contain a drinkable sap. You need to slice off the top and crush the inner pulp, but it's often bitter and not recommended except in an emergency.

- Other cacti should be left alone.

Rose Hips

- Wild rose hips have more vitamin C than any other fruit.

- You can chew them for the nutrients or crush and boil them to make a tea. You'll get more nutrition from chewing.

- Boiled spruce needles make a tea that is also rich in vitamin C. Use only fresh, green needles.

- The flowers of clovers can be boiled for a fine-tasting tea, and the leaves can be eaten sparingly as well.

FOOD

STUFF SACKS

Keep gear more organized, less bulky, and cleaner with stuff sacks

A stuff sack, generically speaking, is any sack or bag into which you can stuff gear or clothing. Why can't you just stuff everything into your pack? Well, you can, and a growing number of backpackers, deeply concerned with traveling as light as possible (see page 76), are carrying fewer of them. But there are reasons to consider the use of stuff sacks.

Stuff sacks organize small items for quicker and easier access. Imagine rummaging inside your pack for spare batteries for your flashlight, a ballpoint pen for journaling, or that extra book of matches—not necessary if such things are kept together in an easy-to-find little sack. When all your grub is kept in one sack, you simply grab the food bag at mealtime.

Stuff Sacks

- Stuff sacks help you keep your gear and clothing organized and easier to access. Keep your small items together in one sack. Keep your food in one bag.

- Stuff sacks of different colors help you grab the stuff you want with the first try.

- Stuff sacks keep dirty things from soiling clean things.

- Stuff sacks do add a little bit of weight, something unappealing to some hikers.

Large Plastic Bags

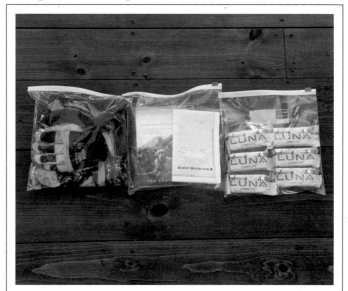

- Clear plastic bags serve as stuff sacks but cost less and weigh less.

- In addition to keeping items organized and easy to find, they keep them clean and dry.

- Fold your map with the area you're hiking across on top.

- You don't have to take it out of a clear plastic bag to read it.

- Do not discard the plastic bags after a hike. You can use one on several trips, as long as it hasn't ripped.

Stuff sacks make large things smaller. Your sleeping bag came with a stuff sack, so did your tent, and, perhaps, your down jacket. Synthetic (fleece) garments, though light in weight, are notoriously bulky. A stuff sack can, however, reduce the amount of space they take up in your pack.

The stove will inevitably collect a residue of fuel on the outside, and pots, despite washing, tend to collect a bit of food residue, and stuff sacks contain the grim and keep the rest of the contents of your pack cleaner. A stuff sack, on longer trips, after a change of socks and underwear, will keep the dirty garments separate from cleaner clothing.

For the best results, stuff sacks should be waterproof or at least highly water-resistant, adding a layer of protection in case of rain. They are available in a variety of sizes, colors, and even shapes and in a variety of prices, sometimes surprisingly high. But you can get by with a selection of plastic bags from the local supermarket.

Small Plastic Bags

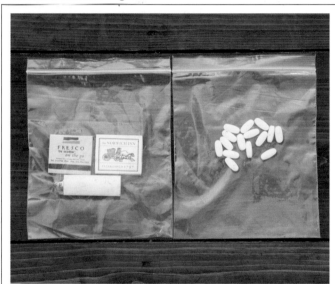

- Small plastic bags, virtually weightless, allow you to save even more weight and organize even better.

- If you carry a medication, as an example, carry only the amount you will need and not a whole bottle.

- Measure out exactly the amount of sugar you will need instead of carrying a large container.

- Small bags can organize small items inside a larger plastic bag, shortening access time.

Stuffing a Stuff Sack

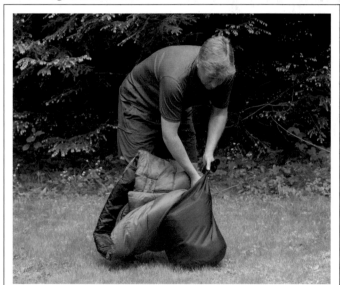

- Stuff sacks make large things smaller. You get more use out of the cubic inches of your pack, and/or you can carry a smaller and lighter pack.

- A stuff sack reduces the space a sleeping bag takes up many times over.

- Bulky fleece garments will stuff down far smaller than if you simply cram them into your pack.

- Your tent will take up less space in a stuff sack than out of one.

WHAT GOES WHERE: PART 1
A place for everything (in your pack), and everything in its place

KNACK HIKING & BACKPACKING

Cramming everything indiscriminately into your pack is, simply put, a bad idea. You are likely to find yourself, on one end of the spectrum, inconvenienced and uncomfortable or, on the other end, in pain and off balance to the point where the chance of a slip or fall increases. There are no hard and fast rules, and you may actually alter the arrangement of the items in your pack, especially heavier pieces of gear, to allow for alterations in the terrain (see page 74). As your backpacking experiences rise in number, you will develop personal preferences in how you pack, and you may join an elite group that thinks everyone else does it wrong. There are, however, general guidelines for packing, and here are a couple:

Step 1: The Sleeping Bag

- Large and bulky, the sleeping bag is usually the first item to go into your pack.

- Most packs today have a sleeping bag compartment built into the bottom.

- Stuff your bag directly into this compartment and not into a stuff sack first.

- If your pack has no sleeping bag compartment, stuff the bag into its sack and place it at the bottom of your pack. It will be the last thing you need to remove.

Step 2: The Tent

- Also large and bulky, your tent usually goes in after the sleeping bag. Tent poles are usually packed separately.

- It will take up a lot less room if you stuff it into its sack first.

- If it's small enough to fit sideways across the top of the sleeping bag compartment, put it there.

- If it's too large, pack it upright. It might be easier to balance the pack's weight if the tent is in the middle of the pack.

1. Avoid tying gear to the outside of your pack. There are exceptions, of course, but you do not want your water bottle, camp shoes, and other such items dangling from cords where they bounce around, make noise, snag on bushes, pulling you off balance, or tear off, leaving you in camp that night without an insulated mug. Besides all that, you look bad. If you need to carry something on the outside of your pack, tent poles for example, lash them securely in place, a job that pack compression straps do well.

2. Everything that you think you might want on short notice needs to be accessible. You do not want an extended search for your lunch or your raingear if a sudden squall blows in, but your sleeping bag and tent can be buried deep. More than just accessibility, keeping your gear handy can be an act of consideration. Your group usually doesn't want to wait while you dig around for your camera or sunglasses.

Step 3: Clothing

- Clothing can go on top of a small tent or around a larger tent.

- Small articles of clothing—socks, underwear, extra bandanna—are sometimes stuffed into a small sack first to keep them organized.

- Be sure to pack clothing into the corners of the pack so you don't waste space.

- Keep an insulating layer, such as a fleece jacket, near the top in case of a sudden drop in temperature.

Step 4: Food

- The food bag, at least at the start of your trip, will be the heaviest bag in your pack.

- Add the weight of stove, fuel, and kitchenware, and your kitchen is the biggest part of the weight.

- It should all ride at approximately the height of your shoulder blades for men, at the bottom of the ribs for women.

- If you have a fuel bottle, keep it in a leak-proof bag and/or in an outside pocket.

WHAT GOES WHERE: PART 2
Pack right for increased comfort on shoulders and hips and better stability on the trail

A thoughtfully packed pack of fifty pounds will ride more comfortably than an ill-packed and unbalanced load of quite a bit less weight. Part of the balancing act can be handled with the pack's hip belt and straps (see page 72), but a lot of it is managed by how you load the pack. Here are a few more things to think about:

1. Utilize all the space inside your pack. Even though that sounds like something everyone would do, space is often overlooked. Fill your empty pot with small items. Stuff an extra pair of socks into you camp shoes. Look for unused corners of your pack where bulky items such as the tent create pockets of space.

Step 5: Parka

- It is wise for hikers to have an outer layer (shell) as one of the final items in the pack, kept handy in case of rain, snow, or wind.

- It can go on top of the other gear in the main compartment.

- Or it can go in a large lid pocket if your pack has one.

- It can also go under compression straps on the outside of the pack.

Step 6: Tent Poles

- You do not want your tent poles gouging into other gear or clothing or into your back.

- You can shove them down alongside the rest of your stuff in the main compartment, away from your back.

- Or carry them under compression straps on the outside if they can be secured. You don't want them slipping out.

- You can roll them in your sleeping pad before strapping it on.

2. Nothing with sharp or hard edges—tent poles, pots and pans, the corner of a book—should be placed where it can jab into your back. The part of your pack that rests against your back should be filled with clothing or other soft items.

3. The load should be balanced so it rides evenly on your center of gravity. Heavier items—stove, fuel, food bag—are best carried close to your body and somewhere between the top of your shoulder blades and the bottom of your rib cage,

or you will otherwise tend to be pulled backwards. You may sometimes pack the heavy gear higher or lower depending on variables discussed later in this chapter (see page 74).

4. A well-packed pack has the gear and clothing snugly fitted inside so it does not shift around, throwing you off balance when you least expect it and most need it. Packs with compression straps allow you to make quick work of removing any "dead" space that you inadvertently leave inside.

Step 7: Small Stuff

- Small stuff can go into whatever room is left, but you want to think about it first.

- Outside pockets can be used to hold and keep small items together.

- There are some small items you *want* to keep handy in outside pockets—maps, compass, trowel and toilet paper, sunscreen, insect repellent, lip balm.

- Don't forget to use the "hidden" space: inside pots and camp shoes, for example.

Step 8: The Pad

- Most backpackers strap their sleeping pads to the outside of their packs. It can go in the main compartment if there's room.

- Most packs today have straps on the outside of the sleeping bag compartment that work perfectly for the pad. Your pad can also ride under compression straps.

- Roll the pad tightly before strapping it on.

- If your pad has a stuff sack, it may have room to hold additional small stuff.

PUTTING ON THE PACK

There's a lot more to it than just throwing the weight onto your shoulders

Just about everyone who has backpacked long enough has been there when it happened or heard a story about it happening. Sometimes the one telling the story did it: In the act of putting on a pack, a back muscle was torn or a knee strained.

Several methods of getting the load onto a back have been tried and used, or tried and discarded, by backpackers. Some hikers sit on the ground, slip into the shoulder straps, then roll onto hands and knees, and stand up—a method that puts a lot of stress on your knees and back. Others set their pack on a rock or log, slip into the straps and stand, a method with some merit, as long as you have a convenient rock or log.

Step 1: Compression Straps

- Compression straps should be loose when you pack your pack. The space inside your pack is not fully available unless the compression straps are fully loose.

- They will not be tightened until your pack is fully loaded.

- If something will ride under your compression straps, place those things after the rest of the pack is packed.

- Tighten the straps fully to prevent any shifting of weight while you're hiking.

Step 2: Lift Pack to Thigh

- Be sure the shoulder straps are loose before lifting the pack.

- With your feet spread for balance and your knees flexed to reduce back stress, lift the pack onto one of your thighs and balance it there.

- Slip one arm partially through the appropriate shoulder strap, the one that feels most natural.

- Maintain the pack balanced on your thigh with your other hand.

What you never want to do is haphazardly sling the weight of a pack onto your back, putting a great deal of stress on lower back muscles and the ligaments of your knees. The method described below works in any situation, whether you're alone or with a group, and, if followed carefully, prevents injury.

Take it easy on yourself and have someone hold your pack while you slip into the shoulder straps.

•••••••••••••• RED ● LIGHT ••••••••••••
To avoid injuring your back or a knee, keep your feet spread apart and set firmly on the ground for balance, your knees slightly flexed to reduce the stress, and work the weight of your pack, step by step, onto your shoulders.

Step 3: Swing Pack to Back

- Lifting the pack with your free hand, and with the arm that is already partially through one shoulder strap, swing the pack up and onto your shoulder.

- Keep your knees flexed during the tossing, and twist your body to help add momentum to the toss.

- Reach around and work your free arm through the other shoulder strap.

- Center the pack on your shoulders, but don't tighten the shoulder straps yet.

Step 4: Fasten the Hip Belt

- Lean slightly forward and hunch your shoulders up a bit to lift the pack higher on the center of your back.

- Holding the pack there with your shoulders, fasten your hip belt.

- Pull the hip belt comfortably snug but not too tight.

- It should rest on the tops of your hips. When you stand up straight, you should feel more weight on your hips than on your shoulders.

OF HIP BELTS AND STRAPS

The suspension system of a pack allows you to fine-tune your balance and stability

All of your pack's straps, except the compression straps, should be loose before you put the pack on your back. These straps are known collectively as the "suspension system." Adjusting the suspension system properly—just the right tension applied in just the right order—allow you to almost mold the pack to your body for maximum comfort and stability on the trail.

First, buckle the hip belt and chest (sternum) straps. Pull the hip belt comfortably snug so that it rests on top of your hips, not riding down over them. Now tighten the stabilizer straps, the straps that connect the hip belt to the pack. If there are two stabilizer straps on each side, tighten the bottom straps first.

Next, tighten the load-lifter straps, the straps above your

Step 1: The Sternum Strap

- To maximize comfort and stability, the suspension system of your pack should be tightened in a particular order.

- Most packs have a sternum strap (chest strap). With the pack now resting comfortably on your hips, clip the sternum strap.

- The sternum strap, like the hip belt, should be comfortably snug.

- The sternum strap should ride about 3 inches below your collarbones.

Step 2: The Stabilizer Straps

- Packs often have stabilizer straps that connect the hip belt to the lower part of the pack.

- They pull the lower part of the pack snug against your hips, and they should be tightened next.

- If you have two stabilizer straps on each side, tighten the lower ones first.

- Pull on both stabilizer straps simultaneously to balance your pack on your hips.

shoulders that determine how closely the pack is pulled against your shoulders.

Finally, snug up the shoulder straps and chest strap—not too tight but comfortably snug. If the shoulder straps are too tight, you may cut off adequate circulation to your arms, and your hands will go numb and puff up, not typically a serious problem but a big discomfort.

You should now feel the weight on your hips. And when hiking, the load should not shift around on your back.

· · · · · · · · · · · GREEN ● LIGHT · · · · · · · · · · · · ·

When your pack fits your body properly, and when you have tightened the hip belt and straps appropriately, two-thirds of the weight of the pack, or slightly more, will ride on your hips—which is where the weight should be and where it should be most comfortable.

Step 3: The Load-Lifter Straps

- The load-lifter straps connect the shoulder straps to the top part of the pack.

- They should be just above your shoulders, and they adjust how closely the pack rides against your shoulders.

- If your pack fits perfectly, they will angle down toward your shoulders at approximately a 45-degree angle.

- The load-lifter straps are the next to be tightened. Pull on both of them simultaneously to better balance your load.

Step 4: The Shoulder Straps

- The shoulder straps are the final straps to be tightened.

- These straps should not be too tight, or they could cut off circulation to your arms, making your hands swell and go numb.

- After tightening the shoulder straps you may need to adjust the tightness of the sternum strap, and that is normal.

- About two-thirds of the pack's weight should now be carried on your hips, and the weight should not shift around as you hike.

CENTER OF GRAVITY

Where you carry most of your pack's weight can vary with the terrain

This section discusses the distribution—and sometimes the redistribution—of the weight inside your pack. You may wish to vary the distribution of the weight depending on the terrain and whether you are a man or a woman. It may also vary depending on the whimsical values known as "personal preference."

As a reminder, lighter gear, such as the sleeping bag, and clothing are generally packed low in the pack. Heavier gear, such as the food bag, stove, and fuel, is usually packed high, with the weight centered at about the shoulder blades. Packing the weight high creates less strain on the spine but makes you a little tipsy—not a problem when a trail provides

KNACK HIKING & BACKPACKING

Centers of Gravity

- Generally speaking, the load on your back rides best if it is centered on or near your center of gravity.

- If the weight is centered too high, you will feel tipsy and less comfortable on the trail.

- Centered too low, and you increase the strain on your back.

- For a man, the center of gravity is about the level of the diaphragm, and for a woman, about hip level.

Hiking on Moderate Terrain

- When the terrain ahead is moderate, with a rough walking surface but not too steep, you may wish to lower the center of weight in the pack.

- You can often accomplish this by placing the heavy food bag lower in the pack.

- The work of carrying the load will be a bit harder, but you will be more stable.

- If you are new to a trail, you can guess the terrain ahead by looking at your map.

relatively easy walking. And weight packed high places it near the center of gravity for a man, which is about the level of the diaphragm. The center of gravity for a woman, however, is about hip level, so women often bear a load more easily when the weight is centered lower in the pack, below the shoulder blades. Some experimentation may be required to figure out what works best for you.

Generally, packing the load low is a bit harder work but gives you more steadiness when the going gets rougher. Off-trail, on moderately rough terrain, lowering the center of the pack's weight to below the shoulder blades for men and even lower for women provides better balance. On steep and highly uneven terrain, where perhaps there will be scrambling as well as hiking, the weight may ride best at the bottom of the pack.

When facing mixed terrain, you can reduce, even eliminate, the need to redistribute the weight in your pack by using trekking poles or a hiking staff to better maintain balance.

Hiking on Rough Terrain

- Rough terrain is rocky and uneven under your feet, and it is almost always steep.

- You will have to do some scrambling, and you might need to use your hands to help you balance or to help you ascend.

- You will be most stable if the center of weight in your pack is low.

- The heaviest gear in your pack will be in or near the bottom of your pack.

Balancing with Trekking Poles

- On mixed terrain you can compensate for the need to shift the center of weight in your pack by using trekking poles.

- The best trekking poles are adjustable.

- For flat terrain, you want your lower arms to be about perpendicular to the ground when you grip the poles.

- When going uphill, make the poles shorter, and when going downhill make them longer. In both cases, you are keeping your forearms perpendicular to the ground.

MINIMIZE

Trimming off pounds, even ounces, from the weight on your back is important

In the modern backpacking era, there is nothing new about attempts to minimize the amount of weight you have to carry. Fifty years ago hikers were cutting the handles off their toothbrushes, clipping the labels from their clothing, and boring holes through every piece of gear that it was semireasonable to bore a hole through.

Simply put, when the weight is on your back, every ounce counts.

Technological advances have created numerous new ways to shave off pounds—lighter but stronger fabrics, thinner but effective insulation, seemingly weightless metals such as titanium. They cost more, but, if you're willing to pay, you can

Minimize Size and Amount of Gear

- You don't need the weight and bulk of a two-liter pot if a one-liter pot will do the job.

- And you don't need two sets of maps or two compasses for one group of hikers—unless you plan to split up.

- If you have an emergency space blanket, you don't need a ground cloth—or vice versa.

- One first aid kit, thoughtfully packed, will serve an entire group.

Tarp

- You may be fine under a tarp instead of in a tent, especially if it's not the season of bugs.

- A large tarp can provide shelter for four or five backpackers.

- If you don't own a tarp, you may be able to set up your tent fly without the tent. Some flies are designed that way.

- If the forecast is favorable, you could be fine sleeping under the stars on a lightweight ground cloth.

reduce the weight of your pack in leaps and bounds.

The ability to go lighter than ever before has created a new breed taking amazing steps to minimize weight. Much of what they have to teach appears in this chapter. But regardless of your level of dedication to reducing weight, a simple truth prevails: Almost everyone packs more weight than needed. Ask questions of just about every piece of gear and clothing.

Are you packing something that another hiker in your group is also packing? A group that doesn't plan to split up needs only one compass and one set of maps.

Is there something smaller and lighter than what you are packing that will do the job just as well—or maybe better? Lose the two-liter pot if a one-liter pot will do.

Are you packing two things, each for a different purpose, when one could serve both purposes? An emergency space blanket will work as a ground cloth.

Do you need it, or do you just want it? Of course, there's nothing wrong with carrying something because you want to. The fun factor should not be minimized.

Get More Use from Clothing

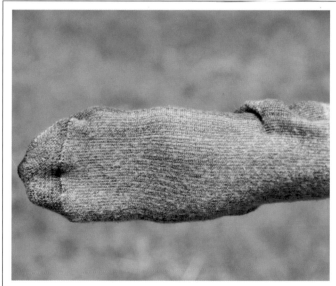

- A common weight error made by backpackers is packing too many clothes.

- You don't need a clean T-shirt every day. If it smells that bad, wash it. Same goes for underwear.

- An extra pair of socks can serve as mittens if the day turns unusually cold. Lose the mittens.

- You can wear the same pair of pants for months. People do it all the time.

To go lighter, ask yourself:

- Do I really need it?

- Have I already packed something that will do the same job?

- Do I have something smaller and lighter that will do the same job?

- Do I need all of this, or can I take just part of it?

- Has someone else in the group already packed one of these?

SUBSTITUTE
Trade heavy gear for lighter gear that does the same job

With every piece of gear and clothing that you consider purchasing, you will have choices in weight. If the products serve similar functions, it's usually best to go lighter. But, as mentioned earlier, the technology that has created "super-

More than ever before, you can save weight by choosing lighter materials.

light" and "ultralight" products comes with a super-high price tag. The cost of outfitting yourself from scratch with high-tech, low-weight stuff can be astronomical.

But you don't have to do it all at once. When it's time to replace an old cooking pot, consider a lighter material. When your parka wears out, think about one of less weight.

Lighter Footwear

- A pound on your feet, goes an old saying, is like five pounds on your back.

- Good, lightweight hiking shoes are made durable as well as comfortable, and the cost may be less than you suspect.

- You can find lightweight shoes that will provide surprisingly strong support for your feet and ankles.

- If you don't need a lot of support, low-cost options are available.

Lighter Water Disinfection

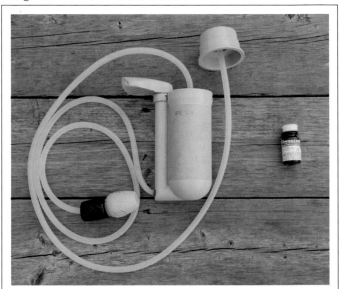

- Water filters are useful, but some of them are heavy.

- You can carry a lightweight filter that removes only protozoa and then treat the water with iodine to kill smaller germs (bacteria and viruses).

- Chlorine dioxide tablets are super lightweight and kill all germs, although they require a long wait.

- Because you packed a stove, you can boil your water to disinfect it. If fires are acceptable, you can boil it over flames.

But substituting is not all about emptying your bank account. Aluminum cookware, for instance, can be lighter and cheaper than stainless steel. You'll need a stove, so get a small one instead of a large one, and the small one doesn't have to cost more. Choose a lightweight method of water disinfection instead of a relatively heavy water filter. You may have always wanted to read *War and Peace,* but save it for the living room and substitute a thin paperback novel. You get the idea.

············· YELLOW ● LIGHT ·············
You may need to take extra care when you carry superlight clothing and some ultralight gear. Despite being of high-quality construction, sometimes "featherlight" may mean it's not as durable as heavier items that serve the same purpose.

Go Light with Technology

- Technology gives you a chance to lose or gain weight in your pack.

- Small digital cameras take excellent photos and can add only ounces to your pack. And they save you the weight and bulk of carrying film.

- A GPS unit, on the other hand, weighs quite a bit more than a small compass.

- Do you really want a cell phone or a radio? They are seldom needed.

Think Small Stove

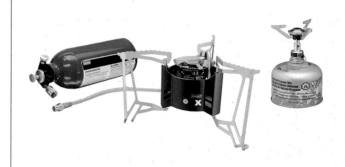

- Some small stoves not only weigh less but also bring water to a boil as fast as or faster than a much larger stove.

- Some small stoves that attach directly to fuel canisters weigh only ounces— and they're easy to operate.

- One small stove will serve a group of four—five if they're light eaters.

- The canisters can be spread among the group, and the weight of the kitchen per person drops dramatically.

DOWNSIZE

In the pack and on the trail, bigger is definitely not always better

You can drop pounds by substituting lightweight gear for heavier gear. Keep shaving off weight with some simple downsizing. The rule of downsizing is this: Don't carry anything that's bigger than you need.

One big weight consideration is your tent. If two of you are off for a weekend with a three-person tent, you may be carrying four or more extra pounds. You can pack an even smaller tent if you choose one that has no room inside for gear. A super-lightweight piece of waterproof nylon (or a super-cheap garbage bag) can cover your gear if rain threatens to fall.

Shelves in outdoor specialty shops are often covered with a wide variety of shapes and sizes of lightweight containers.

If you don't need all of it, don't take all of it.

Three-Quarter-Length Pad

- Three-quarter-length sleeping pads are available, and they all weigh less than full-length pads.

- With a three-quarter-length pad, you can put extra clothing or your empty pack beneath your feet for added comfort and protection from heat loss.

- Self-inflating pads, even though more comfortable, weigh more than closed-cell foam pads.

- If you want a self-inflating pad, you can choose the thinnest, narrowest, lightest model.

Take Only What You Need

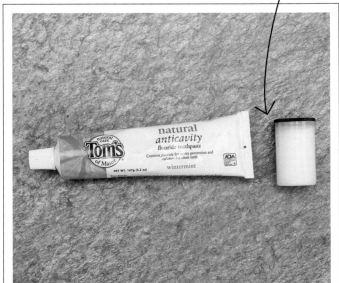

- Squeeze only the toothpaste you'll need into a small canister. You can purchase small containers at outdoor specialty shops or use old film canisters.

- If you have a large bottle of sunscreen, squeeze only the amount you'll need into a small canister.

- Pour only the cooking oil you'll need into a small canister.

- From a large package of grated cheese, take only what you'll need in a small plastic bag.

They are handy, and the lids close securely with screw-tops, but you can use film canisters and small, zip-top plastic bags. Into them goes stuff that would otherwise require you to pack more than you need. Lose the whole bottle of aspirin—shake out enough pills for your trip. You don't need a whole tube of sunscreen—squeeze out enough for your weekend And you need neither a whole bottle of olive oil nor a whole shaker of salt in your food bag—pour what you need into a little container. Forget the whole roll of duct tape in your repair kit—roll off a few yards and wrap it around a pencil stub. You won't even need a whole guidebook to the entire Teton Wilderness Area—carry only the pages that cover your area of travel. And you probably won't need a whole roll of toilet paper; just plan accordingly.

Choose Thinner Clothing

- Advances in clothing technology allow you to pack lighter without losing the services you want the clothing to provide.

- New insulation creates garments that hold in body heat with a loss less bulk and weigh, as pictured.

- Tightly woven material is being used in garments to repel all wind while remaining amazingly thin and light.

- Outer layers that breathe allow you to stay dry without the weight of waterproof nylon.

Take a Smaller Pack

- You can take pounds off your back by choosing the smallest pack that will hold what you need.

- The simplest packs are usually the lightest. Every zipper, outside pocket, strap, toggle, and loop adds weight.

- To save more weight, choose a pack made from lightweight material.

- Remember, however, it is important that your pack fits your body. Do not sacrifice fit in order to carry less weight.

DOUBLE UP
Many of the items you pack can serve you in more than one way

When you're standing beside all that gear and clothing that will soon fill your pack, ask yourself this question: Am I packing two things when one could serve two purposes?

The camp kitchen is an excellent place to double up. You don't need a spoon and a fork. Lose the fork, and spoon up dinner. You don't have to have a hot drink and a bowl of food at the same time. Have a hot drink, then use your mug as a bowl—or vice versa—and then hot tea can be used to "wash" the mug. If you enjoy a hot drink with dinner, eat out of the pot. The lid of a pot can also serve as a plate for a second camper. With three, how about one person eats out of the pot, one eats off the lid, and one uses the frying pan as a

Two Jobs, One Item

- Men can swim in boxer shorts and save the weight of a swimsuit. Women can swim in boxer shorts and a sports bra.

- If you need to sleep in pajamas, sleep in your long underwear.

- Forget the backpacking pillow. Stuff clothing into a fleece jacket or vest.

- If the temperature drops, you can wear your sleeping bag in camp, saving the weight of a heavy parka.

Double Up in the Kitchen

- If someone eats out of the cooking pot, she or he doesn't need a bowl.

- You can eat out of your mug instead of a bowl, if you don't mind waiting for a hot drink.

- The lid of a pot and the frying pan can both serve as plates or bowls.

- If you have a spoon you will not need a fork. Your eating spoon can also be your cooking spoon.

plate? You don't need a serving spoon. Serve the food from the pot with an individual's spoon (before it goes into her or his mouth). You don't need a kitchen knife if you're packing a pocket knife. And you don't need pot grips if you have a multi-purpose camp tool, the type that includes a small pair of pliers.

Here are a few more weight-saving thoughts: If you're carrying a lightweight poncho in case of rain, use it as a ground cloth under your tent or under your food-prep area. Instead of carrying a backpacking pillow, stuff extra clothes into a fleece vest or sweater, and create a pillow of just the right thickness for you. If you just don't sleep well without pajamas, bed down in your long underwear. If you use trekking poles, they work great as poles to hold up the ends of a tarp.

Double Use of Stuff Sacks

- Stuff sacks, after you unpack them, can serve many purposes.

- You can wear them over socks as camp shoes. Waterproof stuff sacks work best.

- You can hang food and other aromatic items out of reach of animals in a stuff sack.

- Turn one inside out and use it to carry sand for a mound fire. (The inside stays clean when the sack returns to its intended use.)

Sleep in Your Clothes

- Sleep in fleece garments and carry a lighter sleeping bag.

- If your feet get cold, zip up a parka and slip it over your feet.

- You can fill a water bottle with hot water and sleep with it for extra warmth. (Be sure the lid screws on tight.)

- You can place extra clothing beneath your bag if your pad is too thin.

83

EAT LIGHT

The minimalist can get by with surprisingly little weight in the food bag

Each day you plan to be on the trail increases the weight of the food bag, and it doesn't take too many days for grub to be the highest percentage of the weight. If you have never lifted a week's worth of food, you may be stunned by the pounds. As an eater, you may decide to become a minimalist.

Most of the weight of food comes from water, and the mini-

malist chooses foods from which the maximum amount of water has been removed, a process known as "freeze-drying." On the trail, boiling water is added back to freeze-dried fare, and, after a few minutes of setting or simmering, dinner is ready. The manufacturers of freeze-dried food have grown more and more inventive with their offerings, crossing the

Freeze-Dried Food

- The lightest food bag for backpackers is filled with freeze-dried food—and it will last almost forever.

- Breakfasts, lunches, dinners, desserts, and snacks, in choices that are seemingly endless, are available freeze-dried.

- Advances in freeze-drying technology have made the food more tasty and more nourishing than ever before. Some have added vitamins and minerals.

- Freeze-dried foods are usually among the most expensive backpacking foods.

Eat from the Pouch

- Read the label. Many freeze-dried meals can be rehydrated in the pouch, saving the washing of a pot.

- If you are not carrying anything with which you can measure the amount of water you add, add more rather than less. Watery

- freeze-dried food is edible. Underhydrated food is not.

- If you eat from the pouch, you don't need a bowl.

- Eat it all. Otherwise you're packing out the heavy weight of uneaten hydrated food.

spectrum of meals with numerous different breakfasts, snacks, dinners, and desserts. You'll find these meal options at most outdoor stores, in the camping section of larger stores, online, and in mail-order catalogs. And many of the meals are amazingly tasty. On the downside, they can also amaze you with their high cost.

You can go almost as minimal and cheaper by shopping for light foods at your local grocery store. Look for rice- and pasta-based dinners and instant soups that require only boiling water.

•••••••••••••••••• RED●LIGHT ••••••••••••••
A package of freeze-dried food tells you how many people that package will feed. Beware: After a long day, you might find it easy to demolish a two-person meal by yourself. The only way to know is to experiment. Until you know, carry more freeze-dried food than you think you'll need. Better safe than hungry.

Shop Light at Supermarkets

- Dehydrated foods are available in every grocery store. You'll find a vast variety: cereals, soups, entrees, desserts.

- They are not as light as freeze-dried, but they are lighter than other foods.

- Many of these foods are "instant," requiring only the addition of hot water and a few minutes of waiting.

- Some of them require a short amount of cooking. You need a stove that simmers to make these turn out right.

Carry Less Water

- Water adds a great deal of weight to your pack—2.2 pounds per liter.

- If you're hiking where there's plenty of water, such as a trail that follows a river, you can carry a small water bottle.

- A half-quart bottle, for instance, holds only one pound of water.

- Most water disinfection tablets will have to be broken to match the chemical to the volume in your container. With other means of disinfection it doesn't matter (see page 42).

LEAVE IT AT HOME

When it comes to saving weight, there are a lot of things you can do without

As mentioned earlier, if you just really want something along, no matter how unnecessary, there is absolutely nothing wrong with tossing it into your pack. But, yes, the weight can mount stunningly fast, so ask one more time: Do I *really* want that?

Think again. Do I really need to carry that?

A few ounces can and should be saved by discarding unneeded packaging at home. You don't need, for instance, the wrappers of candy bars, granola bars, energy bars, cheese sticks, and sticks of chewing gum. Unwrap them and put them into a lightweight plastic bag. Inside boxes of crackers are bags of crackers, inside boxes of pancake mix are bags

Leave Wrappers at Home

- You can save weight and bulk by leaving the wrappers of many foods at home. And there's less trash to pack out.

- Unwrap granola bars, candy bars, energy bars, and fruit bars and carry the bars in a plastic bag.

- Individually wrapped pieces of candy and gum can be unwrapped before leaving home.

- Individual packets of instant cereals and soups can be dumped into one plastic bag. You can estimate the amount to take out for each serving.

Leave Boxes at Home

- Boxes are bulkier and heavier than bags and more difficult to pack.

- Dump the contents of quick-cooking grains, such as rice and pancake mix, from the box into a bag.

- If you need the directions, cut them off the box and put them into the bag.

- Remove crackers, cookies, and such from their original containers and carry them in a zip-top plastic bag. They are also easier to access that way.

of pancake mix, and you don't need the boxes. You may not need an entire box of anything, so measure out into a zip-top plastic bag the amount you do need.

Sure, you may want to shampoo your hair or use deodorant, but you don't need to. You don't even need toothpaste on a weekend hike—just brush without it.

Look at your backpack. Are there straps, even removable pockets you don't need on this trip? Do you need the sack your mess kit came in? Leave them behind.

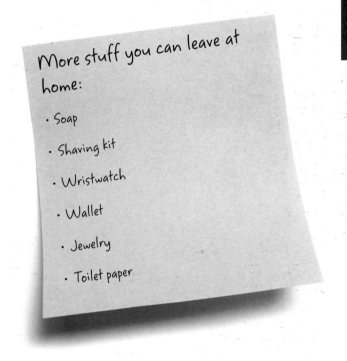

⋯⋯⋯⋯⋯⋯⋯⋯ RED●LIGHT ⋯⋯⋯⋯⋯⋯

Don't think so light that you leave something necessary at home, something that you might need for safety or comfort. The weather might not look like rain, but it can still rain. You may have never needed a first aid kit, but this trip could change all that.

ON GOING LIGHTER

Leave Toiletries at Home

- Look at the size and weight of deodorant. Leave it at home. Most hikers don't notice how they smell until they get home anyway.

- You don't really need to comb or brush your hair every day.

- Your hair will do fine if you don't wash it for a few days. In fact, it's probably good for your hair to take a shampoo break.

- And you can still cut the handle off your toothbrush.

More stuff you can leave at home:

- Soap
- Shaving kit
- Wristwatch
- Wallet
- Jewelry
- Toilet paper

MAPS
A good map, like a good novel, tells a good story

For hiking, you want a topographical map, a one-dimensional spread of paper that tells a three-dimensional story about the ups and downs of the land. If you plan no cross-country, off-trail hiking, you can get by with casual map reading. The casual map-reader has a general idea of north and can orient a map, pointing the top of the map close to north. With a map oriented, you can see your direction of travel, find topographical features such as cliffs and peaks, know approximately where you are on the trail (if you have been referring to the map often enough), and know which way to turn at unmarked trail junctions.

Swirling across the topographical map are contour lines

Contour Lines

Small circular contour lines indicate the summits of peaks.

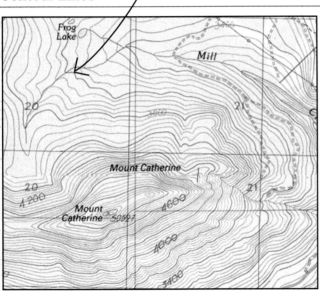

- Contour lines on a topographical map indicate the elevation above sea level and "show" you the shape of the land.

- Contour lines connect points of equal elevation. The distance between any two contour lines is called the "contour interval."

- Darker brown contour lines have the elevation printed on them at some place on the map.

- Lighter brown lines between the darker lines break the elevation and terrain down into even more detail.

Water on Maps

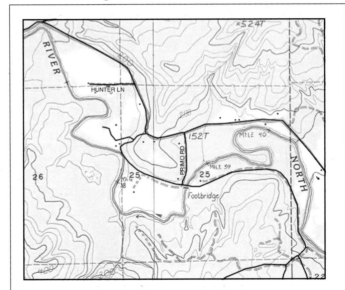

- Blue on topographical maps indicates water: rivers, creeks, streams, lakes, ponds, ice—even contour lines on glaciers.

- A thick blue line indicates a year-round flow of water, or at least water that almost always flows year-round.

- A thin blue line indicates a seasonal flow of water, most often running in spring and early summer.

- Old maps sometimes show seasonal streams as a dotted blue line.

connecting points of equal elevation. The spaces between contour lines are called "contour intervals," and they tell you the vertical distance between the contour lines. On every fifth contour line, printed in a darker color, you can find a number telling you the actual elevation above sea level the line represents.

But keep in mind that the vertical distance between contour lines is not the same on all maps. If 500 feet separate two darker lines, as an example, and four lighter lines stand between the darker lines, separating the space between the darker lines into five sections, then the contour interval for that map is 100 feet. Contour intervals may be as short as 10 feet. Maps with small contour intervals show greater detail than maps with large contour intervals.

On all maps, however, contour lines close together represent steep terrain, and lines very close together represent cliffs. The summits of peaks show as small circular lines, and they're often labeled as to exact elevation. Contour lines far apart represent terrain that gains elevation gently. Sections of maps with no contour lines represent flat land.

Trails on Maps

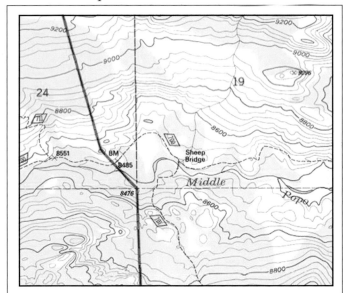

- Trails are shown as black lines, usually dotted. By noting the contour lines over which a trail crosses, you can see if your hike will gain or lose elevation.

- If you see a double-dotted black line, you are looking at a rough road, four-wheel-drive recommended.

- Solid double black lines mean the road is more substantial.

- Boundary lines are often black lines, although newer maps show wilderness boundaries in red.

Vegetation on Maps

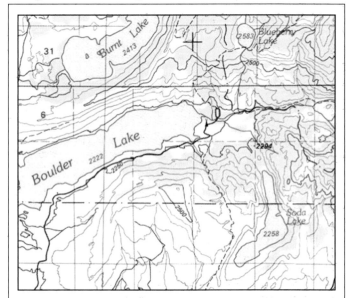

- Green on topographical maps indicates vegetation.

- A solid green area indicates a forest. The density of the forest, how close the trees are to each other, can vary greatly. You won't know until you get there unless you ask someone first.

- A patchwork of green shows you scrub, likely shrubs and/or low bushes.

- White areas indicate the absence of vegetation. It could be sand or ice, but grassy meadows are usually shown in white as well.

COMPASS

There are numerous models, but one will be just right for you

All compasses serve the same basic purposes: They tell you direction, help you decide on a route, and aid you in staying on the route.

Your compass needs to have a rotating component, called a "bezel," and the dial on the bezel will be divided into 360 degrees, the degrees in a full circle, in 2-degree graduations. The bezel is set in a base plate that does not rotate, and the base plate should be clear—you can see through it. The base plate should have at least one line, called the "direction arrow," and it will point in the direction you will hike when navigating with a compass. There will be a needle in a fluid-filled capsule. The fluid slows down movement and prevents unnecessary movement. One end of the needle is red or orange, and the other end is white or black. The bright end

Simple Compass

- You will not need an expensive compass, but it should have a rotating dial with the 360 degrees of a circle marked on it.

- It should have a clear base plate, one that you can easily see through.

- The needle should rotate freely inside of a fluid-filled capsule.

- There should be a direction-of-travel arrow on the base plate. This arrow will point you in the direction you want to travel when following a compass bearing.

Compass with Sighting Mirror

- For more accuracy, choose a compass with a sighting mirror.

- You hold this compass up at eye level, line up your chosen landmark (say, a peak) in the notch at the top of the mirror, and read the bearing in the mirror without moving the compass.

- With a simple compass, you anticipate about 5 degrees of error. With a sighting mirror, the degree of error drops to about 2.

- The 3 degrees of error difference are inconsequential to most backpackers.

of the needle points, more or less, always toward magnetic north, not true north.

True north is a line pointing toward the North Pole. Magnetic north, where the compass needle is pulled by Earth's magnetic field, is located below the North Pole. The difference between true north and magnetic north is known as "declination," a fact that matters only when more precise navigation skills are required (more on that below).

A bearing is one of the 360 degree directions of the compass, and they are always taken clockwise from magnetic north, which is at 0 and 360 degrees. That puts east at 90 degrees, south at 180 degrees, and west at 270 degrees. Accurate maps are extremely important, but a compass can be a bit off. A four-degree error in a compass, for instance, will put you 368 feet off a straight line after 1 mile. That degree of error is insignificant to the average hiker, so you don't need an expensive compass.

Declination

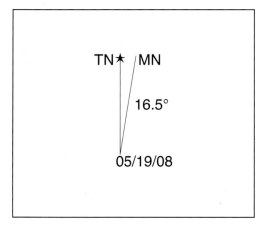

- The difference between north at the top of your map and north as indicated by the compass needle is known as "declination."

- This difference is noted at the bottom of USGS topographic maps, as pictured.

- If the magnetic north is on the left of true north, you are west of true north, and you add the declination to find a true compass bearing.

- If magnetic north is on the right, you are east, and you subtract the declination.

Sighting a Compass

- "Sighting" with a compass means pointing the direction arrow on the base plate at a distant landmark you want to hike to or at least toward.

- With a simple compass, hold the compass flat at about waist level.

- Rotate the entire compass until the direction arrow is pointing at the landmark.

- With a sighting mirror, as mentioned earlier, you hold the compass at eye level and line up the landmark in the notch at the top of the mirror.

ORIENTING MAP AND COMPASS

Both map and compass must be oriented in the same direction to maximize their usefulness

First, orienting a map and compass provides little practical advantage unless you know roughly where you are on the map. You will know this if you have been paying attention to the map and your surroundings since starting on the trail.

Then you need to orient the map accurately to north. Arrows on the map itself will point the direction of true north and magnetic north relative to the map. Your job is to hold the map flat with the arrow on the map pointed to true north. Do this by laying your compass on the map with the long side of the compass aligned with the arrow indicating magnetic north on the map. Be sure the north-south lines and the arrow of the rotating dial on the compass point in

The Lay of the Land

- You need to know approximately where you are on your map.

- The only way to do this is to refer often to your map as you hike.

- Note the lay of the land. You'll know when you cross

a stream on the map, pass a meadow, find a junction of trails, or spot a distant peak.

- To match the lay of the land precisely to the map, you need to orient the map to north.

Finding North

- Hold your compass flat and rotate the dial until the needle is inside the north-south indicator (the orienting arrow), which is a part of the base plate.

- If you are west of true north, rotate the dial to the right, adding the number of degrees of declination.

- If you are east of true north, rotate the dial to the left, subtracting the degrees.

- Now your compass points precisely to north when the needle is in the orienting arrow.

the same direction as the base plate's direction arrow. Now you have all the lines—the map's magnetic north line, the north-south line on the compass, the arrow on the dial of the compass—pointing the same way. Then rotate the compass and map together until the red half of the needle sits squarely inside the faceplate arrow. Your map is now accurately oriented to north.

Once the map is oriented, the terrain features such as ridges, peaks, and cliffs that you see on the map lie in the same places relative to your position on the map as those features actually lie in relation to where you are actually standing. Now you can decide exactly where you are on the trail. When you know exactly where you are, you can figure out exactly how far you have to go to reach your destination, and in what direction.

If you are hiking off-trail (see page 104), you are ready to take a compass bearing (see below) and head out.

NAVIGATION

Orienting the Map

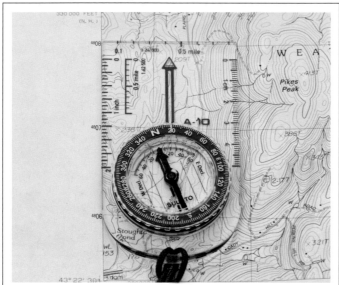

- The edges of your map are aligned with true north in relation to what is depicted on the map.

- Lay the compass on the map. Align the edge of the base plate with the printed edge of the map and hold it firmly there.

- Rotate map and compass until the needle is inside the orienting arrow.

- Your map is now oriented precisely to north. The lay of the land you see will match the map.

Taking a compass bearing:

Hold compass flat.

Point direction arrow.

Rotate dial.

Read bearing.

Hike.

- Hold your compass level and point the direction arrow on the base plate at the distant landmark you are headed for.

- Rotate the dial until the colored end of the needle lies inside the north-south (orienting) arrow of the compass.

- You can now read your bearing at the index line on the center of the base plate.

- When the needle is inside the orienting arrow on the base plate, the direction arrow will point the direction you should hike.

ALTIMETERS

These tools will help you know your exact elevation at any given moment

As an aid to navigation, an altimeter can come in very handy. It tells you your altitude, your elevation above sea level at the point you are standing. It does this by measuring barometric pressure and converting it into an elevation reading. As you climb up in elevation, the barometric pressure falls, and the change is reported on the face of the altimeter. If you sort of

know where you are on a topographical map, and you know your exact altitude, you can find the point on the contour lines on the map that matches your altitude—and you know exactly where you are. You can then see exactly how far you have to go to reach your destination, or if you hiked past the spot you're looking for.

Elevation on the Map

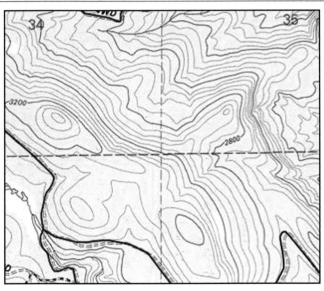

- The contour lines on a topographical map, remember, connect points of equal elevation.

- And the darker brown contour lines have a number on them that tells you the exact elevation of the points connected by that line.

- The light brown lines connect points of equal elevation between the dark brown lines.

- If you know your exact elevation, you can find your exact location on the map—or at least very close to exact.

Altimeter

- An altimeter is a device that tells you the elevation at the point where you are standing.

- To work for you, an altimeter should tell you elevation in increments of no more than 50 feet.

- The altimeter should register elevation to within 100 feet of precisely accurate.

- This mechanical altimeter is more accurate but less durable than an electric altimeter; electric devices are easier to read.

Altimeters, however, vary in their reliability. The incremental readings they give, for instance, may be far apart. You want an altimeter with increments of 50 feet or less, and you want it to be accurate to within 100 feet. And if yours does not compensate for changes in temperature, a sharp rise or drop in temp will alter the reading.

You'll have a choice, also, of a mechanical device or an electronic one. Mechanical altimeters have a needle that points at a number on a dial. They are more accurate but less du-rable. Electronic altimeters are easier to read (the altitude is displayed on a screen), but they require batteries that could fail. In most cases, a mechanical device is a better choice.

And because altimeters respond to barometric changes, you can sometimes stand still and watch your altitude rise or fall when a weather front passes. You need to learn how to recalibrate your altimeter, something you can do when you're at a known point on the map that gives you an exact elevation.

GPS

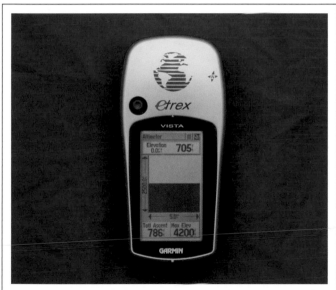

- A global positioning system (GPS) unit will tell you your elevation, displaying it on a screen as pictured.

- Unlike an altimeter, a GPS unit will not be affected by temperature changes and barometric pressure changes.

- A GPS unit, therefore, does not need to be recalibrated to account for temperature and pressure changes.

- GPS units typically cost quite a bit more than altimeters.

Altimeter Used as a Barometer

- An altimeter reads relative changes in barometric pressure to determine elevation and can therefore help you predict changes in the weather.

- If you are stationary for several hours, and your altimeter says you are dropping in elevation, a high pressure system in coming in with good weather.

- A drop in barometric pressure shows as a rise in elevation and says a low pressure system is coming in with deterioration in weather.

- Your predictions, however, will be guesses.

NAVIGATION

GPS

You can know exactly where you are with the push of a button

Here the backcountry hiker meets technology of the most advanced kind: the global positioning system. Thanks to the United States government, a network of twenty-four satellites circling the Earth twice every day sends signals picked up by a GPS receiver, a device that will fit neatly into your pocket. The receiver measures the interval between when the signal was sent and when it was received, and it determines the distance between you and the satellite. When three satellites are accessible, the receiver triangulates the messages and tells you exactly where you are, your location—latitude and longitude—appearing on a little screen. If four satellites are accessible, and four usually are, you will also know your elevation above sea level.

A basic GPS receiver will give you a fix on your position

GPS

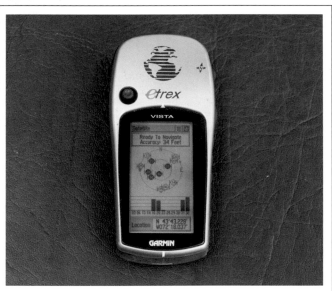

- A global positioning system (GPS) works by picking up satellite signals and translating them into information about your position.

- Receive signals from three satellites simultaneously, and the GPS unit will tell you your latitude and longitude.

- Add the signal from a fourth satellite, and you get your elevation as well.

- GPS units work only as long as the batteries work. If you will depend on the unit, pack an extra set of batteries.

Using the GPS

- GPS units are not affected by rising heat (unless it gets really hot) or any changes in the weather.

- They do not require any calibration or fiddling of any sort by you.

- They work almost instantly, giving you the information

- you want within seconds of being turned on.

- It will, however, require some time for you to learn how to operate the GPS unit of your choice. Detailed instructions are included.

within seconds, and that may be all you need. And it will do its job without any help from you. Some GPS receivers can tell you what map quadrant you're on and help you find your precise location on the map. Depending on the model you choose, a GPS receiver may be able to store hundreds of locations, report the distance you've hiked and your average hiking speed, and even point you in the direction you wish to go if you have programmed that location in earlier.

The system will work twenty-four hours a day, despite the worst weather, including a blinding fog, and in most landscapes (although some land features may temporarily block the signals). You will, however, need to read the instruction book carefully and practice to master the wonders of the global positioning system. On the downside, they require batteries (that, of course, can die), and, although they are becoming more affordable, a GPS receiver will be relatively expensive.

Relating the GPS to the Map

- Knowing your latitude and longitude will be useless information, of course, unless you have a detailed map that allows you to plot the numbers to find where you are.

- You also need to be able to use the map to find a route to your destination.

- More sophisticated GPS units, however, will tell you much more, including the names of map quadrants and measurements that help you find your location.

- The more sophisticated the unit, the more you will have to pay.

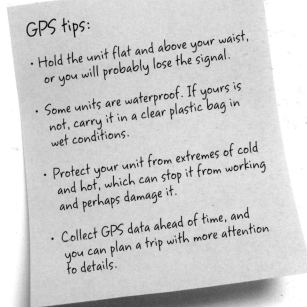

GPS tips:

- Hold the unit flat and above your waist, or you will probably lose the signal.

- Some units are waterproof. If yours is not, carry it in a clear plastic bag in wet conditions.

- Protect your unit from extremes of cold and hot, which can stop it from working and perhaps damage it.

- Collect GPS data ahead of time, and you can plan a trip with more attention to details.

GETTING FOUND
Do not assume that getting lost always happens to other people

Even the most experienced hikers run the risk of getting lost. If you do, how you act will add or subtract from getting found.

This is worth repeating: Be sure to tell someone where you are going and when you expect to return. And tell that someone to initiate a search if you do not return on time.

If you become disoriented, sit down, admit that you are not sure where you are, and evaluate your circumstances as calmly as possible. It is critically important to avoid panic, your greatest enemy. Mentally retrace your steps. You will probably realize your situation is not as serious as it seemed at first.

Avoid unnecessary movement; it will burn up essential energy, and wandering might take you out of the area in which

Marking Your Route

- As soon as you realize you are lost, sit down, relax, and think through your situation.

- Do not panic.

- If you realize you know where you are, mark your path with arrows of sticks or rocks on the ground or arrows drawn deeply in soft soil. If you need to, you can follow them back, or searchers can use them to help locate you.

- As soon as you realize you'll be out overnight, begin to prepare for it.

Rest Often

- If you move, hike slowly and thoughtfully. Do not waste precious energy rushing through the wilderness.

- Rest often, sitting down without your pack on your back.

- If you are setting up an improvised camp for the night, first take stock of everything you have with you. You could be in a better position than you first thought. During camp setup, rest often.

- The energy you conserve might well be the energy that keeps you alive.

the search for you will take place. Empty the contents of your pack and pockets, and inventory what you have with you. If you packed thoughtfully, you will have what you need.

As soon as it seems as if you'll be out overnight, seek shelter. If you have a tent, pitch it while the sun shines. Without shelter, your chance of surviving an unexpected night out is minimal in many environments. If there is nothing else available, bury yourself in leaves, pine needles, or other forest debris. In snow, burrow a hole just big enough for your body. The smaller a shelter, the more easily it is heated by your body.

Find water. Your body will suffer first from exposure and second from lack of water. Water is required for mental and physical energy.

Signal your position. Bright fires at night and smoky fires during the day may alert searchers. Sets of three signals are a universal appeal for help: three fires, three blasts on a whistle, three flashes from a signal mirror.

Fire

- A fire can be psychologically as well as physiologically beneficial. It will boost your spirit as well as protect you from dangerous loss of body heat.

- A fire can also be a signal to searchers—smoke by day, light by night.

- Gather plenty of firewood in daylight so you can keep the fire going through the night.

- Build your fire safely. Out of control, it could be the thing that destroys you.

- The Ten Essentials have been proven worthy by years of use.

- On day hikes or backpacking trips, you should always have them with you.

- You should also know how to best use the Ten Essentials.

HOW TO WALK
Walking on a trail is not the same as walking on a street

Along a street, on a sidewalk, even crossing your front yard, you walk, most of the time, unconsciously—you don't have to think about it. On the trail, your mind needs to spend a lot of the time with your feet.

Every trip, slip, and fall will waste valuable energy and increase the risk of injury. By paying attention to where your feet will land, you can avoid most stumbles. This doesn't mean you'll never see the scenery. You will learn to divide your attention between the vistas and the rocks on the trail.

Walking for most people involves landing first on their heels, which is fine on flat ground. On rougher terrain, learn to land more flat-footed, which will reduce strain on your feet, reduce soreness, and keep you better balanced. A flat-footed stride is easier when you take shorter steps, and shorter steps

Watch Your Feet

- A trail is not a sidewalk. You need to pay attention to where your feet will land next.

- Avoid stepping on rocks, pieces of wood, mounds of soft soil, or anything that could slip or roll out from under your feet, causing you to stumble or fall.

- Avoid stepping on mosses or other delicate trailside plants.

- Your shoe should land flat, firmly gripping the ground, without tipping one way or the other.

Pace Yourself

- It's a hike, not a race. You want to arrive at your campsite with plenty of energy. Walk at a pace that does not require panting.

- If you can't walk and talk, you are walking too fast.

- A hiker should seldom be challenged to keep up. In a group, the pace should be set by the slowest hiker.

- Rest breaks are not a sign of weakness; they are a sign of wisdom.

require less energy than a long stride. And a flat-footed step causes less impact on the land.

Conserve your energy by moderating your speed. Your breathing, the best aid in determining your pace, should be deep and regular, not shallow and fast. As another indication of an appropriate pace, take the "talk test." If you can hike and maintain a conversation, you are hiking at an acceptable pace for your level of fitness. If you cannot talk and hike at the same time, you are walking too fast, using too much energy, and upping the chance of an accident.

Clothes can add to or take away from efficient walking. What you want is freedom of movement. Clothes that restrict your movement not only decrease comfort but also increase your workload. Your choice of pants is particularly important. Generally, the lightest and loosest pants offer the most energy conservation.

Trekking Poles

- Trekking poles (hiking staffs, ski poles)—one or two—greatly benefit almost everyone who uses them.

- They give you better balance on the trail. There is less chance of incurring an injury, including blisters from your shoes slipping and then your feet rubbing against the inside your shoes. They reduce the energy required to hike.

- They ease the stress on joints including hips, knees, ankles, and shoulders. You will also arrive less sore.

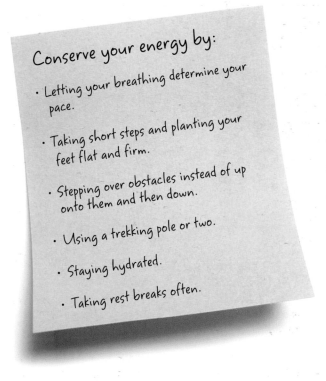

Conserve your energy by:

- Letting your breathing determine your pace.

- Taking short steps and planting your feet flat and firm.

- Stepping over obstacles instead of up onto them and then down.

- Using a trekking pole or two.

- Staying hydrated.

- Taking rest breaks often.

FOLLOWING TRAILS

Staying on a maintained trail is not always as easy as it sounds

Many hikers, probably most of them, start out at Point A and end up at Point B, following a trail without any problems. But sometimes it isn't all that easy.

Trails may, for instance, join other trails, and the trail you want may not be marked with signs. Side trails, created unofficially by users and not by trail makers, often lead in the wrong direction. Unofficial side trails may be heavily used, causing you to think you are on the correct path. The answer lies in carrying an accurate map and paying attention to where you are on it (see page 88).

When you can clearly see the trail, stay on it. It has been built by knowledgeable trail builders who have chosen the

KNACK HIKING & BACKPACKING

Following a Map

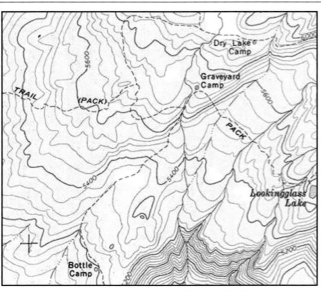

- Trails are not always easy to follow. Your best aid is an accurate map, one that has been updated as recently as possible.

- Topographical maps that cover a small area with a lot of details are the best maps to choose.

- When trails divide, signs do not always tell you which way to go—a map does.

- Refer to your map often so you always know approximately where you are on it.

Well-Maintained Trail

- Well-maintained trails are designed and built by knowledgeable trail makers. They may not be the shortest route, but they are best for your safety and best for the environment.

- Well-maintained trails are easy to see.

- As long as you can see the trail, stay on it, except for the times you step off for a rest break.

- Avoid shortcuts. They almost always require more energy, and they always harm the environment.

path of least resistance and/or the path that is best for the land. What looks like a shortcut may not be one, and, even if it is, shortcuts most often harm the environment.

Sometimes you cannot clearly see the trail. Trails may cross large expanses of bare rock or gravel. In this case, look for cairns, small rock towers marking the path. If cairns are not visible, leave one person on the known trail while the rest of the group searches for the trail's continuation.

Wind or other natural events may drop trees across a trail.

Lingering snowbanks or snowfields can block a trail. If you can see the trail beyond the obstacles, you are good to go. But if you can't, once again leave someone on the trail while others search.

On trails that see little use and little maintenance, the path can disappear. Standing at the last point where the trail is visible, an accurate map can help you choose the direction to go. And, yet again, leave someone . . . well, you know the rest.

Obstacles on the Trail

- Obstacles, such as fallen trees, drifts of old snow, landslides, and rockslides, sometimes block a trail.

- If you can see the trail beyond the obstacle, work your way around and continue.

- If you cannot see the trail beyond the obstacle, leave someone on the trail while others search for where it continues.

- If the obstacle proves insurmountable, the best plan, usually, is to turn back.

Indistinct Trail

- Trails that are not well maintained sometimes become indistinct or, worse, disappear.

- Trail makers often mark a trail's route prior to building it by pinning small signs to trees or cutting blazes into trees. Look for and follow those.

- If you must search for the continuation of the trail, once again leave someone on the trail until you find where it continues.

- This is another example of when an accurate map could be indispensable.

HIKING OFF-TRAIL

When you leave the trail, you will need to follow a compass bearing

For a short distance, you may find your off-trail destination without a compass. In most cases, you will need to take an accurate compass bearing and follow it. First, you will need to orient your map and compass (see page 92).

Now set the compass on the map with the base plate's direction arrow lined up between where you are on the map and where you want to go.

Rotate the dial until the colored end of the needle is inside the north-south arrow on the faceplate, and the needle and north-south arrow are pointing in the same direction. The north-south arrow on the faceplate of the compass is now pointing to magnetic north. And now you can put the map away.

With the compass held flat in your hand, the base plate di-

Using a Map Off-Trail

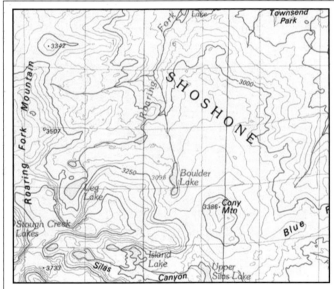

- When you hike off-trail a map is necessary to get where you want to go.

- If the distance is short, you may find your destination using only the map as a guide.

- Before you step off-trail, look for obvious natural features—a river, stream, peak, or cliff—that are on the map and visible from your location.

- Hike toward the natural feature, keeping it in sight at all times until you reach your destination.

Using a Compass Off-Trail

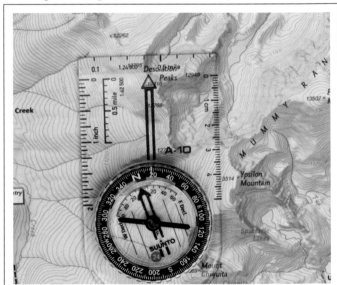

- Without natural features to keep in sight, you will need to use a compass.

- Begin by accounting for the declination on your compass and then orienting your map to north.

- Orient your map by holding your compass flat in your

hand. The needle will point north.

- Lay out your map with the top of the map, which is drawn with north at the top, pointing in the same direction your compass needle points.

rection arrow will point you toward your destination while you walk, provided you keep the north-south arrow on the face plate pointing to magnetic north.

When you are following a bearing, you may run into an insurmountable obstacle such as a cliff. You need to get around it and back on your bearing—and this is not that big a deal. Start by noting the compass bearing of the direction you have to travel to get around the obstacle. As you travel in that new direction, count your steps or otherwise guess at the distance you are hiking. Once past the obstacle, reverse the distance you traveled off-course, following the exact reverse bearing to the direction you just walked off-course. If, for instance, you walked east (a bearing of 90) to get past the obstacle, you will walk back west (a bearing of 270) to get back to your original line of travel. Now you can return to following your original bearing to reach your destination.

Compass Bearing to Destination

- With your map held firmly oriented to north, set your compass on your map.

- Line up the direction arrow on the base plate of the compass so that it points from where you are on the map to where you want to go on the map.

- Rotate the dial of your compass until the colored end of the needle is inside the north-south arrow of the compass.

- Now you can put away the map.

Following the Compass Bearing

- Hold the compass flat in your hand.

- As long as you keep the needle inside the north-south arrow of your compass, the direction arrow on the base plate will point the direction you should hike.

- To save staring at the compass all the time, line up the compass with your bearing and find a prominent landmark along your route—such as a tall tree or nearby peak.

- Hike to that landmark and use your compass to find the next landmark.

ON STEEP TERRAIN

When the terrain goes steeply up or down, alter how you walk

When your route takes you up and down, you will save energy if you change how you walk. The shortest distance between two points may be a straight line, but going straight up a hillside is extremely tiring. On maintained trails you will most often find "switchbacks" on steep terrain, sharp turns back and forth across the fall line. When you hike off-trail on steep terrain, follow a similar switchback pattern, zigzagging

back and forth. Switchbacking makes for longer travel time, but it conserves the most energy.

With no trail, and as you traverse, you can reduce fatigue even more by "sidehill-gouging" as you ascend or descend a hillside. Instead of placing your foot flat on the angle of the ground, which rolls your ankle downhill, kick your foot slightly into the ground to create a partial platform to step on. It takes

Switchbacks

- Trail makers do not build trails that go straight up and down a steep slope.

- Trails that make sharp turns back and forth across the face of a slope are called "switchbacks."

- Switchbacks cause you to hike a longer distance, but

they require less energy, so off-trail you are wise to ascend a steep slope in switchback fashion.

- Switchbacks, despite the longer distance, cause less environmental damage because straight downhill trails channel water, causing erosion.

Take Short Steps

- It takes less energy to climb a flight of stairs one at a time than two at a time.

- It takes less energy to ascend a steep slope taking short steps.

- Likewise, taking short steps going downhill requires less

use of your muscles than taking long steps.

- Short downhill steps cause less stress on your joints. You reduce the chance of injury from a fall or overuse of body parts.

far less energy to walk with your ankles straight. If you are wearing fairly stiff-soled boots, sidehill-gouging tends to be more successful.

As mentioned previously, shorter strides require less effort, and this is especially true on steep ground. It takes more energy to climb stairs taking two steps at a time. It takes more energy to climb hills with long strides than short strides.

MAKE IT EASY

All uphill trails lead eventually to downhill trails, and going downhill increases abuse to your body. Knees crunch under the impact, ankles may twist, muscles and tendons and ligaments get loads of stress. The answer: Take shorter steps. They are less stressful on joints and muscles than long downhill steps.

The Rest-Step

- On very steep slopes, the rest-step provides the most energy-efficient form of ascent. It is a technique used by high-altitude mountain climbers.

- Straighten and bear your body weight on one leg.

- Plant your other foot uphill while maintaining your body weight ("resting") on the downhill leg.

- Step up and shift your body weight to the new downhill leg, and rest on that leg for a moment while you plant the other foot uphill.

Cutoffs

- A "cutoff" is a trail created by use, not by trail makers, that connects two segments of a switchback.

- Hikers of the past, in other words, grew tired of following the longer distance of a switchback and made a shortcut, probably while descending.

- Cutoffs add another scar on the landscape and inevitably lead to erosion, which scars the land even more.

- Do not use cutoffs.

ON ROCKY TERRAIN

Rocks ranging from very large to very small may separate you and your destination

When you travel on foot in the mountains, rocks of all sizes might cover the ground you want to cross. On relatively flat terrain, rocks might slow you down, but they won't be a problem unless the rocks are boulders, a name reserved for large rocks. Boulder fields will require you to choose the path of least resistance, crossing the most flat and smaller boulders, avoiding the route that necessitates precarious climbing.

On steep terrain, all rocks are problematic. When you climb up steep, rocky terrain, you should, once again, seek the path of least resistance. If you find yourself looking for handholds as well as footholds in the uphill battle, test every hold before

Steep Boulder Field

- Boulders, in this context, are large rocks.

- You should cross fields of boulders slowly and cautiously, testing first the next boulder to be sure it won't shift when you throw your weight onto it.

- Choose the path of least resistance, looking for the flattest and smallest boulders to step on.

- If you are uncomfortable ascending a boulder field, you will find descent even more problematic—so you are wise to find another route up.

Talus

- Medium-sized rocks covering a steep slope are called "talus."

- Talus will almost always shift when you step on it.

- Ascend or descend slowly, stepping on the tops of the rocks and not between them.

- If you see lichen growing on one of these rocks, it indicates that rock has not shifted for a long time. As tempting as it is, please do not step on the lichen. There might be room for your foot beside the lichen.

you rely on it. Pull or kick down to see if the rock shifts. Large, loose rocks should be avoided whenever possible.

When you are descending steep rocks, and you feel unsafe standing, face away from the slope and climb down like a crab, using your buttocks for friction. If the descent steepens even more, face sideways to the slope. This allows a good view of holds and the route below. When the route is nearly vertical, face directly into the cliff, as if you were climbing down a ladder. Or find another route.

•••••••••••••••••• RED ● LIGHT ••••••••••••••

On steep rocks, scrambling upward is safer and less awkward than climbing down. If you are comfortable going up, keep going—unless you will need to climb down the same route you ascended. If you do not think you can comfortably and safely descend, find another way up.

Scree

- Small rocks, sometimes mixed with loose dirt, covering a steep slope are called "scree."

- There is little risk from going up or down a scree slope.

- Going up is laborious because every step up involves a partial slip downhill. For maximum efficiency, kick-step up, ramming your toe into the slope.

- You can plunge-step going downhill by taking long strides and plunging your downhill heel into the slope. This involves a possible risk to your knees.

Classifications of steep terrain:

- Class 1: An easy trail

- Class 2: Rough terrain. You may reach out a hand to grab a boulder for balance.

- Class 3: You use both your hands for balance and perhaps to help pull yourself higher.

- Class 4–6: You should be relying on climbing gear such as a rope, harness, helmet, and climbing hardware.

TRAVELING BY FOOT

ON SNOW

In the mountains, even the best of summer routes could involve crossing snow

If you travel high enough into mountains, even in summer, you will find snow, and you might have to cross it. Although crossing snow could be no problem at all, it might be. Several steps can be taken to make travel easier and safer.

In spring, the snow you find, even when deep, can often be easily crossed on its frozen surface without snowshoes or skis if you travel early in the morning, before the sun softens the white stuff. If the snow is already soft, look for a route along the edge where it is usually shallower, or in shade where the rising warmth of the day takes longer to soften the snow.

The snow of summer is almost always old and therefore often hard. Slopes covered in summer snow are most easily

Crossing Snow

- In high country, you might have to cross snow any month of the year.

- Snow will be the firmest early in the morning, so you sink into it less and cross more easily.

- If the snow is soft, crossing close to the edge of a snowfield is usually better because the snow will be shallower there.

- If part of the snowfield lies in shadow, that part will be the firmest.

Crossing Steep Snow

- To ascend a steep snow-field, use the kick-step.

- Kick your uphill boot into the snow until you have created a platform at least half the width of your footwear. On softer snow, you can kick directly into the slope with your toe. On harder snow, you will have to kick your foot sideways into the slope.

- Step gently up onto that platform, keeping your weight toward the slope and not downhill.

- Repeat this process until you reach the top.

crossed in stiff-soled boots and a travel technique known as kick-stepping. Stand up straight to reduce the chance of slipping. Take short steps, and kick each booted foot firmly into the slope until you have a platform to stand on that is at least half the width of your boot. Step up onto the platform gently, pressuring your uphill boot edge. Then kick the next step.

Snow that has melted and refrozen can be icy and treacherously slick. Always note the runout, the area you will slide into if you cannot stop soon enough from a slip. If it looks dangerous, a cliff or a field of sharp rocks, for instance, your best bet is to find another route.

Descending steep snow can be fun if the runout is safe. You can, as an example, glissade. To glissade, point your toes downhill and shuffle along in a sort of skiing motion. If your balance is good, you can glissade down long distances in a short time, using very little energy.

Post-holing

- When there is nothing to do but cross deep, soft snow, you may end up "post-holing."

- When you post-hole, you sink into the snow up to your knees or higher with each step.

- Keep your weight on your back leg, step halfway into your next step, and wait a few moments for the snow to firm up a bit.

- In the end, you will find nothing pleasant about post-holing.

Runout

- Snow that is steep, hard, icy, and therefore slippery poses a threat that can be fatal if you take a slide.

- The greatest danger comes from the runout, the area that lies immediately below the snow slope.

- Large rocks, sharp rocks, and cliffs that drop off steeply are obviously dangerous runouts.

- If the runout is not safe, do not ascend or descend a steep snow slope without technical equipment and know-how.

BEACH HIKING
The world of ebb and flow offers a whole new realm of hiking

In addition to a whole new world of enjoyment, hiking a beach brings a whole new set of challenges. A mile walk inland could take you to dry heat, but beach hikers need to be prepared for cool, moist, and windy conditions at any time, with sand, pebbles, mudflats, or expanses of driftwood underfoot. The clothing you pack should reflect the possibility of a dramatic change in the environment. And your footwear should be chosen with the understanding that your feet will probably get wet.

Sand, the element of beaches, can vary from firm to soft, but all sand tends to slow you down, adding to the hours it takes to reach your destination.

Without a tide table, you could be stranded for hours.

The Surface of Beaches

- Beach backpacking opens a wondrous new world to those who haven't tried it.

- Sand is not all created equal. It can vary from very soft, where the hiking is slow, to firm, where the hiking is relatively easy.

- You may have to cross pebbles, mudflats, or expanses of driftwood. In all cases it usually takes longer than you think to make a mile.

- As the tide ebbs, tide pools may reveal a myriad of fascinating life-forms.

Tide Table

DATE	TIME	HIGH TIDE HT (ft)	TIME	HT (ft)	LOW TIDE TIME	HT (ft)	TIME	HT (ft)
1 T	12:15	7.4	11:03	9.3	5:11	3.6	6:04	-0.7
2 F	12:47	7.6	11:46	9.1	5:56	3.3	6:39	-0.5
3 S	1:18	7.8	12:26	8.8	6:37	3.1	7:11	-0.2
4 S	1:46	7.9	1:05	8.4	7:17	2.8	7:40	0.3
5 M	2:14	8.0	1:45	7.8	7:58	2.6	8:08	0.9
6 T	2:41	8.0	2:27	7.1	8:40	2.5	8:35	1.6
7 W	3:08	8.0	3:14	6.4	9:26	2.3	9:02	2.2
8 T	3:37	8.0	4:12	5.8	10:18	2.2	9:31	2.9
9 F	4:10	7.9	5:30	5.2	11:19	2.0	10:03	3.5
10 S	4:51	7.9	7:16	5.1	12:29	1.7	10:49	4.1
11 S	5:44	7.9	9:00	5.3			1:40	1.3
12 M	6:47	8.0	10:00	5.8	12:06	4.5	2:42	0.8
13 T	7:52	8.3	10:39	6.2	1:38	4.5	3:33	0.2
14 W	8:52	8.8	11:11	6.7	2:51	4.3	4:17	-0.4
15 T	9:46	9.2	11:41	7.2	3:49	3.9	4:57	-0.8
16 F	10:37	9.6			4:39	3.3	5:36	-1.1
17 S	12:12	7.8	11:26	9.7	5:28	2.7	6:12	-1.0
18 S	12:43	8.3	12:15	9.5	6:16	2.0	6:49	-0.7
19 M	1:16	8.8	1:06	9.1	7:05	1.4	7:26	-0.2
20 T	1:50	9.1	1:59	8.3	7:57	0.9	8:03	0.6
21 W	2:26	9.4	2:58	7.5	8:52	0.5	8:42	1.5
22 T	3:06	9.4	4:05	6.6	9:52	0.4	9:24	2.5
23 F	3:51	9.2	5:28	5.9	10:59	0.3	10:14	3.3
24 S	4:44	8.9	7:08	5.7	12:14	0.3	11:21	3.9
25 S	5:49	8.5	8:43	5.9			1:32	0.2
26 M	7:04	8.3	9:49	6.3	12:52	4.2	2:41	0.0
27 T	8:17	8.3	10:34	6.7	2:21	4.1	3:39	-0.2

- Beaches constantly change as the tide ebbs and flows.

- High tide against steep cliffs may make forward progress impossible—and/or retreat impossible.

- Beach hikers should carry a local tide table. It tells the times and heights of every low and high tide for every day of the year for the beach you're hiking on.

- Without a tide table, you could be stranded or, much worse, washed out to sea.

And the amount of sand you have to walk on constantly varies as the sea ebbs and flows. You must carry a local tide table and adhere to its advice. Many a beach hiker has ended up high on rocks waiting for the tide to go out and hoping a rogue wave did not drag him or her off.

When hiking near the water, do not turn your back on the sea. You don't want the unusually large wave washing into you or, worse, washing you out to sea.

It is best for the environment if you spend as much time as possible in the intertidal zone, the region between high and low tides. It is probably the most durable hiking surface in the world (see page 138). Above the high tide mark, you'll find dunes and backshore regions that are fragile and easily damaged.

You should, however, set your camp above the high tide line. It would be most unpleasant to wake up in water.

High Tide Mark

- The high tide mark is the visible evidence—usually debris washed up by the sea—of where the last highest tide reached.

- The intertidal zone, the beach between the edge of the sea and the high tide mark, is probably the most

- durable hiking surface in the world.

- One of the most fragile environments in the world often lies above the high tide mark on unspoiled beaches.

- Stay below the high tide mark whenever possible when hiking.

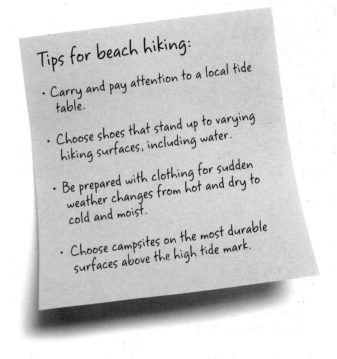

Tips for beach hiking:

- Carry and pay attention to a local tide table.

- Choose shoes that stand up to varying hiking surfaces, including water.

- Be prepared with clothing for sudden weather changes from hot and dry to cold and moist.

- Choose campsites on the most durable surfaces above the high tide mark.

CROSSING RIVERS

If you have to cross moving water, do it as safely as possible facing upstream

There are risks in crossing moving water, but sometimes you have to get to the other side.

Before forging ahead, step in slowly and assess the power of the flow. A strong current only calf-deep can throw you face down. There will be quieter water up or down the river.

A narrow channel may look like an easy crossing point, but a wide, smooth flow is usually easier to traverse. Avoid the outside of a bend in a river where the current tends to run deepest and strongest.

A smooth-flowing surface usually means the bottom of the river is relatively smooth. Cross there instead of where the surface boils due to underlying rocks.

Scouting the Crossing

- Do not assume that the point where you meet a river is the best place to cross.

- Scout up and down the river before choosing a crossing point.

- When you have chosen a crossing point, scout down-river from that point before crossing as well.

- If you end up swimming, you don't want to swim into rapids or over a waterfall. A crossing point is not safe if it is not safe below that point.

Crossing Alone

- Unbuckle your pack's hip belt and sternum strap, and loosen the shoulder straps. You need to ditch the pack if you swim.

- Face upstream. Your balance will be better, and you can see objects floating down toward you.

- Use a trekking pole or the limb of a tree as a third leg. You can also probe ahead with it for holes.

- Take short steps, shuffling your feet and feeling ahead with your foot for the surest footing.

Unbuckle your pack's hip belt and sternum strap and loosen the shoulder straps so you can easily get out of the pack if you're swept off your feet.

Face upstream as you cross. Your balance will be better, and you can keep an eye open for debris floating downstream. Find a long stick, or use a trekking pole as a "third leg" for even better balance. Probe ahead with the pole for holes and hidden rocks.

Foot entrapment can be painful as well as fatal. Shuffle your feet instead of taking steps to minimize the risk of entrapment.

•••••••••••••••••• RED●LIGHT ••••••••••••••••
Do not wade into a river barefoot. The risk of foot damage is high, and the risk of foot entrapment increases. Wear your camp shoes, or remove your socks and boot insoles and cross in your boots. Your boots will dry faster if your socks and insoles are not soaked.

Crossing as a Group

- Groups may choose to cross together, weaker members utilizing the strength of stronger ones.

- A group should hold hands, with the strongest hiker in the lead and the second-strongest hiker going last.

- Groups may cross side by side or in tandem, with the strongest hiker upstream blocking some of the current.

- All packs, once again, should be free at hip belt and sternum strap and loose at the shoulders.

Tips for crossing rivers:

- Step in slowly, assessing the power of the flow.

- A smooth surface of the river often means a smooth bottom.

- In a strong current, work downriver, diagonally across, instead of straight across.

- Never tie into a rope before crossing.

- If you fall, ditch your pack; do not try to stand; swim for shore.

TRAVELING BY FOOT

115

CHOOSING A CAMPSITE

The prime directive in campsite selection is choosing a spot free of hazards

A campsite requires a place not only for your tent but also for your kitchen and your bathroom, and, ideally, you have a great view, with a touch of privacy if other campers are nearby. When choosing a spot to settle down for the night, you are wise to remember the old adage: Great campsites are found, not made.

The most important thing you want to find is a safe spot. If, for instance, a thunderstorm is a possibility, do not camp in the open where you could be a lightning target (see page 160). If you see signs that rain runs through or puddles at a site, look for ground at least a bit higher. A great site, in addition to being relatively flat, drains well in rainfall. A thick

(see page 160)

Choose a Safe Site

- The prime directive in campsite selection is choosing a site free of hazards to you and those with you.

- Stay away from the bottoms and tops of steep cliffs. Rocks could fall on you, or you could fall off.

- Avoid tall, isolated trees that could attract lightning, and avoid large open places in thunderstorm season.

- If it's windy or might become windy, find a campsite with natural protection from wind: dense trees, large rocks, the leeward side of ridges.

Choose a Private Site

- A view is nice, but privacy might be preferable if other campers are nearby.

- If an established trail passes near your campsite, try to set camp where other hikers cannot see it from the trail.

- Look for flat ground at least where your tent will set, and be sure the ground will drain in case of rain.

- Set your camp at least 200 feet from your source of water.

covering of forest debris (needles, leaves, etc.) drains well, as do sand and gravel. Compressed soil and soggy or marshy ground do not drain well.

Avoid spots near the top and bottom of cliffs. You could fall off the top in the coming darkness, and, at the bottom, a rock could fall off onto you.

In most cases, you will need a source of water. But to prevent contamination of the source, your site should be at least 200 feet away.

MAKE IT EASY

Always choose a campsite while there is plenty of daylight left. Not many people can set up camp well in the dark. Your efforts will be complicated by the lack of light and by fatigue, and the risk of accident and of harm to the environment increases.

Choose a Durable Site

- Look for a durable surface to set your kitchen, a spot that you won't compress to death with the high traffic a kitchen needs.

- A great site will catch the morning sun, unless it's the season of scorching heat.

- If the night will be cold, avoid low places where colder air collects.

- If you intend to build a fire, check for the availability of down and dead firewood and an acceptable spot to build the fire.

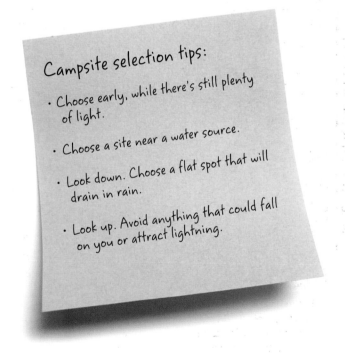

Campsite selection tips:

- Choose early, while there's still plenty of light.

- Choose a site near a water source.

- Look down. Choose a flat spot that will drain in rain.

- Look up. Avoid anything that could fall on you or attract lightning.

SETTING UP CAMP

CHOOSING A TENT SITE
A poor choice of tent site can ruin an otherwise fine campsite

Think about it: You will be in your tent for hours, eight or maybe more. You want your tent site to be as perfect as possible. Experienced campers usually choose a tent site before declaring a campsite acceptable.

You want your tent pitched with the same safety considerations you gave to your campsite, and you want to be sure your site will drain well in case of rain (see page 116). As a

safety bonus, look up. Be sure you don't pitch your shelter under large dead limbs or dead trees that could fall on you in the middle of the night.

Keep using your eyes. Look for ground that seems flat. Once you find a spot, walk around it and look from different directions. A site that at first appears flat might show a fairly severe angle from a different point of view.

Flat Ground

- You will almost always spend a lot of time in your tent, so choose the site thoughtfully.

- You want ground that is flat or close to flat without large, half-buried rocks and tree roots.

- Look at the site from several angles. It might look flat from one perspective but not from another.

- Dead leaves and other debris that collect on the ground under trees can add to your in-tent comfort.

Safe Ground

- As with campsite selection in general, you want a safe tent site.

- Be sure you're not under large dead limbs or standing dead trees that could fall in a wind.

- Tents have been struck by lightning. Set yours away

from lightning attractants and not in a large open area where it could be the attractant.

- If a high wind is possible, set your tent near a windbreak or on the leeward side of a ridge.

But don't rely totally on your eyes. Lie down on the ground or your tent before pitching it. If you detect a slight tilt to your bedroom floor, be sure you orient your shelter to keep your head higher than your feet. Lying down also allows you to find hidden roots and rocks. If surface rocks or logs compete for the otherwise perfect sleeping place, move them, but replace them before you leave if moving them left scars. The next camper does not want to look at ugly bare spots you have left. And future campers will not be encouraged to camp in exactly the same place.

If it feels like a cold night lies ahead, choose a site that is high rather than low. Cold air sinks, keeping the upper end of a valley slightly warmer than the lower end. Select a site, if you can, that will catch the early morning sun, adding warmth to the joy of your own rising.

If Rain Falls

- If there are signs that water has run through or puddled in your site, it will do so again if rain falls. Look for another site.

- A great tent site is on forest debris, sand, or pea gravel that will drain well in a rain.

- It is no longer acceptable to dig trenches around a tent to drain water away.

- Thick grass will recover quickly after a night with a tent on it, but small shrubs and other woody plants will not.

After you've chosen a site:
Change from sweaty clothes into dry clothes.
Change into camp shoes.
Disinfect water for the night and morning.
Pitch tent and fluff up sleeping bag.
Fire up the stove and make dinner.
Store food and gear for the night.

- Dry clothing makes you more comfortable and prevents the loss of body heat.

- Soft camp shoes make your feet comfortable and are easier on the land.

- Water is necessary for health and to keep you functioning at your best.

- You need to fall asleep assured your food is protected from animals and your gear from inclement weather.

PITCHING THE TENT
Setting up your tent should be as easy as one-two-three

With the all-important tent site chosen, you are ready to pitch (set up) your tent. To speak specifically of how to pitch a tent is impossible: Every brand and model pitches at least a bit differently, often in substantially different ways.

Here then is the most critical guideline for tent-pitching: Be comfortable setting up your tent before you hit the trail. You don't want to spend an hour at it on your first night out or,

worse, fail to be able to do it. Every tent comes with instructions for pitching. If you borrowed a tent, you should ask the lender for a quick lesson.

In general, the first step in tent-pitching is to spread out the tent body. With most models, the poles will slip into sleeves in the body. With the poles in their sleeves, the tent sort of "pops" up as you set the pole ends into grommets. Some-

Practice

- Every tent pitches at least a bit differently depending on brand and type.

- If you have purchased a new tent, it came with pitching directions, and you should read them.

- If you borrowed a tent, ask the lender for help setting it up the first time.

- Practice at home. You do not want to learn the idiosyncrasies of pitching a specific tent while you race the setting sun—or, worse, discover you're missing an essential part.

Step 1: Lay It Out

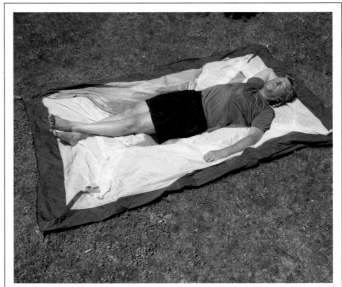

- Before pitching your tent, lay it out flat on your chosen site.

- Lie on it, and roll right and left a couple of times, searching for missed sticks, rocks, pine cones, or roots.

- If there is a slight incline to the site, be sure you'll orient the tent to sleep with your head on the high end.

- If you're using a ground cloth, lie on it instead of the tent.

times the poles will be set in grommets at the corners of the body first, and the tent clipped to the poles.

The fly is the waterproof roof of a tent. A few models come with the fly attached to the body, but most tent flies are set in place after the tent is up. The fly must be set taut to repel water adequately.

MAKE IT EASY

A ground cloth is any waterproof material that sets on the ground. Underneath a tent, it will add a waterproof layer beneath you and reduce abuse to the tent's floor. A ground cloth must not extend beyond the edge of your tent. If it does, rain will collect beneath you.

Step 2: Pitch the Tent

- If your tent has sleeves for the poles, slip all the poles into their proper sleeves.

- "Pop" the tent up by placing the ends of the poles into the proper grommets at the edges of the tent.

- If your tent clips to the poles, place the poles in their proper grommets and clip the tent to the poles.

- With a freestanding tent, you can now move it around to orient it best before pushing in the stakes to draw it tight.

Step 3: Pitch the Fly

- With most tents the fly is a separate piece set up after the main body is pitched taut.

- Most flies attach to the main body of the tent, but some require separate stakes.

- If the fly provides a vestibule, it is the last piece of the tent staked out.

- In all cases, the fly should be made taut to best shed rain and wind and to allow air to circulate between the fly and the main body.

SETTING UP CAMP

KITCHEN AND COOKING TIPS
The kitchen is the heart of a home and the heart of a campsite

Although you spend more time in your tent, you spend more awake time in your kitchen. It tends to be the site of enduring conversations. The kitchen needs to be set up thoughtfully.

If you think your tent site causes the greatest impact on the environment, you are mistaken. It is your kitchen, where people gather to sit, kneel, stand, shift, and shuffle around. That means your kitchen site should be on a durable surface such as rock, sand, gravel, or the forgiving natural litter of a forest floor. Your site could be a short walk from your tent, and that's fine. More than fine in bear country, it could be the best choice. If there are large logs or rocks nearby to serve as seats, so much the better.

When the surface beneath your stove is flammable, you'll need to move the flammable material to the side (to be re-

Kitchen Site

- The kitchen site receives the most abuse in your camp, so it should be chosen with care.

- Choose a spot with a durable surface: a large flat rock, sand, gravel, or soil that has already been heavily compacted by previous campers.

- If you choose to move logs or rocks into the kitchen site for seats, put them back where you got them before leaving the site.

- The kitchen does not need to be near your tent.

Kitchen Setup

- Do not set your stove on flammable material. If you need to scrape flammable material aside, brush it back over the stove site when you break camp.

- A flat rock will serve well as a place to set your stove.

- Some backpackers carry a lightweight square of nonflammable material to set their stove on.

- If you do your food prep on a piece of plastic it will catch the crumbs, making cleanup easier.

placed later), or you'll need a flat rock beneath your stove. A few backpackers carry a small piece of nonflammable material to set their stove on.

You may also consider carrying a small piece of cloth as a "kitchen table." On it you can set your pots and do food preparation. It will catch crumbs and reduce the chance that dirt and debris will end up in your dinner.

"A watched pot never boils," goes the old saying, but watch you should. You don't want the pot to boil over—you may lose part of the meal and/or clog your stove—and you don't want food to cook too long, a route to burned grub.

Do kitchen cleanup right after eating ends, before food residue solidifies on cookware and utensils.

Kitchen Tips

Cooking and cleaning are much easier if done in daylight.

- A burning stove, like a campfire, should never be left unattended.

- Wind will reduce the efficiency of your stove. Use a windscreen and/or set up a windbreak on the windward side of your stove.

- Lids on pots speed up cooking and reduce the amount of fuel you'll use.

- As soon as dinner is finished, heat water for cleanup. The longer you wait, the more difficult cleanup of pots and personal kitchen gear will be.

Tips for preventing burned food:

- Use plenty of water in the pot. Watery is better than burned.

- Butter burns more easily than margarine or oil. Butter is good but requires constant attention.

- Add milk and cheese last and watch carefully. They burn easily.

- If a pot of cooking food seems too hot, lift it off the stove a minute to cool.

- Add a little water to the pan when frying. Food is less crispy but less likely to burn.

THE BATHROOM

Fecal matter is the greatest source of contamination of the backcountry

More accurately referred to as the "potty" or "toilet," the "bathroom" in this section refers to where you deposit your fecal matter. Feces contain a world of germs, some of them healthy, and some of them not—and all of them a potential contaminating element in the wild lands. Improper management can lead to water pollution and the spread of illnesses.

You want a site, of course, that provides privacy. Privacy can be enhanced by announcing to others in your group that you're headed for the bathroom. The slight embarrassment you might feel will be much less than having someone walk up on you during the act.

Cat Hole

- Look for a private spot at least 200 feet from camp, trails, and sources of water.

- Brush forest debris aside and dig down about 8 inches. This is much easier with a backpacking trowel. Do not use the trowel to move fecal matter into the hole. Use a stick or rock if necessary.

- After use, refill the hole with the dirt you removed.

- If a stick is handy, stir some of the dirt in with the fecal matter to speed decomposition.

Latrine

- Groups, especially if small children are members, may choose to dig a latrine.

- Once again, look for a private spot at least 200 feet from camp, trails, and natural sources of water.

- A latrine about 8 inches deep and about 2 feet long should work for almost any group.

- After each use, dirt should be spread over the fecal matter, and the latrine filled back in completely before leaving camp.

Fecal matter needs to be deposited in soil where microbes in the soil will speed decomposition. Pick a spot at least 200 feet from water sources, trails, and your camp. Dig down about 8 inches, which should be enough to prevent animals from digging up the matter later. Digging will be much easier with a small, lightweight trowel. Use the trowel for digging and filling in the hole after your deposit and not for moving fecal matter. When the hole is filled, spend a moment brushing the site or further hiding it with leaves, pine needles, and such. It is better for the environment if you pick a different site each time.

If you use toilet paper (some backpackers prefer natural "paper" in the form of leaves or other material), it is by far best to put it in a plastic bag and pack it out. If you can't, use as little paper as possible and bury it with the fecal matter. Although once considered a viable option, attempting to burn the toilet paper first is not recommended, for fire-safety reasons.

Bathroom Cleanup

- The depth of 8 inches seems to be enough to keep animals from digging up fecal matter, keeping the environment cleaner.

- Eight inches is shallow enough for some air and moisture to reach the fecal matter, encouraging decomposition.

- Dirt used to refill cat holes and latrines should not be compacted by stamping.

- Finally, disguise the hole by roughing up where you dug, scattering twigs and forest debris over the site.

Toilet Paper

- Once hikers were encouraged to burn their toilet paper at the site and bury the ashes with the fecal matter—but it didn't work.

- And occasionally fires were started.

- Conscientious hikers pack their soiled toilet paper into plastic bags and pack it out or burn it later in a campfire.

- Buried toilet paper in the cat hole or latrine takes years to decompose.

125

THE CAMPFIRE
Your fire should have the least possible impact on the environment

When regulations allow a fire, and when the local area has the resources to support a fire, campfires can create some of the most memorable moments on the trail. The ethics of fire-building and alternatives to the standard campfire are discussed later (see page 146).

You will need three types of material to start and sustain a fire: tinder, kindling, and fuel. Tinder is small stuff that ignites easily and burns quickly. Paper works well. In the natural world, look for dry grass, dry leaves, small twigs, and balls of pitch leaking from resinous trees. Kindling is small pieces

Never leave a fire unattended.

Fire Ring

- Fire rings—rings of stones surrounding a fire place—are ubiquitous in America's outdoors.

- If a fire ring exists at your campsite, you should use it if you choose to have a fire.

- Do not build a new fire ring if one does not exist or if the one that does exist is not where you want it.

- Fires in fire rings need to be completely dead before you leave camp.

Fire Pit

- If sand, gravel, or soil without vegetation exists where you want a fire, you may choose to dig a fire pit.

- Do not dig a pit where there are roots of trees and deep layers of forest debris that could ignite.

- The material removed from the pit should be piled nearby.

- Do not place the material from the pit in a place where it will be trampled and compacted by fire enjoyers.

of wood, usually no larger than a pencil, dry and dead. Fuel consists of all larger pieces of wood, also dry and dead, and you won't need any piece larger than about the diameter of your wrist. Gather plenty of kindling and fuel before striking a match.

In addition to fuel, a fire needs air and heat. Take any of these three away, and the fire dies—or it won't even start.

Mound the tinder in the center of your chosen fire place, and stack the kindling on top. Crisscross the kindling, or brace piece against piece teepee-style, so that air can circulate freely.

Now apply heat with a match or lighter to the tinder. As it burns, the kindling will ignite. With the kindling burning, add fuel, starting with small pieces, until the flame reaches the size you want.

Stop adding fuel in time to allow the fuel to burn completely to ash before bedtime. Be sure the ashes are completely drowned to death with water when you're breaking camp. You can scatter the drowned ash broadly without harming the environment.

Fire Pit Cleanup

- When the fire is completely dead, the ashes drowned with water, and anything that needs to be packed out removed from the ashes, scatter the ashes by broadcasting them widely around the area.

- Refill the pit with the material you removed.

- Disguise the site with twigs, leaves, dirt, or anything naturally occurring in the area.

- Leave the site looking as if a fire was never there.

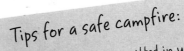

Tips for a safe campfire:

- Be sure fires are permitted in your area of travel.

- Never leave the fire unattended.

- Be sure wind will not blow sparks far away from the fire.

- Don't start a fire under low, overhanging branches of trees.

- Be sure the fire is completely drowned and dead before you leave the campsite.

HAND WASHING

Dirty hands are the leading source of illnesses in hikers and backpackers

Hands are typically covered in germs, some coming while others go, some lying on the surface, and some wedged into cracks. They can be divided into two general categories: the germs that serve a healthy purpose and the germs that cause diseases—and both categories are invisible to the naked eye. A clean-looking hand, in other words, may be germ-laden, and the germs might be bad. Most experts agree germy hands are the source of most of the illnesses that people get outdoors.

Hand washing prior to food handling or attending to wound care, even with detergents, does not remove all the nasty things residing or trespassing on hands, but it does significantly reduce the chance of contamination.

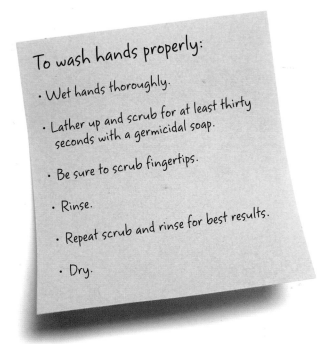

To wash hands properly:

• Wet hands thoroughly.

• Lather up and scrub for at least thirty seconds with a germicidal soap.

• Be sure to scrub fingertips.

• Rinse.

• Repeat scrub and rinse for best results.

• Dry.

Wash Your Hands

- Unclean hands are the leading source of illness on backcountry trips due to the germs that live there and the fact you can pass them to other people.

- You should wash your hands well at least once a day and preferably before every meal.

- With a pot of water, move at least 200 feet from natural water sources to avoid contamination.

- After scrubbing and rinsing, dry your hands to get rid of germs that may be still living in the moisture.

And it's not just the fact that you wash but also how you wash your hands. To get rid of a maximum amount of germs, you need hot water, soap, and thirty to sixty seconds of scrubbing. Hot water is usually in short supply, but you'll do fine substituting a germicidal soap for hot water. A recommended process of hand washing is on the previous page, and it includes drying your hands, an important aspect of the quest for cleanliness because germs can hide in the moisture on wet hands.

Keep your fingernails trimmed short so germs can't hide as well underneath.

········· • GREEN ● LIGHT • ·········

Outdoor life can really dry out your skin, but carrying, and using, a small bottle of moisturizing lotion with an ingredient such as glycerin will help keep the skin of your hands healthy. Keeping your skin healthy will be far more effective than gallons of germicide.

Fingernails

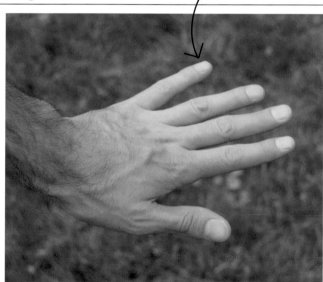

- Germs on hands are often thickest underneath your fingernails. That's not just dirt collecting there.

- Be sure to start backcountry trips with your nails trimmed short to reduce the space germs can hide in.

- When you wash your hands, scrub your fingertips with special attention.

- Clean underneath your fingernails at least once a day to maximize the your health during your trip.

Hand Sanitizer

- You can get your hands quickly free of germs with a hand sanitizer.

- If your hand sanitizer uses alcohol as the germ killer, choose one that includes a moisturizer as well. Alcohol dries out your skin over time, eventually promoting germ populations.

- Read the directions on the label and be sure you use the sanitizer appropriately.

- Hand sanitizers do not remove grime. You still need a good hand washing once a day.

129

HAIR AND BODY WASHING
Sometimes you just want to get clean from head to foot

On an outdoor trip, dirt and germs that collect on your hair and on parts of your body other than your hands do not often create a problem—unless your unwashed odor bothers someone. In fact, there are oils secreted by your skin that help protect your skin from drying out and being harmed by wind and sun. There is an exception: the genital area, especially in women who may be more prone to vaginal infections when their most private parts are not cleaned regularly.

All soaps potentially harm the environment, but you can get a lot of grunge off without soap by plunging into a lake, stream, or river. A brisk rub with unsoaped hands, and you can remove a fair bit of dirt and germs.

Soap

- You do not need to wash your hair and body on back-country trips, although the genital area, especially in women, is an exception.

- All soaps are harmful to the environment, but biode-gradable soaps are easiest on the wild land.

- Hot water is nice, but some soaps suds up well in cold water. The label will tell you.

- Some products—such as No Rinse— for hair and body washing require no rinsing.

Bathing

- When you choose to bathe, carry your water at least 200 feet from natural water sources to prevent contamination.

- Choose a spot that will readily drain, a grassy spot on an area covered in thick, forest duff.

- Wet your hair and body. Lather up. Rinse. Getting wet and rinsing are easiest to do if someone helps you.

- Skimp on soap. Use no more than the minimum you need to achieve a light lathering.

130

Soap does get you cleaner, and when you want to use soap, use it in a way that minimizes harm to the wild land. Start by carrying pots, bottles, or collapsible containers of water 200 feet (about seventy adult steps) or more away from any natural water source to prevent contamination of the water source. Biodegradable soaps are strongly recommended as the environmentally sound choice. But even these soaps take a long time to biodegrade, and fish and frogs have a strong preference for soap-less water. Once well away from the water's edge, use as little soap as possible to suds up and rinse off.

Heating water first allows you to really boost the pleasure of the hair and body washing experience, especially if the air temperature rates as chilly to cold. Warm water has the advantage of easier suds, too; many soaps are available, most often in outdoor specialty stores, that suds up well even in cold water. And some require no rinsing (see below).

Wipe Yourself Clean

- You can get your body satisfyingly clean on the trail by using baby wipes.

- In addition to removing grime and odor, they contain a moisturizer, good for your skin as well as for baby's.

- Choose a product in a soft pack instead of a hard case for easier and lighter packing.

- With a large pack, count out what you think you'll need and carry them in a zip-top plastic bag.

Solar Shower

- Warming up wash water before a bath can add much to the pleasure and success of washing.

- Products are available that utilize the sun's energy to warm your bathwater.

- They must be filled and left in sunlight an adequate

amount of time. The amount of time can vary depending on how warm you like your water.

- They can be suspended from the limb of a tree or held high by someone in the absence of trees.

KITCHEN CLEANUP

Just like at home, you need to keep your kitchen gear clean

Start clean: Be sure you pack clean kitchen gear into your pack. In camp, you'll get the best cleanup water by bringing it to or almost to the point of boiling. Heat will disinfect your wash water. You'll especially want hot water when you use, as recommended, biodegradable soaps because they tend to have less ability to remove food scum unless they're in hot water. As soon as you've spooned dinner out of the pot,

scrape it as clean as possible and add water back to the pot and set it on the stove. By the time you've eaten, you'll be ready to clean.

You can scrub hot, soapy pots, bowls, cups, and utensils clean with sand, but an abrasive pad, the kind you may be using in your kitchen at home, will work better. It is cleaner, more effective, and easier to use. And sand scratches the

To clean your cookware:

• Remove the visible food scraps.

• Use hot water and soap to wash, and scrub with a small, abrasive pad.

• Rinse with clean, hot water or water to which you've added a few drops of chlorine.

• Dry it all with a clean bandanna.

• Broadcast the dirty water at least 200 feet from sources of water.

Step 1: Remove Food Scraps

- The heat of cooking kills most germs on pots, yes, but residual scum left from days without washing can form a film that heating does not fully penetrate.

- Cookware should be washed at least every few days.

- Before washing, scrape as much visible food scraps as possible from pots, pans, bowls, and mugs.

- Scrape the scraps into a garbage bag and pack them out. A small amount can also be dumped into a hot fire.

soft plastic articles of your kitchen gear. Scratches make later cleanings less and less adequate and eventually impossible.

Not all backpackers take the time to thoroughly rinse their kitchen gear after washing—but it's better if you do. Rinsing removes soap residue and germs. You can rinse with a second pot of hot water or with cold water to which you've added a few drops of a sanitizer, such as chlorine.

The final step is drying your gear. You can dry with a camp towel (sold for that purpose) or with a clean bandanna, but remember the towel or bandanna will get pretty dirty after a couple of dinners, so wash it out between kitchen cleanups. In most climates, the air is dry enough to make air-drying of your kitchen gear acceptable. Air-drying is, in fact, preferable to drying with a dirty cloth.

Step 2: Wash the Gear

- Bring the wash water for cookware almost to a boil.

- Using a dab of biodegradable camp soap, scrub the cookware with an abrasive pad to remove the visible and invisible scum.

- Rinse in clean, hot water.

- Or rinse in fresh water to which you've added a few drops of chlorine as a disinfectant. If the rinse water smells strongly of chlorine, there is plenty of it in the water.

Step 3: Dry the Gear

- Allowing cookware to sit and dry in open air is usually okay unless the air is highly humid.

- It is best for air-drying to take place in direct sunlight. The drying is faster (good), and the sun's UV light works toward disinfection.

- It is a bit better to dry your cookware with a clean, dry cloth.

- Air-drying is strongly preferable to wiping cookware with a dirty cloth.

FOOD HANDLING

Know what food to carry and how to manage it on your trip

Germs in food—usually not a problem—can multiply to the point of making your food taste bad and/or making you sick if you don't manage your camp food appropriately.

Proper food management starts with choosing what to carry. Three factors determine how well food keeps—the moisture content, the salt content, and the sugar content. If moisture is not there, germs don't have a chance, and that's one reason

the majority of backpacking foods are dry. If moisture is there, along with lots of salt or sugar, the salt and sugar hold tightly to the moisture, and, once again, germs are not able to multiply. And that's why good foods for the trail often have high salt or sugar content.

Once you've cooked food, you've added moisture and bumped up the opportunity for germs to find a home. Left-

Good Food for the Trail

- Germs don't grow when there is no moisture, so dried foods are good choices as backpacking foods.

- Germs don't grow in food with a high salt content or a high sugar content, so salty and sugary foods are good choices for backpacking.

- Small amounts of food in small bags are less likely to become contaminated than large amounts of food in large bags.

- When a dirty hand reaches into a bag of food, the entire bag may soon be contaminated.

Leftovers

- It is safest to pack out food left over after it has been cooked.

- Leftovers may, however, stay safe if they don't get too warm, such as on cold-weather trips.

- When you choose to eat leftovers, they need to be

kept in high heat for several minutes first.

- You can do this by adding water to the pot and bringing the water to a boil, stirring often to prevent burning.

overs, therefore, for the most part, should be bagged and packed out—not eaten.

Finally, people add their personal germs to food when they reach into group bags with their hands—so don't let anyone do that. With things like trail mix, have everyone carry, and eat out of, their own bag. And even if you're still hungry, you're best not finishing your friend's bowl of grub—unless you are willing to eat germs, too.

ZOOM

Even though, as a general rule, you don't eat leftovers, there are times when you can, especially if it's cold outside and the leftovers cooled off quickly. Add a little water, raise the temperature of the leftovers to high, and keep the temp high for several minutes, stirring often to prevent burning.

Say No to Sharing

- Hands and mouths are the greatest source of contaminated food on backcountry trips.

- To be safe, hikers should not share spoons, bowls, and mugs.

- To be safe, you should not finish another hiker's candy bar or bowl of oatmeal. You can do it, but you assume a risk.

- Trail mix should be packed individually, each hiker eating his or her own out of his or her own bag.

To maintain hygiene in camp:

- Wash your hands well at least once a day.

- Wash your hands after having a bowel movement and before preparing food.

- Wash your cookware well at least every few days.

- Carry food that is nonperishable.

- Don't eat leftovers.

- Don't share utensils, mugs, and such with other hikers.

- Don't let hands get into food the group will share.

135

PLAN AHEAD AND PREPARE

Getting ready to "have zero impact" starts before you walk out the door

Many people heading out on a hiking or backpacking trip, and perhaps most of them, are interested, to some degree, in protecting wild land from harm. A large part of the enjoyment of an outdoor experience lies in finding the wild land wild, and here that means unmarked by other people. Many of those same people are surprised to learn that wilderness can be extremely easy to harm. Litter and blackened rocks

around old campfires are easy to recognize, but recreationists in the form of hikers and backpackers often unknowingly pollute natural water sources, trample vegetation, compact soils in ways that promote erosion, and contribute to wild land degradation in other, less obvious ways.

The techniques of the Leave No Trace program (see the Resource Directory for more information) are based on

Books and Pamphlets

- Education is far more effective than legislation in promoting the ethical use of wild lands.

- Hikers who leave the least impact on the land have learned how to leave the least impact on the land.

- Some actions that have zero impact are obvious (pack out your litter), but some are subtle (such as the long-lasting impact of compacted soil).

- Many books and pamphlets are available that will inform you about how to have zero impact on the land.

Avoid High-Use Areas

- Understandably, areas that get the most human use are areas that show the most effects of human use.

- Plan trips into areas that see less human use, and plan to have zero impact of your visit.

- Plan trips to wild lands in seasons that are less crowded with human visitors.

- Plan trips with small groups. Small groups (say, four hikers) are less likely to leave a trace than larger groups.

the belief that a considerable amount of damage can be prevented if users of wild lands are better informed—that education is a key element in preservation. The core of the Leave No Trace program is not only beliefs but also seven principles for reducing the damage caused by outdoor activities, particularly nonmotorized recreation. The principles and practices extend common courtesy and hospitality to nature and to other wild land visitors. They are based on respect for nature and the science behind having zero impact on the land.

Plan ahead by considering your goals and expectations and by taking pretrip steps to preserve the wild places, and prepare by gathering information and skills. Plan to leave no trace and prepare by learning how to have zero impact on the land. Plan, for instance, by reducing the amount of garbage you carry by repackaging food, getting rid of trash you might accidentally leave behind. Prepare by learning specific minimum-impact techniques for the area you are visiting. A desert needs respect in ways that differ from subalpine meadows. It is your responsibility to have zero impact on the land.

Pack the Right Gear

- With knowledge about how to have zero impact, you can choose gear that will help you have zero impact.

- A backpacking stove is far less impactful than a fire.

- A lightweight backpacking trowel allows you to adequately dispose of human waste by digging a hole the proper depth.

- Soft camp shoes, instead of hard-soled shoes, help you move around camp without as much trampling of vegetation and compaction of the soil.

Repackaging

- Hikers who carry less litter into the backcountry tend to leave less litter in the backcountry.

- When you open a candy bar, for instance, a small piece of the wrapper sometimes drops unnoticed to the ground.

- Unwrap candy bars, granola bars, and energy bars and repackage them in plastic bags, leaving the wrappers behind.

- Pour the contents of food boxes, such as rice and other grains, into plastic bags and leave the boxes behind.

STAY ON DURABLE SURFACES
Travel and camp where you will cause the least amount of damage

A footprint in soil of the southern Appalachians will likely be gone within a year. In Glacier National Park it could be visible twenty-five years later. If you step on a cryptobiotic crust in canyon country, more than one hundred years of growth disappears. You need to think about where your feet fall.

When a designated trail lies before you, stay on it. A group should stay in single file to prevent widening the trail, and everyone should resist the temptation to take shortcuts.

If the day's walk ends in an established campsite, as set by previous use or by a land management agency, utilize it. Most of the damage to a site occurs in the first time or two someone camps there. Creating a new campsite often means creating a lasting impact.

If you do travel off-trail, walk on durable surfaces. Spread

Durable Surface

- Durable surfaces, especially sand, gravel, rocks, and snow, bounce back quickly after being walked or camped on. Nondurable surfaces, such as wet ground, may show the impact of human feet for many years.

- Where a trail is visible, you should stay on it.

- A group should hike in single file on a trail to avoid widening the trail.

- Avoid taking shortcuts that connect sections of trail. Shortcuts tend to create pathways for erosion.

Impacted Campsite

- You will have far more impact where you camp than where you hike.

- If you find a campsite that has obviously been used before, use it again. You will have less impact on a used site than on a pristine site.

- If you find a fire ring, and fires are acceptable, use the ring; don't build a new one.

- When you walk from camp to your source of water, take a new route each time to avoid creating a trail.

groups out. Two people walking single file can create a visible trail. Set your camp on a durable surface—forest duff, a gravel bar, a large rock slab—and avoid creating trails around camp, something very possible if you take the same route every time to your water source or to your bathroom spot. Stay no more than one night when you camp in a pristine location.

ZOOM

Durable surfaces—sand, gravel, rock, snow, ice, dry grass, and water—resist impact and bounce back fast when they are used. Nondurable surfaces—riverbanks, muddy ground, and ground covered with fragile vegetation—may show impacts lasting a lifetime in the form of destroyed plants and erosion.

Pristine Area

- When hiking across a pristine area (where there is no trail) do not walk in single file. As few as two hikers in file can leave a visible path.

- If you camp in a pristine area, camp and pitch your tent on durable surfaces.

- Be especially careful to set your kitchen on a durable surface.

- If you need a fire, build a zero impact fire, such as a mound fire (see page 146).

Restoring a Site

- When you leave, take care to clean up and "freshen" up the spot so it appears as if no one has ever camped there.

- Check twice to be sure you have not left litter behind, including visible food scraps.

- If you moved large rocks or logs, replace them in their original spots.

- Brush areas of the ground—a dead limb will serve well— where there is visible evidence of your camp.

WASTE DISPOSAL: PART 1
If you packed it in, you should pack it out—but you can't always

Into every pack, no matter the size of the pack or the length of the hike, should go a garbage bag. You are going to be creating litter—candy wrappers, gum wrappers, spilled food—that you need to pick up and pack out. Even if by some miracle you don't have trash of your own, you're bound to find the litter of someone less careful than you—and you'll pack that out. Thank you.

But usually you will not pack out your fecal matter and urine (although in certain areas—the snow slopes of Denali National Park, for instance—you must). You will, however, deal with your waste products in ways that limit or eliminate pollution of water sources, the spread of diseases, and unpleasant experiences for those who follow you into the wilds.

Pick Up Litter

- Day hikers and overnight backpackers alike should pack at least a small garbage bag.

- Into it will go any litter you created as well as litter you find left behind by others.

- If you build a fire, comb through the dead ashes for unburned trash that will need to be packed out.

- If you dropped a small pocketknife or failed to pull out a tent stake, that, too, is litter.

Outhouse

- The greatest potential source of contamination to wild areas is human fecal matter.

- In most cases (there are a few exceptions) you will not be packing it out.

- If you find an outhouse, you should use it, keeping fecal matter in that immediate area concentrated and controlled.

- If you find the outhouse especially unappealing, report it to the local land manager when you have the opportunity.

If an outhouse or latrine exists where you travel, use it. It may sometimes be less than fully appealing, but it is important to concentrate fecal matter in places where it is intended to be concentrated. Far more often than not, hikers must create their own "toilet," and this is discussed fully on page 124.

Other than fecal matter, one of the most notorious ways to leave a waste-disposal trace is in a campfire. Not everything people throw into the fire will burn, with foil liners to packaging being among the most common campfire litter. Leftover food tossed into the flames typically becomes a charred and long-lasting mass. Plastic does not burn—it melts but remains. If you use a fire to burn trash, sift through the cold ashes before you leave and remove, and pack out, everything left unburned.

Then, before shouldering your pack, check your campsite one more time for small pieces of paper, dropped food scraps, and the tent stake you missed pulling out of the ground.

Packing Out Fecal Waste

- There are a few highly sensitive areas where local land managers require you to pack out your fecal matter.

- Most people are happy to hear that these situations are extremely rare for the average hiker or backpacker.

- On glaciers, some parks require travelers to remove their waste in a clean mountain can.

- In some narrow river corridors, land managers require human waste to be removed in poop tubes, lightweight devices manufactured to transport human waste.

Remove Litter from Fires

- Some hikers still mistakenly believe that anything thrown into a roaring fire is no longer litter.

- Plastic does not burn. It melts, changing form, and it should not be thrown into a fire.

- Aluminum foil and foil wrappers do not burn. If they were thrown into the fire, they are still in there somewhere.

- Large clumps of wet, leftover food seldom burn. They harden into a blackened lump that remains.

141

WASTE DISPOSAL: PART 2
Attention to details can greatly reduce what you leave behind

Here is a fact: The urine that you leave behind is almost never a health problem. The odor of your urine, however, can linger for a surprisingly long time. And urine often attracts wild animals who, if deficient in salt, will defoliate plants to consume your spilled salt. (Staying well hydrated, by the way, reduces the salt concentration in your urine.)

If there is a waterway nearby, and if you have not been instructed otherwise by land managers, urinating directly into rivers, where the urine is diluted, is recommended. Without a waterway, move well away from camps and trails to urinate. Preferable is bare ground or rocks instead of vegetation. If there is a plentiful supply of water at hand, consider rinsing the urination site with a splash.

Waste water other than urine is created when you wash

Urinating in Waterways

- Your urine is almost never a health problem in the backcountry, but it can be an odor problem. No one likes a smelly campsite.

- Wild animals will sometimes dig up vegetation and defoliate bushes to get the salt in urine.

- If you have not been instructed otherwise by land managers, it is usually okay and sometimes preferable to urinate in bodies of moving water.

- In moving water, urine is rapidly diluted to harmlessness.

Urinating on Land

- Move well away from camp and trails to urinate. How far could depend on how much privacy you need.

- Try to find a spot without vegetation such as bare rocks and bare ground.

- If there is plenty of water at your water source, you can splash the spot you urinated to increase dilution.

- If you use a pee bottle at night, mostly a man thing, be sure to empty it in an acceptable spot.

your kitchen gear. The Leave No Trace program advises straining dirty dishwater through a small, fine-mesh strainer. Do this at least 200 feet away from water sources to prevent contamination from the soap, if you used any. In bear country, it is wise to strain dishwater well away from camp because the water will still have a tempting odor available to noses far more sensitive than yours. The particles of food you recover should go into the garbage bag for packing out.

Brushing your teeth produces yet another form of waste water. You can spit into a pot of water and then broadcast— fling over a wide area—the used toothpaste. Or you can broadcast as you spit, spraying the toothpaste instead of dropping a gob onto the ground.

Dilution is the solution to pollution.

Straining Out Scraps

- Small food scraps are usually left in the dishwater after kitchen cleanup.

- These should not be left on the ground where they are litter and a source of unnatural food for some wild animals.

- The scraps can be trapped and packed out by using a small, lightweight strainer, as pictured.

- The straining should take place 200 feet from water sources in order to prevent your soap from contaminating the water.

Broadcasting

- Waste water without food scraps should be broadcast from the pot or pan.

- To "broadcast" means to toss the water widely, as pictured, dispersing it over as large an area as possible.

- Soap and any unstrainable-residue will be diluted by broadcasting. There is little harm to the environment.

- After brushing, you should broadcast your toothpaste by spitting it over as large an area as possible.

LEAVE WHAT YOU FIND

Pass on the gift of discovery by taking nothing from the wild land

When you leave behind all that you find on your hike, you help retain some of the special qualities that make the less-visited areas of Earth attractive. Leaving what you find, in other words, decreases the chance that you'll leave a trace.

And sometimes it's the law. The Archaeological Resources Protection Act and the National Historic Preservation Act demand that structures, dwellings, and artifacts on public lands be left undisturbed in order to preserve the past. It is illegal to harm (sometimes even to touch), to excavate, or to remove anything that has been there for fifty or more years, including potsherds, arrowheads, rusted railroad equipment, dilapidated logging equipment, and the insignificant piece of shattered glass from an old bottle. (The law further protects pictographs and petroglyphs.) And the Migratory Bird

Artifacts

- Some artifacts might once have been trash, but now they are historical and cultural reminders of past civilizations.

- Potsherds, arrowheads, ancient tools (no matter how broken), and ancient dwellings (no matter how dilapidated) are all artifacts.

- Carving on rocks (petroglyphs) and paintings on stone walls (pictographs) are also artifacts.

- Artifacts are protected by law and should not be touched, much less removed from the backcountry.

Natural Objects

- Removal of any natural objects from national parks and wildlife refuges is prohibited by law.

- In other places, you can share the delight you feel in finding natural objects by leaving them for others to see.

- Some objects, such as antlers, play a role in the natural order of things. Mice, for instance, eat antlers for the calcium.

- Many birds use discarded feathers to build their nests.

Treaty Act protects the nests and feathers of some species of wild birds.

Collecting anything in national parks and wildlife refuges is prohibited. (Some public lands, however, do allow the collection of some natural objects, although a permit is typically required.)

Often the gathering and removal of natural objects from wild land are an ethical question—and only you have the answer. If you see something that attracts your interest, that flower, rock, shell, feather, or antler might very well attract the next traveler's attention, if the object is still there. These natural objects may also fill a unique ecological niche that you are unaware of. A field mouse may need to gnaw the antler, or an osprey may need those feathers for a nest. A decorative-looking piece of wood might partially shelter a pika's burrow, or a hermit crab may want for a home the very shell riding in your pocket.

Don't Pick the Flowers

- When you pick a wildflower, you have ended any chance that another hiker will enjoy finding that particular flower.

- When you gather colorful rocks, you have done likewise.

- The question of whether to take it or leave it is often ethical. Most often, the ethical response is to leave it.

- Some areas do allow gathering of some natural objects, such as firewood for your home, but a permit is typically required.

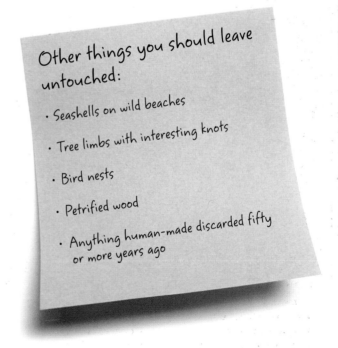

Other things you should leave untouched:

- Seashells on wild beaches

- Tree limbs with interesting knots

- Bird nests

- Petrified wood

- Anything human-made discarded fifty or more years ago

MINIMIZE CAMPFIRE IMPACTS
You no longer have the right to build a fire anytime or anywhere

Once essential for cooking and comfort, fires are no longer necessary. But who doesn't love a campfire? They are companionable, compelling in their light and beauty, warming on a chilly night, and just plain fun. On the other hand, careless fires make lasting impacts on the land, and campfire builders have denuded many wild areas of wood for fires.

Fires are inappropriate in areas where growth is slow. Arctic willows, as an example, are few and far between, taking hundreds of years to mature.

It is not unusual for areas to have fire bans, sometimes to lessen the high danger of wildfire and sometimes to allow trees to grow. It is your responsibility to know and obey fire restrictions.

Fire Ring

Mound Fire

- It is your responsibility to know about and obey fire bans and fire restrictions.

- It is also your responsibility to build a safe fire, one you can extinguish rapidly if it begins to spread.

- If an old fire ring exists where you are camping, use it and don't build a new one.

- If two fire rings exist, and one can be easily and completed dismantled, you may choose to do so, hiding all evidence that a fire once burned there.

- A mound fire is built on a pedestal of sand, gravel, or soil with very little organic material in it.

- Gather the material (you may have to carry it to your chosen spot) and pile in on a piece of tarp or a ground cloth to facilitate cleanup.

- The pedestal should be at least 6 inches high and about 2 feet across.

- When the fire is completely out, return the material of the pedestal to its original spot.

When a campfire is acceptable, you need to ask yourself a few questions: Does the area have enough wood to support a fire? Will a wind take sparks into dry tinder or into the tent? Is there water nearby to put out an uncontrolled blaze? And how can a fire be made with as little impact as possible?

If there's a fire ring, use it, and leave it for others to use. Do not build a fire ring. Without a ring, scoop out a shallow pit in inorganic soil—a sandy spot is usually an excellent spot—in which to build your fire. Or build a mound fire or use a fire pan, both of which are described below.

Keep your wilderness fires small, using only dead and downed wood, never breaking limbs from trees. Use only pieces of wood you can break with your hands. This smaller stuff will burn completely into white ash that you'll later drown with water and broadcast. Then you can fill in your fire pit, or replace the soil you built your mound fire on, and leave the land almost exactly the way you found it.

Fire Pan

- A fire pan is made of metal and used to contain a small fire.

- You can use an aluminum roasting pan, an oil pan, or a metal garbage can lid. Because you will be carrying it on your back, the lighter the metal, of course, the better.

- Set the pan on rocks above a nonflammable, nonvegetated surface.

- Line the pan with a couple of inches of inorganic soil before building your fire.

Firewood

- Before starting a fire, be sure there is an ample supply of firewood.

- Firewood should be down and dead. Do not break limbs from trees.

- Do not gather wood bigger around than your wrist. The pieces should break easily with your hands. Larger pieces are difficult to get to burn completely to ash.

- The use of saws, axes, and hatchets should not be necessary and in most cases is not desirable.

147

RESPECT WILDLIFE
Animals do not need and seldom benefit from encounters with humans

Of all the chance encounters on the trail, few are as memorable as those with wild animals. As special as these encounters are to you, the animals rarely benefit. Around the globe, wildlife is threatened by loss of habitat, pollution, disease, and poaching. The ethical hiker acts in ways that promote wildlife survival instead of adding to their problems.

Some species adapt to humans in close proximity, going about their business as usual and earning the tag "habituated." Some are attracted to human food and trash and become overhabituated. Some species run away from humans, abandoning at times not only their critical habitat but also their young. In all cases it is best for hikers and the animals to avoid habituating animals or driving them away.

Maintain Distance

- Respecting wildlife means, essentially, taking no actions that will make their lives more difficult.

- Observe wildlife from a distance. This is better for the animals and sometimes better for the humans.

- Close encounters sometimes drive animals away from their preferred habitat, sometimes even away from their young.

- Some species become habituated to humans and don't run away. They may be killed by land managers to make life safer for humans.

Don't Feed the Animals

- All wild animals are better off if they never eat human food.

- Their natural diet is nutritious, and human food, for them, is not.

- Lured by human food, animals may congregate in greater number than the immediate habitat can handle. They may become aggressive or destructive, attitudes that you do not want to encounter.

- Small animals may become nuisances, and they may be vectors for disease. You are better off if they are not in your camp.

Watch wild animals from a distance, and do not approach or follow them. Whenever possible, avoid startling them or forcing them to flee. Travel quietly—except in bear and mountain lion country. When you see an animal, do not make sudden movements or shout to attract it. If it's close, you should not make eye contact with most species, an action animals often interpret as a threat.

Do not feed animals, intentionally or accidentally. Feeding alters their natural behavior and may damage their health. Human food is never as nutritious as their natural food. When wild animals become overhabituated, bears certainly being the most newsworthy, you know what the end result will be: the death of the animal.

Keep your camp clean, taking care to pick up food scraps accidentally dropped on the ground. Store your food in ways that prevent animals from reaching it. Hanging your food bag usually works, but the best storage methods sometimes vary with location, and local land managers can tell you how to do it right.

Store Food Properly

- How you store your food in camp often determines whether or not you attract wild animals.

- "Food" includes garbage and anything scented or flavored such as toiletries.

- To avoid attracting small creatures, bag everything and hang it well off the ground and well below the supporting limb of a tree.

- In bear country, hang it at least 10 feet off the ground, 6 feet from the trunk of the tree, and 6 feet from the supporting limb.

Leave Your Dog at Home

- Wild animals and dogs don't do well together, even when the dog is on a leash.

- The barking of dogs is assumed a threat by wild animals (and is seldom appreciated by other hikers).

- The most well-behaved dog might carry diseases that wild animals can contract. If you must hike with your dog, be sure all vaccinations are up to date.

- In terms of respecting wildlife, dogs are best left at home.

BE CONSIDERATE OF OTHERS

Little things will mean a lot to the experience of other visitors

You will most often be sharing the trail with other people. Some of them will be wearing a backpack. Some may be of another recreational persuasion, and may be riding horses, trailing goats, leading llamas, or pedaling a mountain bike. You should always consider the role of outdoor etiquette and whether or not your actions will leave a trace of negativity.

Foremost, ethical behavior suggests that you should choose a cooperative spirit when meeting others—and, as is often the case, little things mean a lot.

It is a simple act of courtesy, when meeting another group, to offer a polite greeting and to yield the trail to others. Step to the side and give them an open path. Before passing

Other Hikers

- How you treat other hikers will have an impact not only on them but also most likely on you.

- Choose to maintain a cooperative spirit with all those you meet on the trail. Remember: Little things mean a lot.

- When meeting others on the trail, offer a friendly greeting and step to the side, yielding them the right-of-way.

- When passing others, announce your presence quietly and proceed with caution.

Livestock

- On the trail, people riding or leading livestock—horses, goats, llamas—have the right-of-way.

- Move to the downhill side of the trail (it is less threatening to the animals), speak softly, and avoid sudden movements.

- If nearby campers have livestock, stay well away from the animals unless invited by the livestock owners.

- If you pass through gates on the trail, leave them open or closed depending on how you find them.

someone slower on the trail, politely announce your presence and proceed cautiously around.

People leading or riding livestock have the right-of-way. Step off the downhill side of the trail and talk quietly, avoiding sudden sounds and movements that might startle the animals.

Do not take rest breaks on the trail. Step a short distance off-trail and rest on a durable surface. If another group has established a camp, avoid picking a site too close to the group for comfort. And try to find a spot for your camp that doesn't interfere with the view of others who are already there or who might arrive later.

Most visitors to wild land come looking at least in part for peace and quiet. Respect that by avoiding the use of radios and other music-blaring devices, using bright lights at night, and, in general, making a nuisance of yourself.

If you hike with your dog, keep it under control, quiet, and out of other people's campsites. This often entails keeping your pet on a leash.

Campsites

- Whenever possible, choose a campsite well away from the trail, a site that can't be seen from the trail.

- If others have already established a camp at your destination, move away to set your camp.

- Set your camp in a spot that doesn't intrude on the other campers' view.

- It's best to camp where the campsites are not visible to each other. It's even better if the campsites cannot hear each other.

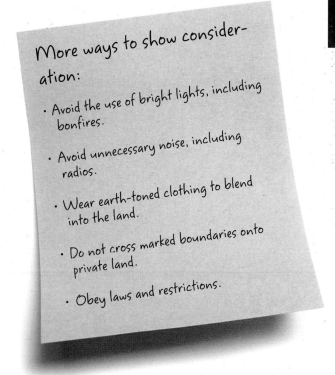

More ways to show consideration:

- Avoid the use of bright lights, including bonfires.

- Avoid unnecessary noise, including radios.

- Wear earth-toned clothing to blend into the land.

- Do not cross marked boundaries onto private land.

- Obey laws and restrictions.

TIPS FOR COLD DAYS
Let the temperature fall outside you but not inside you

Remember: Several layers of clothing are far better on chilly days than one bulky layer (see page 26). But the fact that you are wearing layers is not what protects you. As you exercise, you generate heat and start to warm up. That's when you need to open your outer layer, ventilating to allow cooler air to keep sweating to a minimum. When you warm up too much for ventilation to keep you dry, it's time to peel off a

layer—or two. If you still feel sweaty, slow down to a pace that prevents overheating. And when you stop moving, or the temperature drops, you add layers back on. It's a balancing act and worth every minute.

Store a stocking cap, mittens, and a candy bar or other high-energy snack near at hand, in a pocket of your clothing or an outside pocket of your pack. Cover your head and hands if a

Dress Like an Onion

- Several lighter layers are much better than one or two heavier layers.

- Layers allow you to control the heat and sweat produced by exercise, which allows you to stay dry. You need to stay dry to stay warm.

- As you warm up, ventilate your outer layer or layers. If you feel hot and sweaty after ventilating, remove an outer layer or two.

- When you start to chill off, put the layers of clothing back on.

Hat and Mittens

- Your head makes up almost 10 percent of the surface area of your body. You can lose a lot of heat through your head.

- Keep a stocking cap or a similar head covering handy at all times. Be sure it will reach down over your ears.

- A parka with a hood means you have additional covering for your head if you need it.

- The smallest body parts get coldest the fastest. Keep a pair of mittens handy at all times.

chill develops. Eat to supply your internal furnace with fuel.

At bedtime, you lose more heat into cold ground than into cold air. Be sure your sleeping pad is cold weather-worthy. Or carry two pads. Unpack and fluff up your sleeping bag well before hitting the sack. The fluffier it is, the more insulation it provides.

MAKE IT EASY

It's a lot easier to stay dry than to dry out. When you start exercising, a sudden rush of perspiration can soak your clothing before you realize it. Start the hiking day slightly underdressed. As you exercise, you will warm up. Add a layer if you don't feel warm enough.

Two Sleeping Pads

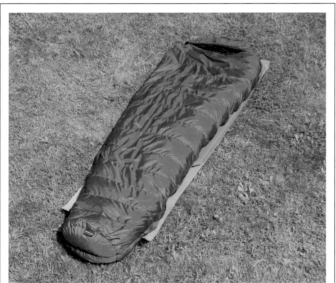

- With an excellent sleeping bag you'll still sleep cold if your pad isn't thick enough.

- You can always carry two pads in extremes of cold to ensure a warm night.

- If there's enough space inside your bag, you can sleep in clothing for additional warmth.

- Beware: If the space inside your bag is too small for additional clothing, the clothing compresses the bag's insulation, and you'll end up colder than before.

Some cold weather camping tips:

- Camp on the high end of valleys or on higher ground—heat rises.

- Set your camp out of the wind.

- Set your tent to catch the morning sun.

- Sleep with a candy bar, and if you wake up cold, a sugary snack will soon turn into internal heat.

- Store full water bottles upside down so you can still open them if the water freezes.

- Or sleep with tightly closed water bottles to prevent freezing.

TIPS FOR HOT DAYS

Let the temperature rise outside you but not inside you

Maintaining adequate body heat in hot weather isn't going to be a problem, but creating too much internal heat can be devastating (see page 194). You might be most comfortable, and safest, dressing in shorts and a T-shirt to shed as much excess heat as possible. In extremes of heat, such as deserts, however, you may find you will feel better wearing lightweight trousers and a long-sleeved shirt that provide

shade from the heat of the sun. You don't see desert dwellers in shorts: They wear billowing robes.

Hot weather clothing, in general, should be something like billowing robes: thin, loose-fitting, and made of natural fibers to allow cooling air to circulate around your body, encouraging evaporation of body moisture. Clothes that fit loosely also prevent biting insects from reaching your skin. Choose

Dress for the Heat

Rest in Shade

- Hot weather clothing should fit loosely and be woven loosely to allow air to move over your skin.

- Hot weather clothing should be of fibers such as cotton that hold moisture near your skin.

- Sometimes shorts work as good cooling agents. Sometimes your skin stays cooler if covered with the proper clothing instead of being exposed to direct sunlight.

- You'll need a hat that shades at least your face. If it shades your neck, too, it's even better.

- Hike early and late in the day to avoid traveling in the most intense heat.

- Rest in midday heat. Rest in shade. The shade can be natural, or you can create it with a tarp. If you can nap, you'll usually feel better after it.

- If there is a breeze, rest where it will blow across you.

- Take off your shoes and socks to allow your footwear and feet to dry.

clothing of a light color. Dark clothing absorbs sunlight, and its heat, while light-colored clothing reflects the sun's heat, increasing the chance of comfort. Black, in heat, is the color of death. Wear a wide-brimmed hat to protect your head, face, and neck from heat and sunburn. If you have enough water, periodically dampen your shirt and your hat. The moisture will cool you as it evaporates.

People who live in hot climates invented the siesta. It makes sense. Plan to spend the hottest part of the day resting in shade. Hike the hardest early and late in the day, taking advantage of cooler temperatures.

Heat rises, so look for low areas to set camp. If you can find an acceptable shady spot for the tent, go for it. If a breeze blows, however, you may be cooler setting camp where the air movement can reach you. An ideal campsite would have shade and a gentle breeze blowing through.

Drink enough water to keep your urine pale or devoid of color.

Wear Wet Cotton

- Evaporation of moisture from your skin is the fastest route to staying cool. If you can keep your skin moist and allow air to flow over it, you'll stay much more comfortable in heat.

- Wet a cotton bandanna and wear it around your neck to cool the blood going to your brain.

- Wear a wet bandanna on your head underneath your hat.

- Soak your cotton T-shirt in water and wear it until it dries.

Some more hot weather tips:

- Water is life—you can't drink too much water as long as you snack regularly.

- Drink enough water to keep your urine light yellow or clear.

- Wear light-colored clothing to reflect the sun's rays.

- Use a sunscreen that won't wash off in your sweat.

- Use a lip balm of SPF 15 or higher to prevent drying out and burning.

WEATHERWISE

TIPS FOR WINDY DAYS
No one can say for sure which way the wind will blow

Although no one knows for sure which way the wind will blow, you can make an educated guess. In areas where high winds are common, trees will lean away from prevailing winds. Wind will bank loose forest debris against the side of large trees and rocks. The weather history of an area often includes the direction of prevailing winds. And winds, from any direction, can be a blessing or a curse to backpackers. The cooling wind on a hot day can blow with enough strength to keep annoying insects away, but if that wind drops in temperature, life in camp can be miserable. Hot or cold, wind can rattle the nylon walls on your tent with sleep-depriving ferocity. Even mild wind of can make your stove sputter.

Friendly Wind

- Wind can be a blessing on a hot and/or buggy day, cooling you and keeping the insects in hiding.

- Look for a campsite in the open.

- If the wind is not blowing and you know the direction of prevailing winds, set your camp on the windward side of natural windbreaks—trees, rocks, ridges.

- Prevailing winds, most often blow west to east in the continental U.S.

Unfriendly Wind

- You will often want your camp set out of the wind, especially if it's chilly.

- A high wind can rattle tent walls, keeping you awake at night.

- Set your tent on the leeward side of a natural windbreak—a large rock, a dense stand of trees, below a high ridge.

- Do not set your tent with the door facing the wind. Pitch the fly tight, using stakes and taut lines, to minimize rattling and to prevent a big gust from blowing the tent away.

If you anticipate high winds, seek a campsite with protection from the wind—on the leeward side of ridges, large rocks, and dense stands of trees. In wind, stake your tent down, at least on the windward side, before putting the poles in place, and be sure the main entrance is not facing into the wind. Once it is up, add taut lines from your tent to additional stakes, rocks, or trees. To reduce rattling, pitch up your tent with as much tension in the fly as possible so wind is shed.

When wind is not expected, it is still wise to always carry a windscreen for your stove. It will shorten cooking time, saving fuel even on a calm day. In wind, set your stove on the leeward side of logs or rocks as additional protection.

In windy areas, pack a lightweight windshirt, a shirt designed to protect you from wind and pretty much nothing else. Unprotected skin dries out in wind, and, even on warm days, a high wind can blow away your body heat in uncomfortable waves.

Wind and Stove

- Wind can reduce the efficiency of your stove to zero.

- Carry and use a windscreen with your stove. The best windscreens reach from the ground to above the flames and entirely around the stove.

- Utilize windbreaks for your stove—things such as rocks and logs.

- You can improvise a windbreak with gear. A camp chair often works well. Or set your stove on the leeward side of your tent—but not too close.

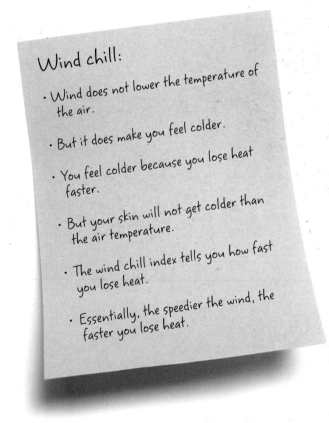

Wind chill:

- Wind does not lower the temperature of the air.

- But it does make you feel colder.

- You feel colder because you lose heat faster.

- But your skin will not get colder than the air temperature.

- The wind chill index tells you how fast you lose heat.

- Essentially, the speedier the wind, the faster you lose heat.

TIPS FOR RAINY DAYS
You need a watertight plan for days when precipitation falls

Some people, farmers mostly, like it, but rain tends to be the ruination, or at least the spoiling, of the plans of backpackers. With some foresight and knowledge, it doesn't have to be that way. Here are some tips for waterproofing your campsite.

Be sure your tent has an adequately large rain fly. If the seams are not factory sealed, seal them at least twenty-four hours before your trip, giving the sealer more time to dry.

Choose a tent that sets up quickly, and practice setting it up quickly. You might be racing a rainstorm someday.

Choose a tent without a mesh ceiling. Condensation can form on the fly and drip into your living space.

Do not pitch your tent in a depression that could collect water or in a spot that shows evidence that water has run

Tent with Vestibule

- A tent with a large vestibule overhanging the door is a big plus in rainy weather.

- A vestibule allows you to enter and exit the tent without getting rain inside. You can take off your rain parka under the vestibule and leave it there.

- Under the vestibule, you can store gear that won't fit inside the tent.

- If you're careful, you can fire up your stove and cook under a large vestibule.

Large Tarp over Tent

- A large, waterproof tarp is another big bonus in rainy weather.

- Underneath a tarp, you'll have a dry area to store gear, cook, and hang out for tea and conversation.

- Suspend a large tarp first above your tent site. You'll

be able to set up the tent out of the rain, and you'll enjoy the added protection, sort of like a second fly.

- A tarp over your tent gives you more protected ground to store gear.

through. Quality tent floors are waterproof, but water can puddle under your vestibule and make access to the tent problematic.

Keep your tent pitched taut. Tighten the rain fly straps and guylines so the fly does not touch the walls. This will allow air to circulate and reduce condensation.

When it rains, keep the tent door slightly open and keep any other tent opening, such as windows, cracked to allow ventilation and reduce condensation.

Choose a synthetic-filled sleeping bag if you anticipate a lot of rain. Synthetics will soak up less moisture and dry faster than other fills. Line your sleeping bag's stuff sack, or the bag compartment of your pack, with a plastic bag. Keep your extra clothing in a plastic bag inside your pack. An ounce of prevention!

In rain, move your bag and clothing away from the tent door before opening it. But don't let your bag and clothing rest against a tent wall in case condensation forms.

Open Vents

- A problem in rainy weather is the condensation that forms on the inside of the tent when you're in it.

- To minimize condensation, keep all vents of the tent open, and keep the door open at least partway.

- Be sure your fly is pitched tight to shed water and to keep the fly from touching the tent.

- A tent with a ceiling vent is not a good idea. Water condensing on the inside of the fly may drip on you.

More rainy day tips:

- Line your pack with a large garbage bag before packing it.

- Use a large garbage bag to store gear outside your tent.

- Seam-seal all stitches in fly and raingear that isn't factory sealed.

- Use a sleeping bag with synthetic insulation because down bags, once wet, are useless.

TIPS FOR THUNDERSTORMS

It is critically important to protect yourself during a lightning storm

The bad part of a thunderstorm comes from the rain and wind. The really bad part appears as lightning. The power in a lightning strike is awesome and somewhat unpredictable, and the danger cannot be overemphasized. Here are some tips on how to maximize your safety.

You need to know local weather patterns. Generally speaking, storms with lightning roll in quickly, usually in the afternoon and typically in the summer months.

Plan your hike so that you are not out in the open, especially above the tree line, during the times when storms blow in.

Watch for and plot storms. When the flash of lightning precedes the boom of thunder by five seconds, the storm is ap-

Lightning

- Lightning strikes most often on summer afternoons. Storms approach rapidly, usually at a speed of about 20–25 miles per hour.

- Lightning tends to reach out ahead of an oncoming storm. It can reach for miles.

- When the flash precedes the boom by five seconds, the storm is approximately 1 mile away.

- Find a safe spot while the storm is still 5–6 miles away. The time between flash and boom will be about thirty seconds.

Safe Tent

- In lightning season, choose a safe camp and tent site.

- Stay away from tall cliffs and tall trees, especially isolated tall trees. A stand of trees of uniform height is generally safe.

- Avoid places where water runs or collects. Once lightning strikes, the current may flow where water flows.

- Do not set your tent in the open where it might be a target for lightning—although a low site in low, open rolling hills is considered safe.

proximately 1 mile away—if you matched the right flash to the right boom. To be the safest, find a safe spot when the storm and the lightning are 5 to 6 miles away.

During a storm, avoid places near solitary tall trees and rocky pinnacles. Avoid those same places when you choose a campsite and a tent site.

During a storm, you don't want to be near metal objects, open bodies of water, or long conductors, such as fences. Look for uniform cover, such as the lowest spot in low roll-ing hills or a stand of trees of about the same size (but avoid touching any of the trees). If your chosen low spot has col-lected water, choose another drier low spot. Deep dry caves are usually safe, but shallow overhangs are usually not.

During a storm, sit on some kind of insulating material—your sleeping pad will work great—in a tight position. And spread a group out so a lightning strike won't get everyone.

Finally, if you're caught in a bad spot when a storm breaks, run fast to a safe spot.

Lightning Safety Position

- If your tent is set safely, stay in it and on your pad during a storm.

- If you're outside, find a safe spot and assume the light-ning safety position.

- Squat or sit with your feet drawn up near your body and close together. Sit on your pack or on your sleep-ing pad in case of ground current.

- Spread a group out. In case of a harmful strike, there will be rescuers for the patients.

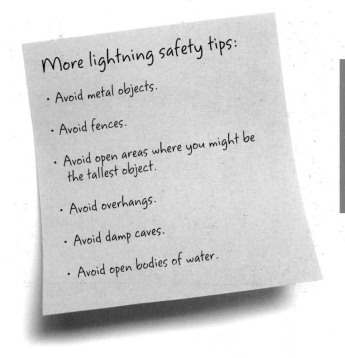

More lightning safety tips:

- Avoid metal objects.

- Avoid fences.

- Avoid open areas where you might be the tallest object.

- Avoid overhangs.

- Avoid damp caves.

- Avoid open bodies of water.

PREDICTING THE WEATHER

With weather forecasting, it will be a guess, but make it a good one

Your best bet in terms of predicting the weather is this: Leave it to the professionals. Check the forecast for the time of your trip and, as mentioned earlier, check into the weather history of the area in which you will travel. Plan accordingly by packing for the worst conditions you might encounter. Knowing regional climate and weather patterns can be at least as useful to you as knowing a specific day's forecast.

Once you're on the trail, pay attention. A few indicators of coming weather have proven relatively trustworthy over the years.

Low-pressure systems often bring rain, and these systems create winds that blow counterclockwise—and that means the wind comes from the south. "Wind from the south brings rain in its mouth."

KNACK HIKING & BACKPACKING

Cirrus Clouds

- Cirrus clouds are high, thin, and wispy, often like a brushstroke of white against a background of blue.

- They are sometimes referred to as "mare's tails."

- They are made of ice crystals and herald the arrival of precipitation in the form of rain or snow.

- Expect some fairly dramatic change in the weather within the next twenty-four hours or so. If you're wrong, at least you are prepared.

Cumulonimbus Clouds

- Cumulus clouds are fat, white, and puffy. They are the clouds that paint pictures in the sky.

- Cumulus clouds might be saying the weather is going to stay the same, or they might tell you a bit of wind is on the way.

- If they darken, thicken, and tower upwards, they are now cumulonimbus clouds, the clouds that bring earth-battering storms.

- Cumulonimbus clouds bring the lightning storms of summer.

Campfire smoke remains near the ground when a low-pressure system is in your area, so rain is possible. In high pressure, the smoke rises straight up, and you can anticipate fair weather.

Clouds often take on a reddish color early in the morning when rain is coming, and the rain usually arrives by nightfall. Reddish clouds in the evening indicate the opposite, a clear sky the next day. "Red sky in the morning, sailors take warning. Red sky at night, sailor's delight."

ZOOM

If you have a barometer or a barometric readout built into your watch, watch for a fall in pressure. A fall can mean that clouds are liable to build and that precipitation will fall. A rise in pressure can indicate the opposite: clearing skies.

Fast-Moving Clouds

- Clouds that hang low in the sky and move fast are being pushed by a hard wind.

- The wind may come down to earth.

- They often signal an overall change in the weather. If they are blown from south to north, there is a better chance of rain than from other directions.

- They could be carrying a storm to you, or they could be carrying it away.

Halo

- Sometimes you will see a hazy halo or wide ring (called a "corona") around the sun by day or the moon by night.

- It usually signals a change in the weather, and it often means rain is on the way.

- The rain usually falls within a day or two.

- If the halo is narrow and tight against the sun or moon, rain may fall in as little as twelve hours.

INSECTS
Protect yourself from the biters and stingers of the natural world

All insects have two things in common: six legs and the habit of spoiling an otherwise wonderful outdoor experience. Most of them, but unfortunately not all, are also kept off your skin with insect repellents.

Studies have consistently shown that nothing repels better than DEET (N,N-diethyl-3-methylbenzamide). Despite negative press, DEET has been applied to human skin literally billions of time without harm, and the EPA has pronounced DEET safe for human use. You should, however, read the directions on labels carefully, and follow them.

Other repellents that have proven their worth include products containing permethrin, lemon eucalyptus oil, and soybean oil. These repellents work but not as long as DEET. If you don't like DEET, use another repellent and apply it more often.

Mosquito

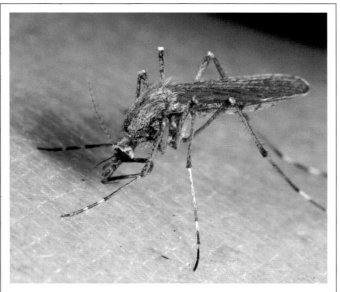

- Mosquitoes are most active at dawn and dusk in areas where you find standing water (in which they lay their eggs).

- Be sure your mosquito netting on tent door and windows is in good repair.

- Apply an insect repellent to exposed skin. DEET works best. Also proven are products containing picaridin, lemon eucalyptus oil, and soybean oil.

- Apply permethrin to your clothing. Not only a repellent, permethrin also kills insects that touch it.

Black Fly

- Black flies are most common in spring and early summer, but they may be encountered later in the summer as well.

- Their eggs are able to hatch in moving water and still water.

- Like mosquitoes, black flies are more attracted to darker clothing than to lighter colors.

- When they swarm hungrily, they may be resistant to insect repellents. Wearing clothing they can't bite through may be your only hope.

But repellents are not your only defense. Other prevention steps include camping well away from water and wet areas, choosing a campsite that takes advantage of bug-deterring breezes, keeping your camp clean of food scraps and other items with bug-attracting aromas such as scented soaps, lotions, deodorant, and toothpaste, keeping your tent door closed whether you're inside or outside, and reducing the use of bright lights at night to avoid the bugs attracted to light.

Remove the stinger of a honeybee as soon as possible by any means. Scraping is not required.

········· RED●LIGHT ··········
The sting of a bee or one of its relatives—wasps, yellow jackets, hornets, fire ants—could cause a life-threatening allergic reaction called "anaphylaxis." If you are severely allergic, you should be carrying injectable epinephrine, and you, and those with you, should know how to use it.

Honeybee

- Bees are attracted to bright colors, including the clothes you might be wearing, and sugary foods.

- Having a clean camp, with containers closed after use, helps keep bees and their relatives—wasps, hornets, and yellow jackets—away.

- Don't swat or make sudden movements. Stand still or back away slowly. They won't sting unless threatened.

- Only the honeybee leaves a stinger in the wound. It should be removed as soon as possible.

Fire Ants

- Fire ants, residents of south-eastern U.S., including Texas, are relatives of the bee.

- They live in mounds and attack furiously if disturbed. They attach themselves with their mandibles and then sting repeatedly with a rear-mounted stinger.

- The sting causes a burning pain. A bump rises, and it itches.

- The application of cold usually reduces the pain. Nothing else has been proven to work.

WILD ANIMALS

TICKS

Worldwide, only mosquitoes pass more diseases to humans than do ticks

With eight legs, ticks are relatives of spiders, not insects. And unlike insects who hit and run when they bite, ticks attach themselves and feed for days. As they feed, they pass germs, if they picked up any from the host of their last meal. Mosquito-borne diseases are passed more often to humans, worldwide, but ticks pass a greater variety of diseases. In the United States ticks make people ill far more often than mosquitoes.

Ticks of the family Ixodidae, the family that passes disease-causing germs to humans, have three feeding stages of life—larval, nymph, and adult—and they almost always drop off their host in between feedings and look for another host when they need to eat again. They will feed on just about

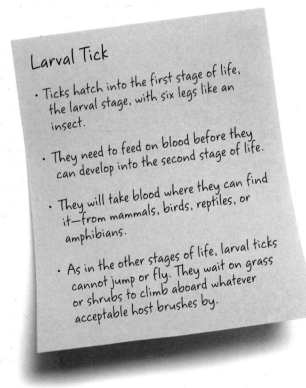

Larval Tick

- Ticks hatch into the first stage of life, the larval stage, with six legs like an insect.

- They need to feed on blood before they can develop into the second stage of life.

- They will take blood where they can find it—from mammals, birds, reptiles, or amphibians.

- As in the other stages of life, larval ticks cannot jump or fly. They wait on grass or shrubs to climb aboard whatever acceptable host brushes by.

Nymph Tick

- In the second stage of life, the nymph stage, ticks have eight legs, clearly identifying them as arachnids, not insects.

- Once again, they need to feed on blood, this time to develop into adults.

- After climbing onto a host, a tick will crawl slowly around until it finds a suitable place to feed.

- Although they can feed anywhere, they attach to humans in places the bitten human cannot see about 20 percent of the time.

anything with blood—mammals, birds, even reptiles. Thus they are well-endowed with the ability to spread germs.

Once they find a host, ticks may hike around slowly for hours before choosing a spot to settle down and, with specialized pincer-like organs, dig a small, painless wound in the host. They then insert a feeding apparatus with a relatively powerful sucking mechanism that allows ticks to ingest blood. Now anchored firmly to skin, ticks feed for an average of two to five days, and sometimes longer than five days, depending on the species. On the plus side, they pass germs slowly as they feed, not sharing enough to cause disease unless they have fed for hours, sometimes more than twenty-four hours.

Of critical importance during tick season is checking yourself twice a day. Because ticks embed often in hard-to-see spots, you will need help or a mirror to perform a thorough check. Immediately remove all free-ranging and embedded ticks (see below).

Another plus: Though not insects, ticks are repelled by insect repellents, those containing DEET and permethrin working especially well.

Adult Tick

- Adulthood is the third and final stage of a tick's life.

- Adult ticks must feed on blood before they can reproduce.

- Ticks anchor themselves by inserting a barbed, harpoon-like structure in their mouth area into skin.

The barbs point backward, making them difficult to remove.

- They will feed until satiated, a point at which they are vastly bigger than when they attached. After feeding, they usually fall off the host.

Tick Removal

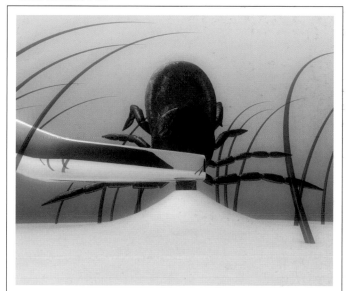

- Ticks pass germs as they feed. If they are crawling around unattached, they have not yet fed.

- Embedded ticks should be removed as soon as possible.

- Grasp the tick near your skin with pointed tweezers

and pull directly out without jerking or twisting. Do not squeeze the tick during removal. If you save the tick, it can be tested for disease later if you get sick.

- No other method removes the tick before it can pass more germs.

SPIDERS

Scary in appearance, spiders frighten many people but seldom harm people

First, for haters of spiders, some bad news: There are billions of them, and almost all of them carry venom that can be injected with a bite from their fangs. All spiders are also carnivorous, spending their waking hours waiting for or searching for living prey. When they bite, their venom paralyzes their natural prey and liquefies the tissues of the prey so the spiders can then ingest their meal.

But now the good news: Only a few dozen species on this entire planet have a bite harmful to humans. Most either have venom that doesn't work on humans, too little venom

Black Widow Spider

- Almost all female black widows have an hourglass shape on the underside of their abdomen. It is usually red.

- Only the female bites, and only when threatened, and the bite is usually painless.

- But as the venom spreads, the pain becomes intense—muscular cramping that tends to center in the abdomen.

- Nothing can be done except the application of cold to the bite site and strong pain-killers. Antivenin is available if needed. Find a doctor. Deaths in humans are rare.

Recluse Spider

- Recluse spiders usually have the shape of a fiddle on their head and back, giving them the name "fiddleback."

- Both sexes are equally venomous, not that it really matters because they look the same.

- The bite is usually painful, followed by the development of a painful red blister. It often becomes "volcanic," open and raw, refusing to heal.

- There is nothing to do but find a doctor. Human deaths are extremely rare.

to bother us, or fangs too weak to bite through our skin. In the U.S., "dangerous to humans" is a tag applied to only three spiders: widows, browns, and hobos (see below).

If you think someone has been bitten by a dangerous spider, it is important to keep that person calm. If the bite site is evident, wash it and apply an antiseptic. For pain, cool the bite site with ice, if possible, or with cold water if that's all you have. Cold also reduces blood flow to the injured area, which slows down the spread of the venom. A pain-killing drug, if you have one, may also be useful. Pain from serious spider bites, a black widow bite being an example, may require more pain-killing power than the normal first aid kit contains.

Forgoing the rest of your trip to find a medical facility is strongly advised, especially if you are unsure what is causing distress in the person you think bitten. But most people bitten by dangerous spiders are released from the hospital after eight to twelve hours with no problems. Youngsters, elderly, and the very sick may be admitted for longer.

Hobo Spider

- The hobo (northwestern brown) spider is light brown, perhaps appearing to have a hint of yellow or green.

- The legs are conspicuously hairy.

- Their legs reach up to 1.5 inches in length, a bit larger than the average recluse spider. But they look like a recluse without the fiddle.

- The bite they inflict causes a reaction similar to a recluse bite, and your response should be the same.

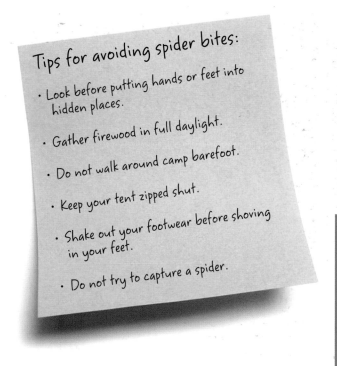

Tips for avoiding spider bites:

- Look before putting hands or feet into hidden places.

- Gather firewood in full daylight.

- Do not walk around camp barefoot.

- Keep your tent zipped shut.

- Shake out your footwear before shoving in your feet.

- Do not try to capture a spider.

169

SNAKES

It is rare for a human to die from a snakebite in the United States

Snakes almost universally bite a human only when they feel threatened. They feel threatened only when they are touched (such as stepped on) or cornered. If one does bite you, your chances of survival are excellent.

One in four bites from pit vipers does not inject venom.

Some experts estimate the number of venomous snakebites in the United States to fall between 7,000 and 8,000 per year. But in many cases the snake's identity remains in doubt, and the number is probably lower. The number of people who die from all those snakebites is remarkably low, as low as five to six per year and often less, according to the American Association of Poison Control Centers. The cause of the low

Diamondback Rattlesnake

- There are at least thirty-four different pit vipers in the U.S. All rattlesnakes are pit vipers.

- Pit vipers have hinged fangs that spring forward and point down at an angle of 90 degrees from the roof of their mouths.

- They inject venom with a muscular contraction that pushes the venom down the hollow fangs.

- They do not always inject venom, but when they do it can vary from a mild to a severe envenomation.

Water Moccasin

- Water moccasins (cottonmouths) are pit vipers that do not have rattles.

- Like all pit vipers, they have triangular heads, catlike pupils, and heat-sensitive pits between the eyes and the nostrils.

- Like all pit vipers, they can strike no more than a little past half their body length.

- When a pit viper envenomates, there is severe burning pain, followed by swelling. The more the pain and swelling, the worse the envenomation.

death rates is attributed to the availability of effective anti-venins and the relatively low toxicity, compared with snakes worldwide, of U.S. snakes.

At least ninety-nine out of every one hundred poisonous bites by indigenous snakes in the U.S.—and many years one hundred out of one hundred—are received from a pit viper: a rattlesnake, a copperhead, or a water moccasin (or cotton-mouth). The other dangerous U.S. snake is the coral snake.

Coral snake venom is more powerful than pit viper venom, but the symptoms of coral snake venom may not show up for twelve hours or more after the bite. For those reasons, anyone bitten should be on the way to a medical facility as soon as possible.

Copperhead

- Copperheads are the only other U.S. pit vipers without rattles.

- As with all pit viper bites, the worse the envenoma-tion, the sicker the patient gets—nausea, weakness, dizziness, among other things.

- Pit viper bites are often made worse by well-meaning rescuers.

- You need do no more than keep the patient calm and find a doctor as soon as possible. It is best if the patient remains still, but if walking gets you to a doctor quicker, then walk.

Coral Snake

- In the U.S. coral snakes are banded in red, black, and yellow. Remember: Red on black, venom lack—red on yellow, kill a fellow.

- They are not pit vipers; their venom is stronger than most pit viper venom.

- Their dull fangs require them to chew before they can break human skin. You may have time to snatch them off.

- The bitten need a doctor as soon as possible, even though the signs and symp-toms of poisoning may take hours to develop.

BEARS

Almost all bear encounters can be prevented if you take the right precautions

Almost everyone fears bears more than they need to. Many people have hiked for years in bear country without ever seeing one. Still, close encounters can go against you and should be avoided whenever possible. It is certainly wise to take steps to prevent a meeting with something so large, powerful, and nearly always hungry.

Probably more important than anything else is staying away from places bears obviously frequent. If you see bear scat, bear tracks, claw marks on trees, a gnawed carcass of a deer or elk, or a bear, keep on hiking.

When an area is reportedly thick with bears, pitch your tent out in the open. Bears do not like surprises, and seeing you

To avoid confrontations with bears:

- Make noise as you hike.

- Do not camp where you see bear signs: scat, tracks, clawed trees.

- Set your tent where a bear can see it from a long way off.

- Camp clean.

- Store all aromatic items out of a bear's reach.

Black Bear

- Black bears may be black or several shades of brown. They weigh up to about three hundred pounds.

- All bears have a well-developed sense of personal space. The size of the space varies. If you enter their space, they will flee or fight. Black bears usually flee.

- Beware the black bear that sees you yet still approaches.

- If a black bear approaches, do not run. Stand your ground. Yell. Clap your hands. Lunge at the bear. Throw things.

a long way off usually results in the bear going a different direction.

In bear country, talk, sing, and otherwise make some noise as you travel and camp. The bear who knows you're there is the bear you don't see.

Camp clean. Any garbage—leftovers, trash—is a potential attractant. Keep your garbage separately bagged. If you burn garbage, throw it on the fire early in the day, and bag anything that does not completely burn.

At night, store all your food, garbage, and anything else fragrant—toothpaste, soap, chewing gum—in ways that do not attract bears. Carry it 300 feet or so from your camp, and hang it at least 10 feet off the ground and at least 6 feet from the trunk of a tree. You can hang your bag from a limb, but it's even better to tie a rope between two trees and suspend the bag from the middle of the rope. When trees are scarce, double bag your food in plastic and store it on the ground at least 300 feet from your tent.

Grizzly Bear

If attacked by a bear:

- If a black bear attacks, fight back aggressively.

- Hit a black bear in the eyes and nose.

- If the bear is a grizzly, fall on your stomach, arms around your head, and play dead.

- Keep playing dead if the grizzly rolls you over.

- But keep rolling until you're facedown again.

- Grizzly bears of the Rocky Mountains may reach over five hundred pounds in weight.

- Their personal space is larger than a black bear's space. The grizzly you catch suddenly up close is the one most likely to charge.

- Groups are far less likely to be charged than an individual.

- If a grizzly charges, do not run. Stand your ground. The bear may suddenly stop. If the bear stops, stand still. Don't yell. Then move very slowly, angling away from the bear.

MOUNTAIN LIONS
The number of mountain lion attacks on humans is on the rise

Bear attacks, primarily grizzly attacks, often come from a bear that feels threatened. Mountain lions—also known as "cougars" and "pumas"—attack humans as a source of food and for no other known reason. And while the number of bear attacks has been relatively constant, lion attacks are on the rise—probably because those lions are having trouble finding anything else to eat. You need to be prepared.

If you see a mountain lion, do not run. Face it, and stand up tall. Make and maintain eye contact. Because a lion typically attacks in stealth, knowing you have seen it could prevent a charge. Pick up rocks or sticks, and strike an aggressive pose.

Adults should pick up small children. Larger children should crowd against an adult. Lions prefer a smaller target, and you want to eliminate the smallness of children. Mountain lions

To avoid mountain lion confrontations:

- Travel with a group and never alone.

- Limit your activities at dawn and dusk.

- Don't go jogging, especially alone, in lion country.

- Avoid lion kills—partially eaten carcasses covered in dirt and debris.

Relaxed Mountain Lion

- Mountain lions can weigh 140 pounds and reach more than 7 feet in length, including the tail. They can reach speeds of 45 miles per hour, faster than any bear.

- They lead secretive lives and are seldom seen by humans.

- Deer and elk are their primary food sources.

- Attacks on humans are on the rise, probably due to loss of their normal habitat and usual food sources.

have charged into groups of people to snatch a small child.

If the mountain lion does not back off, lift your arms or your pack to make yourself look bigger. Move slowly toward higher ground.

If it moves toward you, scream or make other noises that might sound intimidating. If it's close enough, throw things at the lion. Show your teeth. Your goal is to appear dangerous.

A mountain lion getting ready to attack holds its body near the ground. Its rear legs begin to pump, and its ears turn with the furry sides away from you. Swallow your fear, and attack the lion. If you have a stick, stab at its face. If you have no stick, charge but stop before its claws can reach you.

If it attacks, fight back with all your strength, directing blows at the lion's face and ears. It may comfort you to know mountain lions rarely counterattack someone on the attack.

Tense Mountain Lion

- Mountain lions sneak up on their prey, then suddenly rush in from behind and attempt to bite and break the neck.

- Preparing to attack, a mountain lion stays low to the ground, crouching or creeping forward.

- The tail twitches, and the ears are erect.

- Just before attacking, the rear legs begin to pump, moving up and down, and the ears are turned with the furry sides away from you.

If you encounter a mountain lion:

- Don't run.

- Stand tall and keep facing the lion.

- Maintain eye contact.

- Pick up a weapon—a stick or rock.

- Yell and show your teeth.

- If the lion moves toward you, step toward it, brandishing your weapon.

- If it attacks, fight aggressively, striking at the eyes, nose, and ears.

PLANTS THAT CAUSE ITCHING

Avoid contact with these plants—but if you don't, treat yourself correctly

Not everybody reacts to the resinous oil, urushiol, inside poison ivy, oak, and sumac, but more than 85 percent of people do—and the itching is usually ferocious. If you make contact, what you do next is extremely important.

In addition to recognizing and avoiding the plants, washing may prevent the reaction, washing as soon as possible after you realize you may have touched one of these poisonous plants. Even the extremely sensitive have an estimated five to ten minutes to wash off the urushiol before it soaks in enough to cause trouble. Those of low sensitivity may have two hours. Cold water, lots and lots of it, inactivates urushiol, so plunging into a nearby stream or lake

Poison Ivy as a Shrub

- Poison ivy is a common plant found in most parts of the U.S.

- Its appearance varies greatly, but it has two primary forms. One form is a small shrub.

- Although it can grow as an individual shrub, it most often grows in patches of many plants, some plants reaching 30 inches in height.

- As with poison oak and sumac, urushiol is found in the leaves, stems, roots, berries, and flowers, and the oil is active throughout the year.

Poison Ivy as a Vine

- The second form of poison ivy is a "hairy" vine that grows up trees.

- Both forms have leaflets that grow in threes at the ends of the stems.

- As with poison oak and sumac, you can get the oil on your skin by brushing the plant or by touching something—such as your shoes—that has touched the plant.

- When these plants are burned, the oil, still active, can be carried in particles of smoke.

would be a reasonable act. If you have plenty of cold water available, especially within the first three minutes of contact, soap does not help. Avoid hot water that may spread the oil around more than take it off.

The use of soap is recommended after the three-minute period ends. As to what kind of soap, the experts vary, but detergents—such as your camp soap—seem to work as well as anything. Of greater importance than what kind of soap is how you use it. Use repeated rubbings, not scrubbings, with sufficient rinses in between.

············ RED ● LIGHT ·············

Poison ivy can grow as a ground cover, a small shrub, or a woody, ivy-like vine, all rich in the oil that causes the unpleasant reaction. To protect yourself, you need to know what it looks like in your area of travel—and avoid contact with all parts of the plant.

Poison Oak

- There are actually two varieties of poison oak: eastern and western. The western plants cause more reactions in humans because they are far more ubiquitous.

- The plants have leaflets in sets of three, but the leaves are more oaklike in appearance.

- Poison oak grows most often as a viney, woody shrub.

- As with poison ivy and sumac, the offending oil stays active for years after being removed from the plants.

Poison Sumac

- Poison sumac is a tree growing in the eastern U.S. in wet or flooded ground, most often in swamps.

- It reaches heights ranging from 6 to 20 feet.

- It has compound leaves of five to seventeen leaflets. The leaflets grow to about 5 inches from veins that are red in color.

- As with poison oak and ivy, the oil that causes an allergic reaction is found in all parts of the plant.

PLANTS THAT POISON

Identifying and avoiding poisonous plants can save your life—or another's life

The most important guideline for avoiding ingestion of a poisonous plant is this: Never eat a wild plant unless you are absolutely certain it is safe. The people who do die are usually children who haven't been taught better or adults seeking a recreational high who pick the wrong plant. Fortunately, death by wild plant poisoning is rare. But knowing what to do in the case of accidental ingestion can be critically vital.

If you think someone has eaten a poisonous plant, and it happened within the past few minutes, induce vomiting—but only if the person has not altered in level of consciousness. Have the person drink a large mug of water and then lean forward, mouth open wide. Reach in gently with a finger

Water Hemlock

- Many experts consider water hemlock the most poisonous plant in the U.S.

- It is a perennial herb, a member of the carrot family that grows throughout North America along streams and in wet meadows.

- The leaves are compound, comprised of leaflets that are narrow, toothed, and pointed. The flowers are small and white, growing in flat-topped clusters.

- All parts of the plant are toxic, especially the roots and young growth.

Jimsonweed

- Jimsonweed (or datura) is a coarse, weedy herb that grows throughout the U.S.

- The leaves are large and sort of oval-shaped with wavy margins, the stems are stout, and these parts of the plant have an unpleasant odor. It develops large, lovely, trumpet-shaped white to purple flowers that smell nice.

- All parts of the plant are poisonous, especially the leaves and seeds.

- Bits of this plant are sometimes ingested for the hallucinogenic effect—not a good idea.

or two, and tickle the back of the throat to stimulate vomiting. As the minutes pass, vomiting becomes less and less useful, and its usefulness ends at approximately thirty minutes.

Some hikers, especially parents, choose to carry activated charcoal in their first aid kits. Its efficacy is unsupported by hard scientific evidence, but it might help.

The poisoned person should drink as much water as reasonably possible while being removed from the trip and to a doctor. Bring along a part of the plant for positive identification. The doctor's treatment will be aided if you can report how much of the plant was eaten, when it was eaten, and how long after ingestion the victim started to feel sick (if, of course, the person started to feel sick).

If you enjoy plants and would like to try eating some of the tastier species, hike with a plant expert and/or carry a guidebook that provides photos and precise descriptions of local plants—and still think twice before taking a bite.

Deadly Nightshade

- The deadly nightshade (or belladonna) is a branching perennial found extensively in the U.S.

- It grows to 5 feet in height with leaves that reach 7 inches. Its flowers are bell-shaped and dull purple with a faint scent.

- The green berries turn black and have a slightly sweet taste when they're ripe.

- It is a very deadly plant indeed: Ingesting two berries could kill a child, and ten berries or one leaf could kill an adult.

Monkshood

- Monkshood is a perennial herb that can grow to 6 feet in height in moist meadows and along streams of the western U.S.

- The flowers are dark blue, with the upper sepal draping over very much like a small hood.

- Later the seeds develop inside a short, beaked capsule.

- All parts are toxic, especially the seeds and roots. It is a truly dangerous plant: Small amounts, under the right growing conditions, have proven lethal to humans.

MUSHROOMS THAT POISON

Many toxic fungi have edible cousins that are very similar in appearance

Almost all humans who have died from eating a bad mushroom have been adults who mistakenly identified the offending fungi as a safe one.

The mushroom most likely to kill if ingested is a member of the Amanita species (death cap, death angel, or destroying angel), responsible for 90–95 percent of all human deaths by mushrooms. A member of this species can produce fatal liver and kidney failure in two to three days. Typically growing under deciduous trees in the United States, Amanitas show a yellowish to white cap 1.5 to 6.5 inches (4–16 centimeters) in diameter and a thick stalk 2–7 inches (5–18 centimeters) in length with a large bulb at the base. The gills under the cap

Deadly Amanita

- The deadly Amanita is a member of a group of mushrooms called "destroying angels."

- It is a chalky white mushroom with a bulbous base that grows in open woodlands throughout the U.S. with the exception of the Pacific Coast.

- The entire plant is toxic, and this mushroom accounts for somewhere between 90 and 95 percent of all human mushroom poisoning deaths.

- One mushroom, raw or cooked, may prove fatal.

Fly Amanita

- The fly Amanita has a wide red to yellow cap, white scales, and a whitish stalk. It may reach 10 inches in height.

- It is often found growing in circular groups, called "fairy rings," in woods and meadows.

- Deranged, manic behavior, delirium, and a deathlike sleep are common reactions to ingestion. Some people report a feeling of elation. Explosive diarrhea is possible.

- Although the effects are severe, death is rare.

are usually easily visible and white to green in color.

Onset of gastrointestinal distress—severe nausea, vomiting, abdominal cramps, diarrhea—with Amanita, and with all potentially death-causing mushrooms, usually occurs six to twelve hours after ingestion. As a general rule, remember this: If symptoms develop within approximately two hours of ingestion, it is unlikely that the mushroom is one of the potentially fatal varieties. In other words, if stomach discomfort soon follows mushroom munching, the chance of serious mushroom poisoning is extremely slim.

Here's the main point: By the time signs and symptoms show up in serious mushroom poisonings, it's too late to do anything except hurry to a hospital where supportive care might save the life of the person. That means if you think someone has eaten a bad mushroom, start treatment quickly. If you're in doubt, start treatment quickly. You don't want to wait for signs and symptoms. Each moment that passes lets more and more poison be absorbed into the person's system. Treatment—give water, induce vomiting, give water—is the same as for poisonous plants (see page 178).

False Morel

- True morels are coveted for their tasty edibility. But false morels, a name given to several similar mushrooms, are questionable dining options.

- True and false morels share a cap that looks somewhat like the wrinkled surface of a brain.

- True morels are hollow, and almost all false morels have a solid or cottony mass inside.

- The toxicity of false morels remains in question, but most experts agree they should not be eaten.

Galerina

- More than three hundred species of the mushroom Galerina are known to exist. You can find them growing almost everywhere.

- In general, they are the "little brown mushrooms" of the world. And at least one species contains the hallucinogen psilocybin.

- Because they are small and relatively unattractive, they are seldom eaten.

- But most, though not all, of the Galerinas contain a toxin that could make you very sick and possibly dead.

PLANTS THAT BOTHER

Some plants hurt or irritate your skin without causing a serious problem

Contact with some plants causes trauma to the skin or skin irritation that almost always resolves harmlessly. But in the meantime you can be terribly bothered. In all cases, it's worth your time to learn to identify those plants in your area of travel—and avoid touching them. If that fails, here are some suggestions.

Contact with cactus spines seldom comes in singles. With large spines, settle down with your tweezers (which should be in all first aid kits) and laboriously pick them out, one by one, despite the protestations of the victim. They need to come out. If, however, you have glue on hand, glue such as Elmer's or rubber cement (both of which have been tested

Cactus

- Cacti come in all shapes and sizes imaginable, are adapted to hot and arid environments, and have sharp spines.

- The spines, being organic, are sources of infection and should be removed from human skin as soon as possible.

- You can pull them out with tweezers or the small pliers often found as a part of a multipurpose tool.

- The spines of some species of chollas come off in clusters that may be pried out with a comb.

Stinging Nettle

- Stinging nettles are covered in hairs. The tips of the hairs break off and lodge in skin when touched.

- The hair tips become like tiny syringes injecting several irritants that cause a stinging burn and itching.

- The length and severity of the reaction depend on individual sensitivity.

- There is not much to be done, although some people report relief from applying baking soda mixed with a little water.

and found functional), smear it on the affected body part. Press on a piece of gauze—or paper will work—while the glue is moist. After drying, the gauze can be peeled off, taking with it a very high percentage of the spines, as much as 95 percent in experiments. This method is especially effective when the spines are small. It makes a small bottle of glue in your first aid kit a reasonable addition in cactus country.

Some plants contain chemical skin irritants in their fluids. This group includes buttercups, mustard seed plants, and the spurges (which include snow on the mountain, crown of thorns, and milkweeds). Individuals vary in their reaction from mild skin redness to large lesions (an obvious skin injury). As soon as you notice something going on, wash that area of skin with soap and water. This is not an allergic reaction, so anti-allergy medications will work only a little bit or not at all. You can periodically soak the area of skin in cold water or apply a cold, wet compress for some relief until the reaction resolves.

Buttercup

- The buttercups, numerous in species, grow in woods, meadows, and along streams over much of the world.

- The flowers are almost always buttery yellow and may be cup-shaped.

- The leaves and sap contain a skin irritant that causes anywhere from a little to a lot of redness and itching.

- The entire plant is poisonous if eaten, but the toxins become harmless when the plant is dried.

Wild Mustard

- Mustards of the genus *Brassica* grow as broad-leafed herbs or small shrubs.

- They have yellow flowers that bloom in long clusters.

- The oil of these plants is irritating to skin, causing redness and itching, the severity depending on the concentration of the oil. In your eye, enough oil could cause blindness.

- Although mustard in a bottle is tasty and obviously safe, eating these plants causes vomiting and diarrhea.

WOUNDS
Scrapes and small cuts cause the most visits to the first aid kit

Wilderness wounds seldom bleed badly enough to cause concern. But if you are concerned, apply direct pressure to the wound. Direct pressure may be augmented with elevation of the wound to higher than the bleeder's heart. Stopping blood loss rarely requires anything else.

Next, you need to clean and bandage the wound to prevent infection. But first, wash your own hands and put on protective gloves. Start the cleaning process by scrubbing around the wound with soap and water and then rinsing the soap off with disinfected water. Remove any foreign matter embedded in the wound by using disinfected tweezers or by gently brushing the matter out of the wound.

Scrapes often have foreign matter firmly embedded, and you'll need to scrub the surface of the wound itself to get it

Step 1: Stop Serious Bleeding

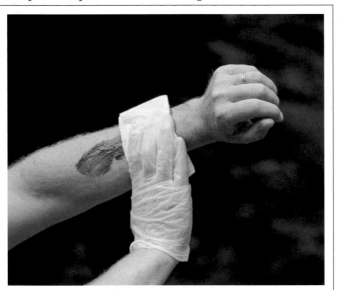

- Small wounds may be allowed to bleed to a stop. Minor bleeding is harmless and actually cleans out the wound a bit.

- Pressure directly on the wound will stop almost all serious bleeding. The bleeding person can often apply the pressure. If you apply pressure to another person, wear the surgical gloves found in many kits.

- You must press firmly enough to stop the flow of blood.

- Elevation of the wound above the bleeder's heart will encourage bleeding to stop.

Step 2: Clean the Wound

- With a clean cloth or gauze and soap, scrub the skin around the wound.

- Do not scrub inside the wound itself unless the wound is an abrasion (a scrape).

- Irrigate the surface of the wound using an irrigation syringe found in many kits. Use at least a half liter of water.

- Without an irrigation syringe, you can improvise. You can, for example, use a plastic bag filled with water with a tiny hole punched in it.

clean. Otherwise the best method for cleaning the wound is mechanical irrigation. Irrigation involves a high-pressure stream of an acceptable solution directed into the wound, best directed from an irrigation syringe. For almost all wounds, the best cleaning solution is plain disinfected water. Draw the water into the syringe, hold it about 2 inches above the wound and perpendicular to the wound, and push down forcefully on the plunger. Keep the wound tipped so the solution runs out. Use at least half a liter, more if the wound still looks unclean. Without an irrigation syringe, you can improvise by using a biking water bottle, melting a pinhole in the center of the lid of a standard water bottle, or punching a pinhole in a clean plastic bag filled with water and then squeezing out the water.

After cleaning, apply a sterile bandage to the wound. An adhesive strip bandage will cover smaller wounds. Larger wounds will need a larger bandage, such as a gauze pad and tape.

Step 3: Close Wounds that Gape

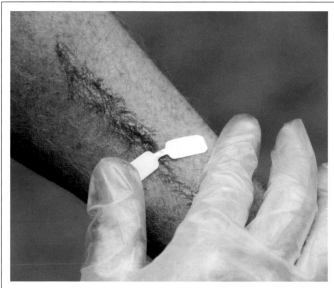

- After cleaning, wounds that gape open will heal best if taped shut.

- The edges of the wound need to be taped in exactly the place where they were before the injury. Take your time.

- You can use butterfly adhesive strips or any sticky tape cut into thin strips.

- If, however, the wound gapes open more than 0.5 inch, cover it with sterile gauze and find a doctor. This wound needs stitches.

Step 4: Bandage the Wound

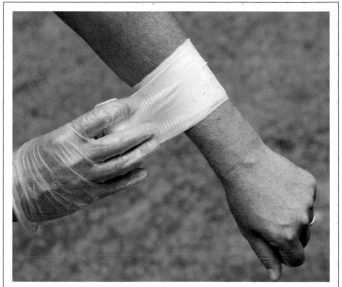

- All open wounds should be covered with a sterile bandage.

- An adhesive strip (a Band-Aid, for example) is a sterile bandage for small wounds.

- Larger wounds can be covered with gauze pads that are held in place with tape or an elastic wrap. You can also cover wounds with roll gauze.

- Wounds should be checked every day and the old bandage replaced with a new one. If you see signs of infection, find a doctor.

BLISTERS

The single most common outdoor injury can be prevented in most cases

Injury-wise, nothing troubles hikers more often than a blister on a foot. The hot spots that, if ignored, later become fluid-filled bubbles form when friction causes a shearing away of the tough outer layer of skin from the sensitive inner layer. Only where skin is hardened is it thick enough for this to happen—heels, toes, soles, palms. Loose skin just wears away with friction, leaving an abrasion. Blisters range from unpleasant to terribly debilitating. But they are not a serious problem unless they become infected.

What should you do? Blisters feel better when the bubble is deflated, and controlled draining is far better than having them rupture inside a dirty sock. Clean around the site

Step 1: Wash the Site

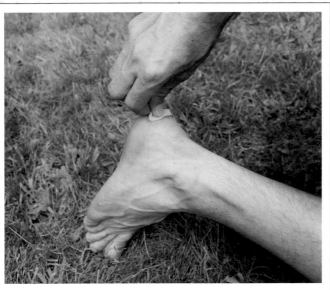

- Before you drain the fluid-filled bubble, wash around the entire site, including a gentle washing of the bubble.

- You can wash with soap and a soft cloth or gauze. If you use soap, rinse the site after washing.

- Or you can wipe the entire site with an alcohol prep pad found in many first aid kits.

- Some kits include a wet, soapy pad inside a foil packet. They work well.

Step 2: Drain the Bubble

- You will need to gently open the bubble to drain it.

- You can use anything with a sharp point such as a knife or a safety pin.

- The sharp point needs to be disinfected first. You can wipe it with alcohol or heat it with a flame. The

- black stuff left after heating is sterile. Don't wipe it off, or the disinfection will be voided.

- After opening, gently massage out the fluid with a gauze pad.

thoroughly. Sterilize the point of a needle or knife with heat from a match or lighter or by wiping the tip with alcohol, and break the bubble. Massage the fluid out. Leaving the roof of the blister intact will make it feel better and heal faster. If the roof has been rubbed away, treat the wound as you would any other (see page 184). Apply a dressing that limits friction: a bandage designed especially to cover a blister site or a moleskin "donut" (a rounded piece of moleskin with a hole cut in the center) filled with ointment, or ointment and a gauze pad over the blister.

Blisters can be prevented by: 1) wearing boots or shoes that fit and are broken in, 2) wearing a thin inner sock under a thicker outer sock (the socks will move against each other, reducing friction on the skin), 3) treating hot spots with moleskin, a special blister-preventing product, tape (duct will work), or tincture of benzoin compound before they become blisters, and 4) taking off your boots to let your feet cool off and dry when you take a break from hiking.

Step 3: Bandage the Drained Bubble

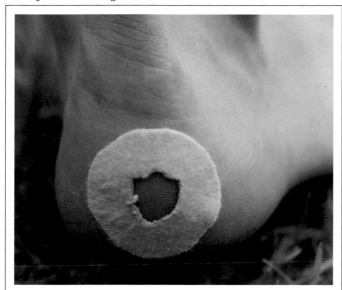

- The bandage for a drained blister needs to protect the site from further friction.

- A moleskin donut works well. Cut a piece of moleskin into a circle, fold it, and cut out the center. The donut needs to be big enough to fit around the drained bubble.

- Stick the donut over the drained bubble with the wound in the hole.

- Fill the hole with an antimicrobial ointment to further protect against friction.

Step 4: Tape over the Hole

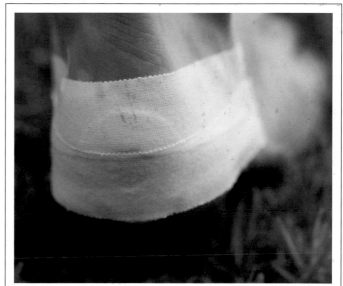

- To keep the ointment in the hole and to further protect the site, place tape over the donut.

- The strip of tape should be long enough to reach around the heel and down about halfway to the toes on both sides of the foot.

- If your tape is narrow, you can use more than one strip.

- Place a strip of tape around the foot, not too tight, to hold the ends of the longer strips of tape in place.

SPRAINS AND STRAINS

Properly treated, musculoskeletal injuries do not have to sideline the victim

Not far behind wounds, including blisters, the next most common injuries to hikers are musculoskeletal and usually involve ankles or knees.

Sprains are tears in ligaments, and strains are overstretched muscles and/or the tendons that attach muscles to bones. They may be impossible to tell apart, but you don't have to know for sure because they are both treated the same. They can range from a mild annoyance to debilitating. Pain should encourage sensible action, and sensible action involves proper first aid.

First aid is RICE: rest, ice, compression, and elevation. But RICE should be applied after an initial evaluation of the injury.

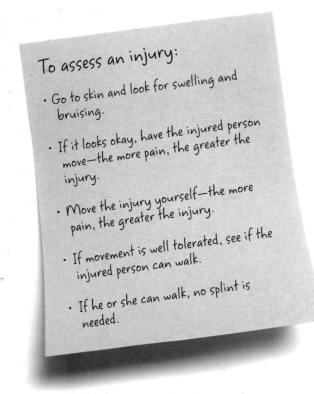

To assess an injury:

- Go to skin and look for swelling and bruising.

- If it looks okay, have the injured person move—the more pain, the greater the injury.

- Move the injury yourself—the more pain, the greater the injury.

- If movement is well tolerated, see if the injured person can walk.

- If he or she can walk, no splint is needed.

RICE the Injury

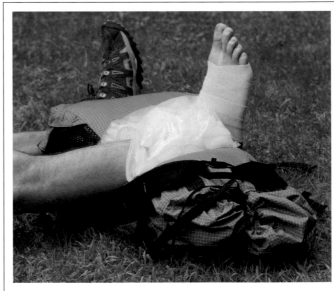

- Rest: Keep the injured person comfortably at rest during the RICE therapy.

- Ice: Place cold on the injury—ice or snow in a plastic bag will work, or soak the injury in cold water, or wrap it in wet cotton.

- Compression: Apply an elastic wrap around the injury, working from the toes toward the calf if the ankle is injured.

- Elevation: Prop the injury up at or above the level of the injured person's heart.

The primary goal of the evaluation is to determine if the injury is usable or not. The injured person should be at rest, relaxed. Take a look at the injury. Look for deformities and rapid swelling and discoloration. Have the person actively move the joint and evaluate the amount of pain involved. Move the joint more aggressively with your hands and evaluate the pain response. Finally, if the injury appears usable, have the person test it with his or her body weight. A usable injury can be, well, used. And it should be used to walk slowly out and find a doctor.

············· RED ● LIGHT ·············

Apply an elastic wrap toward the heart—from the toes toward the heart or from the fingers toward the heart— and not the reverse. Never put a wrap on tighter than about 50 percent of its stretch. If it's too tight, it can cut off circulation and cause a serious injury.

Wrap the Injury

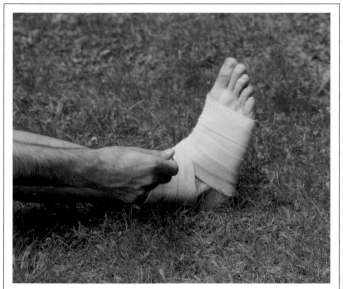

- After twenty to thirty minutes of RICE therapy, remove the cold and the compression and give the area time to warm back up.

- This is usually complete in twelve to fifteen minutes. The injured person should remain at rest.

- After rewarming, allow the person to walk again to be sure she or he still can.

- Before hitting the trail, reapply the elastic wrap. Use the wrap for the remainder of the hike, taking it off during sleep periods.

Monitor the Injury

- If possible, lighten the load on the injured person's back—share the load—and find a hiking staff to improve the victim's balance.

- The injured person needs to stay tuned to the injury.

- If numbness or tingling develops, a break is necessary, and the injury should be looked at and propped up.

- If the pain becomes too much, you will need to get a rescue team to carry the injured person.

FRACTURES

If the bone could be fractured (broken), it needs a splint

Sprain? Strain? Fracture? The general rule is: When in doubt, splint! A splint should immobilize the broken bone(s), prevent further injury, and maximize patient comfort until a medical facility can be reached. To do this best, a splint needs to be made of something soft to pad the injury comfortably and then something rigid enough to provide support. Padding should fill all the spaces within the system to prevent movement of the injury. Avoid the void! In addition, a splint should be long enough to immobilize the joints above and below a broken bone or immobilize the bones above and below an injured joint.

Splints should immobilize the injury in the position of function or as close to position of function as possible. Functional positions include: 1) spine, including neck and pelvis, straight

Step 1: Pad the Injury

- To splint an injury, you need lots of padding.

- The padding can be extra clothing, a light sleeping bag, or anything soft and bulky. With only a little extra clothing, you can increase the padding by filling it with leaves and other soft forest debris.

- Moving gently, wrap the padding completely around the injury site.

- It will be difficult to continue with too much padding. A couple of inches thick should be enough.

Step 2: Apply Rigid Support

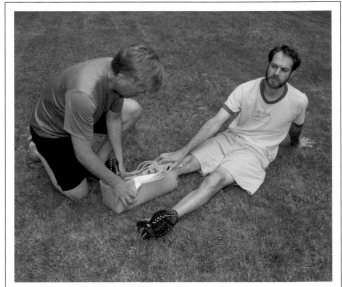

- A sleeping pad, once tied firmly in place, will be rigid enough for a broken leg.

- The pad should be slipped beneath the leg. It should reach from near the groin to past the foot.

- If the pad is too wide, it can be folded up on one or both sides.

- The part of the pad extending beyond the foot should be rolled up to the bottom of the foot.

with padding in the small of the back, 2) legs almost straight with padding behind the knees for slight flexion, 3) feet at 90 degrees to legs, 4) arms flexed to cross the heart, and 5) hands in a functional curve with padding in the palms.

In choosing materials for splinting, you are limited only by imagination: sleeping bags, foamlite pads (and they can be cut to fit the problem), extra clothing, soft debris from the forest floor stuffed into extra clothing. For rigidity there are items such as sticks, tent poles, ski poles, ice axes, Crazy Creek Chairs, internal and external pack frames. Lightweight commercial splints are available as additions to your first aid kit (e.g., SAM Splint, wire splints). Splints can be secured in place with things like bandannas, strips of clothing, pack straps, belts, and rope. Useful items in your first aid kit for securing splints include tape, elastic wraps, and roll gauze. Large triangular bandages are helpful in creating slings and swaths.

Step 3: Secure the Rigid Support

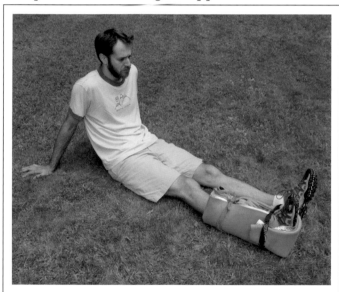

- Starting at the foot, tie the rolled-up end of the pad to the foot. The foot should end up supported at about 90 degrees to the leg.

- You can use bandannas, pack straps, pieces of rope, shoelaces, or whatever you have.

- Continue up the leg, tying the pad firmly in place. Remember: Firm ties make the pad rigid.

- Use knots that are easy to loosen. You may have to remove the splint periodically for comfort or to check the injury.

Step 4: Go for Help

- You will need a litter to carry the injured person out.

- If your group is large enough, some members can stay with the injured person while others go for help.

- With a group of two, make the injured person as com-fortable and protected as possible. Leave water and food within reach.

- Rescues are better managed if you carry out a written description of what happened and exactly where the injured person is.

COLD ILLNESS

When you lose internal heat faster than you gain it, you get hypothermia

Hypothermia, by far the most common cold illness, is a lowering of the body's core temperature—usually at 98.6° F—to a point where normal brain and/or muscle function is impaired. This condition may be mild, moderate, or life-threateningly severe.

In mild cases, the cold person shivers, fumbles when trying to perform complex tasks, grumbles about anything and everything, mumbles with slurred speech, and stumbles when walking. These signs are collectively referred to as the "umbles."

Moderate cases are indicated by a worsening of the "umbles" and uncontrollable violent shivering.

In severe cases, shivering stops. There is increasing muscle rigidity, increasing loss of contact with the world, and de-

Ways to lose body heat:

- When you're in contact with cold ground via conduction

- When the wind blows via convection

- When your skin is wet with sweat via evaporation

- When you're just sitting there via radiation

Mild Hypothermia Treatment

- Change the person out of damp clothes into dry clothes. If the person is not too damp, you might need only to add layers of dry clothes.

- The outer layer of clothing needs to be a shell to stop heat loss from wind and to turn back heat loss from radiation.

- Insulate the person from the cold ground.

- Give the person plenty of water to drink and simple sugars to eat. Warm water is only slightly better than cold water.

creasing heart rate and breathing rate. Heart and lung activity can drop so low as to be undetectable.

Management of the cold person can be divided, for simplicity, into two categories: 1) treatment for mild and moderate hypothermia and 2) treatment for severe hypothermia.

The mild-moderate hypothermia patient is still trying to warm up internally. Change the environment so the heat being produced internally is not lost. Get the person out of wet clothes and into something dry, out of wind and cold and into some kind of shelter, even if the only shelter available is the protection of waterproof, windproof clothing. If the person can take food and drink, and eat and drink, give her or him simple carbohydrates to stoke the inner fire. Fluids are more important than solids to a cold person. A warm (not hot) sweet drink will add a tiny bit of heat and a lot of simple sugar for energy. Even cold fluids are better than no fluids. If the patient can still exercise easily, you may keep him or her moving after initial treatment.

The severe hypothermia patient has lost the ability to rewarm. Carefully follow the directions below.

Severe Hypothermia Treatment

- This person needs to be handled and moved very gently. Rough movement can seriously damage the person.

- This person needs to be undressed and placed in a sleeping bag.

- Insulation protecting the person from the ground needs to be thick.

- Wrap the person in a layer that turns back wind and moisture and holds in body heat. A tarp or tent fly will work fine. Now you need to find help.

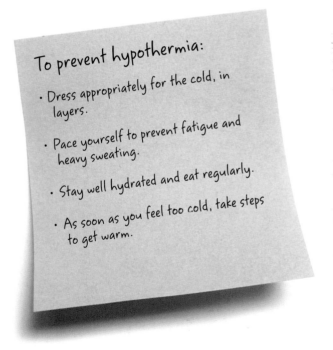

To prevent hypothermia:

- Dress appropriately for the cold, in layers.

- Pace yourself to prevent fatigue and heavy sweating.

- Stay well hydrated and eat regularly.

- As soon as you feel too cold, take steps to get warm.

HEAT ILLNESS

Problems range from mild exhaustion to serious stroke

Heat exhaustion, on the mild end of heat illness, as the name implies, involves someone who is greatly fatigued. This person may also complain of a headache, perhaps nausea, and sometimes vomiting. Thirst is typical, as is a decreased urine output. Dizziness may strike when the person stands quickly.

The problem is a volume problem—not enough internal water—and it is typically not serious. The cure is suggested by the name: Exhaustion calls for rest, preferably in a cool, shady spot. Replace fluids with water and salt with a pinch added to a liter of water or by some salty snacks. Oral rehydration salts or a sports drink will work. Do not use salt tablets—they are

When people are too hot:

- They complain of great fatigue, headache, perhaps nausea.

- They seldom urinate, and urine is dark and low in volume.

- They are very thirsty.

- They may have a dramatic change in level of consciousness.

- They may have red and hot skin.

Treatment for Heat Exhaustion

- People with heat exhaustion need to rest out of direct sunlight. A shady, breezy spot will work best.

- They need to drink plenty of water. The water should be sipped and not gulped down. They will probably benefit from a salty snack.

- They need to be cooled off and can wear a wet bandanna and a wet T-shirt. They can be fanned.

- When they feel okay, they are okay to keep hiking.

too concentrated. To increase the rate of cooling, the person may be wet down and fanned. When the person feels okay, the backcountry adventure may be continued.

Heat stroke occurs when someone is producing core heat faster than it can be shed. Disorientation and bizarre personality changes are common signs. Skin turns hot and red and sometimes (but far from always) dry.

Heat stroke is a temperature problem. Once a human brain gets too hot, it is a true emergency, and only rapid cooling will save the life of the person. Take off any heat-retaining clothes and drench the person with water. Concentrate cooling efforts on the head and neck. Cold packs may be used on the neck, armpits, groin, and on the hands and feet. Fan constantly to increase evaporation. Massage the limbs to encourage cooler blood to return to the core. When, or if, the person is able to accept and drink cold water, give it. A doctor must be found as soon as possible, even if the hot person appears to have recovered.

Treatment for Heat Stroke

- People with heat stroke need to be cooled off as quickly as possible.

- They should have their clothing removed. Leaving cotton underwear on is fine and possibly better.

- They need to be soaked with water and fanned ag-gressively. They will benefit if their arms and legs are massaged while they're being fanned.

- Even if they appear to recover, they should be seen by a doctor. Long-term damage from heat stroke is highly likely.

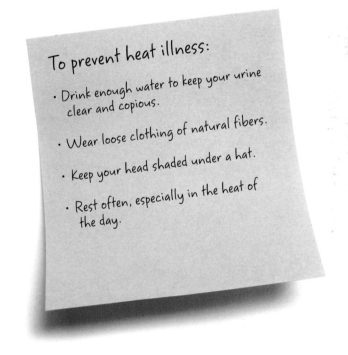

To prevent heat illness:

- Drink enough water to keep your urine clear and copious.

- Wear loose clothing of natural fibers.

- Keep your head shaded under a hat.

- Rest often, especially in the heat of the day.

INFANTS ON THE TRAIL
Most infants can go just about anywhere the parents can go

Baby will add pounds to someone's back, so your ability to travel with the extra weight is the main limiting factor when hiking with an infant. Small infants are typically content in a front carrier, but it should be high enough behind baby's head to support the head. Older infants are usually fine in a back carrier. Experts generally agree, however, that backpacking trips are not wise until the baby is strong enough to

hold up her or his head, usually somewhere between six and nine months of age.

Infants need almost constant attention on the trail, just like at home. If illness develops, you need to have a plan in mind: What is the shortest route to medical care?

Breast-feeding infants are set for safe and convenient food as long as mom remains healthy. Water should be boiled for

Carrying the Baby

- A young infant should be carried in a front carrier, and it should be high enough to support the baby's head.

- Older infants ride fine in a back carrier, but babies must be strong enough to hold their heads up.

- Choose a back carrier with pockets so you can pack things the baby needs with the baby.

- Remember: Baby needs to be protected from heat and cold just like the person packing the baby.

Gear for Baby

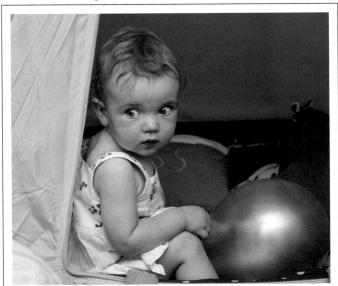

- Just like at home, baby will need some toys, something to chew on, something that makes noise.

- In addition to clothing, you will need a plan for dealing with messy diapers.

- Feces can be buried, just like yours, and wet diapers can be laid in the sun to dry, saving weight.

- Don't forget the basics: wet wipes for cleaning baby, cream for baby's bum, and food that baby likes to eat.

formula and mixed with the powder shortly before feeding baby. Any formula left out for more than about two hours should be discarded.

After four months or so of life, some infants will begin eating cereals and pureed foods. Dry baby cereals handle the trail well and can be mixed with breast milk or formula. Jars of baby food may be carried, but they will spoil quickly after being opened, and the jars, full and empty, add noticeable weight. Somewhere between nine and twelve months, baby may start to eat finger food.

Then there are the diapers. Feces can be removed and buried. Wet, disposable diapers will lose quite a bit of weight if opened and set in the sun to dry before adding them to the garbage bag. You may opt for cloth diapers on longer trips because you can wash and reuse them—but washing diapers is labor-intensive, requiring a lot of hot, soapy water that has to be dumped appropriately to avoid polluting the environment.

Bedtime for Baby

- If baby sleeps well at home, baby will sleep well on the trail—sometimes better on the trail.

- In warm months, baby will sleep fine on a pad under the usual light blanket or two. At nap time, put baby down in shade, not in a hot tent.

- In colder months, baby can have her or his own little sleeping bag.

- Some parents prefer to carry zip-together sleeping bags and sleep with baby between them.

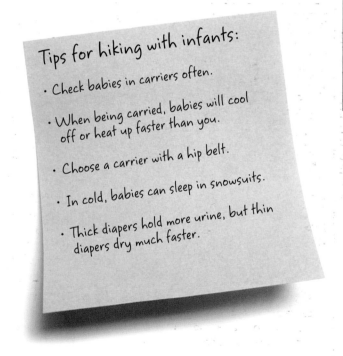

Tips for hiking with infants:

- Check babies in carriers often.

- When being carried, babies will cool off or heat up faster than you.

- Choose a carrier with a hip belt.

- In cold, babies can sleep in snowsuits.

- Thick diapers hold more urine, but thin diapers dry much faster.

FOUR SAFETY LESSONS FOR KIDS

When children are old enough to express independence, they will

By the time children can wander out of camp, toddling or dashing, they become much more difficult to manage on outdoor trips. But that doesn't mean you should leave them at home. Trail time may be some of the best family experiences in your book of memories.

Here are three guidelines: move slow, keep it simple, and stay flexible. Hiking children may have to be the pacesetters,

but they will need patient encouragement to keep moving. Give them time to stop and explore the natural curiosities they encounter. In fact, expect to stop every ten or fifteen minutes, at least briefly. Pushed, rushed, and not allowed some control, kids will be unhappy—and so will their parents.

Small children require a parental "peeled eye" at all times. Dress them in bright-colored clothing so they are easier to

Lesson 1: Know What Not to Touch

- Identify to children plants that can hurt them—stinging nettle, plants with thorns. Tell them what will happen if they touch the plants (see page 182).

- Identify to children poison ivy, oak, or sumac. Tell them what will happen if they touch these.

- Tell children to not touch any dead animal—bird, mammal, reptile. There is danger of disease.

- Tell children to not touch any animal, including insects, unless you are with them. You don't want kids collecting harmful bugs.

Lesson 2: Know What Not to Eat

- Teach children to eat nothing unless you have approved it first.

- In fact, teach children to put nothing on the trail into their mouths unless you have reviewed and approved it.

- Tell them why it is important to avoid eating the bright red berries, the curly leaf, or the pretty yellow flower.

- They can, however, help you gather berries you have identified as safe. It will be a valuable experience.

keep track of. Teach them what to do if they are separated from you: "Hug a tree," stay put, and call for help. At about four years of age, kids can blow whistles. Clip a whistle to your child. Three blows is the signal for help. Blow twice on your whistle to signal that you're on the way.

By five years of age, most kids can carry a small pack. Keep it light in weight, with such things as small toys, snacks, a small water bottle, a hat. A "real" backpack will have to wait until a child reaches 4 feet in height, the height at which a backpack can be fitted to his or her body size.

As soon as kids can be assigned camp chores, give them some. Most of them will enjoy assignments, and all of them will benefit from them, learning to contribute. Even small children can pick up trash and pack their own little packs.

Lesson 3: Drink Often

- Teach children the importance of staying hydrated. They may not understand at younger ages, but they will benefit from hearing.

- Children should all have their own water bottles. Choose a colorful bottle that is easy to drink from.

- Flavor their water with a drink mix that they like to encourage drinking. Let them add it to the bottle and shake it up.

- If you model good drinking behavior, they are far more likely to adopt good drinking behavior.

Lesson 4: Use Sun Protection

- Teach children the importance of avoiding overexposure to the sun.

- Show them how to apply sunscreen. Let older children apply their own as you watch. (Wash their hands afterwards to prevent them from putting it into their mouths.)

- Children should all wear hats with brims that protect their faces and necks from direct sunlight.

- Children should have sunglasses as soon as they're old enough to wear them.

FUN CAMPING PASTIMES FOR KIDS
Motivating your older children is a challenge that offers great rewards

By the time children are ready for school, their ability to focus and participate in camping activities is greatly expanded. They are sponges ready to soak up knowledge. They are now also old enough to get bored. Parents need to plan to keep their kids motivated.

Before leaving home, create anticipation by talking about the lake they can fish in and swim in, the animals they might see. Allow children to choose many of the things they want with them: books, toys, games. Read about where you're going—the geology, the flora and fauna, the history—and fill the trail and the campsite with interesting stories and tidbits of information.

Older children often enjoy helping with the overall plan for the trip. They can understand maps, so go over your route

Books

- Children benefit from books in camp just as they benefit from books at home.

- Pack books for younger kids that you know they will enjoy having read to them.

- Let older children choose the books they want to read. Help them choose another book if they pick the complete works of Dr. Seuss in one volume.

- Set up a reading time in camp when the whole family relaxes with a book.

Coloring and Drawing

- Rare is the child who fails to enjoy coloring and drawing.

- Let older children choose the coloring book they want to pack along with their favorite colors in markers or crayons.

- Pack a book of blank pages or at least a few sheets of blank paper. Encourage kids to draw what they see: a tree, the tent, a flower. They can create an illustrated journal.

- Play drawing games such as the child draws it and you guess what it is.

with them. They might take great pleasure in having a map for themselves and keeping track of their location as you travel. Your children may respond well to a reward system: candy for remembering the names of flowers, a cookie for doing their camp chores.

They can understand why you chose the campsite you did, why you are careful to avoid pollution, why you lay out the sleeping bags in time for them to fluff before crawling in, how the human body loses heat and gains heat. They can understand the importance of staying close to you. Teach them well.

Enthusiasm is contagious: If you are enthusiastic, they tend to be enthusiastic. Let them climb trees and rocks; just stay close to catch them if they slip. On the trail, point out bits of wonder: a bird, a caterpillar, a flower, a colorful rock. Consider giving each child a camera (inexpensive, disposable ones are fine), and encourage them to record the trip on film. But moderate your expectations: They are, after all, kids.

Playing Cards

- A deck of playing cards is well worth the weight.

- Children can play Crazy Eights and Go Fish. They can play Slap Jack and Spoons. Remove all but one queen, and they can play Old Maid.

- Lay the deck out face down, and they can play the Memory Game, turning over two cards and keeping matched sets. If the cards don't match, they go back face down.

- Build houses out of cards.

Fishing

- All children want to try their hands at fishing, at least for a while.

- You will end up doing a lot of casting, but most older children can do the reeling. And you can help younger children work the reel. Successful little anglers can help cook the fish for dinner.

- Beware: Some kids will want their own rod and reel. And kid-sized rods and reels, of course, are available.

- They don't need a license.

GREAT IDEAS FOR WOMEN HIKERS
There are concerns on the trail that tend to be unique to women

On the trail, women have to deal with, and sometimes worry about, a few things that don't usually trouble most men.

Women, for instance, often find urination more problematic. Look for a spot where you can squat with your arms extended out in front as counterbalance—or, even better, look for a spot with a branch or rock you can hang on to as you squat to make urination more relaxed. Use natural formations to help stabilize your body and keep yourself even more relaxed and avoid a mess. Natural formations also help with privacy.

Drink plenty of water to keep your system flushed, especially if you are susceptible to urinary tract infections. Be sure

KNACK HIKING & BACKPACKING

Washing Up

- Women remain generally healthier on the trail if they wash their nether region daily.

- This is quickly accomplished with a pot of water, a bottle of camp soap, and a bandanna. Wash with the soapy bandanna and rinse with the rest of the water.

- Allow the washed area to air dry for the best results. Loose-fitting clothing will assist with air drying.

- Wear cotton underwear whenever possible. Synthetics promote the growth of germs.

Bear Concerns

- There is no evidence at all that bears are attracted specifically to menstrual odors. And menstrual fluid is odorless inside the body.

- Bears are, however, attracted to interesting odors, and a soiled tampon might be considered interesting by a bear.

- So you should double bag in plastic all soiled tampons and pads to minimize the waste odor.

- Keep the bags with your garbage, and hang the garbage at night.

to relax and empty your bladder each time you urinate. Consider a talk with your doctor about packing an antibiotic in case of an infection.

You can forget many of the usual daily washing rituals, but cleaning your nether regions should not be one of them. Good hygiene guards against yeast infections, minimizes odors (especially if you are menstruating) that may arouse the curiosity of bears and other animals, and it just helps you to maintain that "fresh feeling." Wear tampons, if possible, instead of maxi-pads. Use unscented sanitary supplies. Wash regularly with unscented wet wipes; you may also want to bring along a little squirt bottle to serve as a backcountry bidet. Bring changes of clean underwear and/or wash your underwear frequently.

If you dislike oily hair, and a shampoo is not possible, massage corn starch into your hair to absorb the oil, and then comb it out.

The Pregnant Hiker

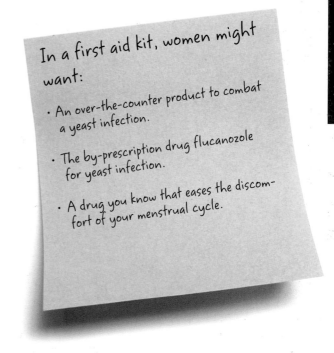

In a first aid kit, women might want:

- An over-the-counter product to combat a yeast infection.

- The by-prescription drug flucanozole for yeast infection.

- A drug you know that eases the discomfort of your menstrual cycle.

- Walking is a healthy thing for pregnant women to do, and healthy women who are backpackers do not need to stop if they are pregnant.

- Many experts suggest it is not a good idea to take up backpacking for the first time during pregnancy.

- During the third trimester it is not a good idea to hike a long way away from your doctor.

- During a normal pregnancy, women can hike to 8,000 feet above sea level without endangering mom or fetus.

HIKERS OVER SIXTY-FIVE

There is no age at which you should stop going on hikes

It is becoming increasingly difficult, and well it should, to define "elderly." More and more of the "gray group" are on trails, many of them learning to love hiking when they were younger and seeing no reason to stop. That doesn't mean you can't start a hiking life at sixty-five, or fifty-five, or seventy-five. As the old saying goes: Age is all in the mind—if you don't mind, it don't matter.

If, however, you're considering starting out later in life, you need to consider a couple of things: How good is your overall health, and are you fit enough to function well on the trail? An examination by a physician will give you the overall answer. Let the physician know you're planning a hike, if you're planning to go overnight, and about the environmental conditions you might encounter—the heat, cold, or higher alti-

Older Hikers

- If you are an older backpacker, there's no reason to stop until you physically can't hike anymore. If you stay active on the trail, you might never stop.

- If you plan to start backpacking as an older adult, get a checkup first. Tell the doctor what you have in mind.

- Start small: short hikes, easy trails, light loads.

- In fact, start walking around town first. Your endurance will build quickly with regular walks.

Gaining Strength

- Lifting and moving—activities that require muscular strength—are involved in backpacking.

- You are never too old to gain strength.

- Your best bet is to join a gym or athletic club where you can do resistance train-ing (weight lifting, exercise machines) under the guidance of a trainer.

- Concentrate on your legs, hips, back, and shoulders. Three workouts a week with rest days in between will give you the best results.

tude. If you have been diagnosed with specific conditions, such as cardiovascular disease, ask for specific guidelines. If your fitness is a bit low, you, at any age, can work on improvement (see below).

As you age, it becomes increasingly important to maintain a reasonable body weight. To lose weight—and slow aging—eating less is not nearly as important as exercising more. Dieting, in fact, may rob you of valuable nutrients. You need less protein and more carbohydrates as you age. Sixty to seventy percent of your food intake should be complex carbohydrates (pasta, breads, beans). Stay lean to feel young.

You may need supplements in your diet, especially antioxidants, which some experts suspect may slow the aging process. Of special value are vitamins C and E and beta-carotene. Amounts of these nutrients, if taken on a daily basis, are difficult to determine. Rough estimates are 500–1000 milligrams of vitamin C, 100–400 international units of vitamin E, and 15–25 milligrams of beta carotene.

Flexibility

- To properly and safely lift and move, you will need to increase your flexibility.

- As with gaining strength, you are never too old to gain flexibility.

- Stretching improves your fitness, increases your sense of well-being, and reduces the chance of injury.

- Concentrate on your calves, hamstrings, groin, and shoulders. Ten minutes of stretching every day should give you the results you want.

Tips for older hikers:

- You're not young anymore, so don't try to be.

- Set appropriate objectives in terms of distance and terrain.

- Move at a pace comfortable for you.

- Rest as often as you feel the need.

- Find young companions who can carry the heavy stuff.

PETS ON THE TRAIL

Pets will require as much and often more attention than at home

Dogs are often members of the family, and you wouldn't want to hit the trail without them. If you plan to bring your dog, you need to consider a few things other than regulations concerning dogs.

Are your dog's vaccinations up to date? Your pet could be exposed to germs such as rabies. You might want to check with your vet.

Be sure a tag hanging from your dog's collar identifies your pet. You might get separated.

You need to plan for your dog's meals as well as your own. A dog that scavenges for food could end up eating some very unhealthy stuff.

On some trails, you need to clean up after your dog. Regulations demand it. Some hikers clean up all the time, consider-

Hiking with Your Dog

- Be sure your dog is welcome, or at least allowed, on the trails you intend to hike.

- It is your responsibility to prevent your dog from pestering or challenging other hikers.

- It is your responsibility to keep your dog from chasing wildlife. Uncontrolled dogs are the reason numerous trails are closed to them.

- As hikers yield to horses, dogs should yield to other hikers. Step off the trail with your dog.

Dog with Pack

- Some dogs are able, once trained, to carry part or all of their food on the trail.

- Not all dogs are born hikers. But they will try to keep up with you despite being overheated or in pain. Condition your dog for the trail as you condition yourself.

- Pack a first aid kit that allows you to care for your dog as well as yourself.

- Carry water for your dog when you are hiking between water sources.

ing it appropriate to leave no fecal matter for other hikers to avoid.

On overnight hikes, think about where your dog will sleep. In the tent? Do you need bedding for the dog?

You need to prevent your dog from chasing wildlife. It's bad for the wild animals, and it is often illegal. It could be bad for your dog if the animal is a skunk, a porcupine, or a large and hungry carnivore.

······· YELLOW ● LIGHT ·······

Some hiking and backpacking trails and areas do not permit dogs. National forests, for instance, usually allow dogs, but national parks may not, even on a leash. State parks often require leashes, and U.S. Fish and Wildlife almost never allows dogs to roam. Know before you go.

Camping with Your Dog

- Be ready and willing to clean up after your dog. Bury its fecal matter as you bury yours.

- Plan where your dog will sleep. Most backpackers keep their dogs in the tent at night.

- Dogs that run free often return with ticks, hair smeared with poison ivy resin, or leading angry bears.

- Be sure your dog wears a tag that allows a finder of a lost dog to be a returner.

More tips for hiking with dogs:

- Obey the rules and regulations related to dogs.

- Carry a leash in case you need it.

- Keep your dog under control when meeting other hikers and livestock.

- Be sure your dog's vaccinations are up to date.

CLEANING GEAR

If it needs to be cleaned, clean it before you store it

You want your outdoor gear and clothing to last as long as possible and to serve you as well as possible, and both those outcomes are the result, to a large extent, of adequate cleaning.

Start, in fact, on the trail to maximize the life and service of your stuff. It's dirty out there, and grime hastens the deterioration of any fabric, but you can treat your material in ways that slow down deterioration. Don't drag your tent across the ground or toss your clothing into the dirt. Hang your parka over the limb of a tree or over your backpack in camp, or throw it into the tent when you don't need to wear it. And don't use your expensive clothing as a padded seat by the fire.

There is a false notion that machine-washing waterproof/breathable fabrics damages the material. Washing is good

Cleaning the Tent

- Cleaning your gear will keep it working best for you and make it last longer.

- Tents should never be cleaned in a washing machine (or dried in a dryer). Those acts will destroy the fabric.

- Set your tent up in a shady spot when you return home, and wipe it out with water and a clean cloth or sponge.

- For stubborn grime, use a nondetergent soap for cleaning. Do not use dishwashing liquid or spot remover.

Cleaning the Kitchen

- Use your kitchen sink at home to clean your camp kitchen.

- Even if you washed your gear the last morning on the trail, which you probably didn't, you will get it cleaner at home.

- Waiting until your next trip means grime will harden, making the job more difficult. Plus, you're ready to go next time.

- Wipe your stove off well, and clean the jets with the tip of a small wire (which might have come with your stove).

for these fabrics, and dirt, campfire smoke, and the oil from your skin are not. Washing most often actually restores the effectiveness of these fabrics. You should, however, follow the manufacturer's recommendations. Some specify the use of a nondetergent soap, and some say a detergent is fine. Recommendations may also include the use of a gentle cycle of the washing machine.

Oil from your skin and dirt will collect in your sleeping bag. Bags don't need to be cleaned after every trip, but they do require periodic washing. Follow the directions of the manufacturer. If your bag (or parka) is down-filled, special cleaning is required, a service provided by some dry cleaners.

Soil, sand, and dust will clog your stove and water filter, reducing their effectiveness on the trail and cutting short their life expectancy. When you bought them, you were given printed instructions on how to clean them. In fact, most of your gear came with cleaning instructions, and all are worthy of following.

Cleaning Your Boots

- Use a brush to remove dirt and caked-on mud from your footwear before storing it to prolong its life.

- Manufacturers suggest some materials can be cleaned with soap and water. Read the label before you discard it.

- Cleaning is absolutely essential to preserve leather. Leather-cleaning products are available.

- If your footwear has a waterproof/breathable liner, such as Gore-Tex, swish water around inside the shoe to clean the liner.

Cleaning the Water Filter

- Water filters eventually clog. As it happens, pumping becomes more difficult and water squirts out where it's not supposed to squirt out.

- Some filters can be cleaned by backwashing, some can be cleaned by scrubbing the insides, and the instruc- tions that came with your filter will tell you.

- Some filters should be disinfected by pumping bleach-rich water through.

- If your filter is not clean, you can't be sure it will work.

DRYING GEAR

Moisture needs to be removed from everything before storage

In storage, moisture, even a little dampness that you might not be able to detect easily, leads to mildew on fabrics and to their demise as useful outdoor gear and clothing. On some metals, it leads to rust, and on other surfaces it produces mold and fungus that are just plain nasty.

You can safely assume some of your gear needs to be dried. Your tent collects moisture from the damp air you exhale during the night. Your sleeping bag collects moisture released by your body. Everything you wear needs to be dried.

Your boots need special attention. Take out removable insoles to dry them. If your feet sweat heavily or if your boots get especially wet, stuff newspaper inside the boots for a few hours to absorb moisture. Leather boots should never be dried near a heat source, which can irreparably damage them.

Drying Your Sleeping Bag

- Storing anything damp is completely a bad idea.

- Assume your sleeping bag is damp even if you cannot detect any moisture. In fact, you should spread your bag out to dry a bit before stuffing it on the trail.

- Turn it inside out and lay it out in shade or inside the house and not in direct sunlight. Ultraviolet radiation slowly deteriorates synthetic materials.

- In a humid climate, it is much better to dry your bag inside.

Drying Your Tent

- Your tent should be set up in shade, out of UV light, to clean it. Leave it there until it is completely dry.

- After the walls are dry, turn the tent on its side to allow the bottom to dry.

- Flip your tent fly over to adequately dry the inner side.

- Give your folded tent poles time for the shock cord to dry before storage.

Despite the fact that your water filter is designed to be wet, it will last longer if it is stored free of water, and that means dry inside.

Modern, high-tech fabrics come with drying instructions as well as cleaning instructions. Some labels tell you the use of a machine dryer will damage the material, and some say a dryer, usually on low heat, is good for the material, and you need to follow the instructions. Almost all synthetic fibers are degraded by ultraviolet light and shouldn't be dried in direct sunlight. Hang your wet stuff in the shade or inside the house or garage with, if possible, windows and doors open for ventilation.

If it rains and/or the air is filled with humidity, everything probably needs to be dried. Don't forget the small things: lengths of rope or cord, the first aid kit, the repair kit, the food bag, the camp chair, the flashlight.

Drying Your Footwear

- Moisture will always be inside your footwear after you take it off, the result of sweating if nothing else.

- Open your footwear up fully, with the tongue extended, to better dry it. If it's really damp, stuff in newspaper for a few hours to absorb moisture.

- Remove removable inserts from your footwear to thoroughly dry them.

- Do not place leather boots near a heat source, anything that radiates heat. It will dry the leather out too much, destroying it.

Drying Other Gear

- After shaking the debris out of your pack, prop it up with zippers unzipped and the main compartment and pockets open to dry.

- Spread out your sleeping pad to dry before storage.

- Turn your stuff sacks inside out to dry.

- Mildew not only breaks down the fabric of your gear but also eats away at the waterproof coating on the tent fly, tent bottom, pack, stuff sacks, and raingear.

REPAIRING GEAR
Before storing your gear, check it closely and make needed repairs

Life on the trail is rough on gear, and sometimes repairs are needed. You want everything in good shape before storage so that you're ready for the next trip. And you don't want to toss out something that still works with a touch of repair.

Cuts, tears, even some separated seams can be sewn up. High-use areas of some clothing, such as elbows and knees, may be worn thin but patchable by sewing on a swatch of cloth. For synthetic fabrics such as tents and nylon shells, inexpensive patch kits are available. Some people simply patch with duct tape. Duct tape works in an emergency, but it should not be used as a permanent fix.

The durable, water-resistant finish that comes on many fabrics will eventually wear out. The fabric will begin to soak up instead of repel water. There are several products avail-

Sew It Up

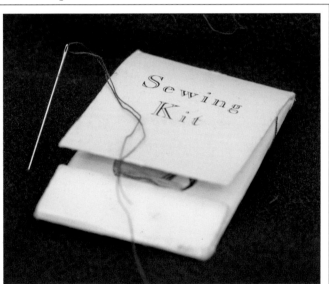

- Check your clothing for cuts, tears, and separated seams, and sew them up.

- If the clothing has worn spots, those that often eventually appear on elbows and knees, you might be able to sew on a patch.

- Check the mosquito netting in your tent for holes that you can sew up.

- For holes in your tent, sleeping bag, raingear, and similar items, you will need a patch that presses on.

Seal the Seams

- For waterproof gear, such as the tent fly and your rain parka, the seams need to be sealed to maintain waterproofness.

- Many of these items now come seam-sealed from the factory, in which case you're good to go.

- For other seams, you should seal the seams at least once a season.

- Apply a seam-sealer when the gear is completely dry, apply it carefully to be sure each stitch is sealed, and allow it to dry for twenty-four hours before use.

able that allow you to replace the finish. Check first with the manufacturer's instructions to see if a specific product is recommended.

Leather boots will need to be treated with a waterproofing agent at least once a season, more if you've hiked a lot. In any case, you can't really overtreat a leather boot.

Your first aid kit often needs "repair" in the form of replacing the used items, throwing out expired drugs and filling up with new ones, and replacing sterile products that inadvertently got opened or wet.

Sometimes gear and clothing cannot be repaired—the items have to be replaced. The time to do that is right after a trip so that you're ready for the next one. But before hiking to the garbage can, check the manufacturer's guarantee. Makers of outdoor gear take pride in the durability of their products, and they may make repairs you can't or replace items that failed if it's reasonable the product should have lasted longer.

Repair the Stove

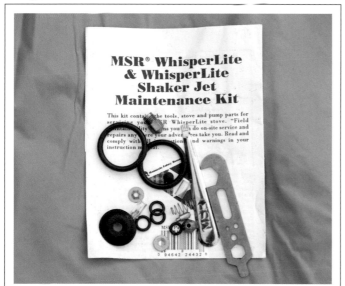

- If your stove was burning poorly, it might have a clogged fuel line. You can often disassemble the stove and clean the line. Use a rag dipped in white gas.

- Use a rag and white gas to wipe carbon residue from the burner. It is a source of clogging.

- Stove pumps that don't work might have a dry O-ring. Lube it with the proper oil.

- All you need to maintain your stove in good repair comes in a stove repair kit.

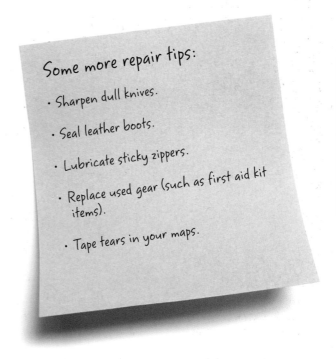

Some more repair tips:

- Sharpen dull knives.

- Seal leather boots.

- Lubricate sticky zippers.

- Replace used gear (such as first aid kit items).

- Tape tears in your maps.

STORING GEAR

How you store gear can add to or take away from its life

Now that you know how to keep your gear clean, dry, and in good repair, there are a few more storage tips that, if used, will prolong the life of your stuff.

But first, avid backpackers often have a storage area set aside specifically for outdoor gear. They like to have it together, organized, stored properly, and ready to go on the next trip.

You may not have the space or the inclination, but it's worth considering.

Items that fit neatly into stuff sacks, making them as small as possible for packing, tempt you to store them stuffed—but don't do it. The creases in tightly stored fabrics, including your tent, become weak spots over time. The insulation in

Things That Stuff

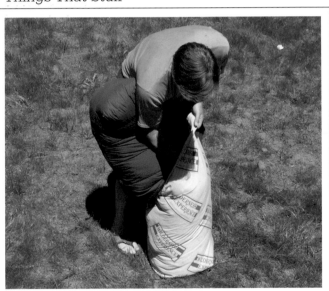

- Long-term compression kills gear and clothing.

- Never store a sleeping bag compressed. You will lose the value of the insulation. Store bags hung up or, even better, loosely stuffed into a large cotton or fishnet sack.

- Do not store a tent in its stuff sack. It will break down along the folds. Store it loose on a shelf or in a large cotton bag.

- Store clothing hung up or folded on a closet shelf and not stuffed into a bag.

Things You Sleep On

- Self-inflating pads need to be stored with the valves open to allow moisture to escape. Otherwise mildew will grow inside the pad.

- Self-inflating pads need to be stored flat because long-term compression will destroy their ability to self-inflate.

- Once they are dry, they can be stacked on top of each other.

- Closed-cell foam pads can be stored loosely rolled after they are dry.

some items—sleeping bags, parkas—loses its loft if compressed for long periods of time. That's why you see sleeping bags in outdoor specialty shops hanging fully loose from pegs or hangers on the wall. Fabrics, like people, also do best when they can breathe. Store your fabrics in large, cotton bags where they are not compressed, folded loosely on closet shelves or in cardboard boxes, or hanging in a closet.

Stove fuel degrades over time from condensation and buildup of residue—and your stove suffers. Start each season with a fresh supply of fuel. Empty your stove before storage,

and leave the cap off the fuel tank for a several hours to allow evaporation of the little fuel that remains inside.

If you live in a humid climate, store your footwear with fresh, dry newspaper stuffed inside to absorb moisture.

Some items may need a dab of protection to prevent drying out in storage, such as the O-ring on your stove and the hinge of your pocketknife. Use a product—silicone or oil—designed for the purpose.

Things That Hold Fuel

- Empty the fuel from your stove before storage unless storage time will be short.

- If you have a stove with a pump that inserts into a fuel bottle, do not store the pump in the bottle. Fuel bottles with fuel in them should be stored upright.

- Do not store fuel for more than one year. It breaks down and will contaminate your stove.

- Fuel bottles with old fuel should be emptied and then rinsed with fresh fuel.

Things Stored a Long Time

- Lubricate the hinges of your knife with the proper oil before long-term storage.

- Lubricate the O-ring and pump cup (if your stove has a pump) on your stove with the proper oil or silicone before long-term storage.

- Take the batteries out of your flashlight before long-term storage.

- The longer any of your gear and clothing will be stored, the greater the importance of storing it correctly.

STRETCHING THE LOWER BODY
Stretching is the link between your inactive life and your active life

Fitness for the trail, or for anywhere, can be divided into three areas: flexibility, endurance, and strength. To gain and maintain flexibility, you need to stretch, and stretching needs to involve the appropriate body parts in the appropriate way. When done often enough, stretching keeps your body supple, and ready for action, and flexibility helps prevent injuries.

A few gentle stretches before vigorous exercise are benefi-

cial, loosening and warming stiff muscles, but a stretching workout should be saved until after vigorous exercise. Too much stretching before a period of hard exercise may actually weaken your muscles, decreasing the benefit of endurance and strength training.

Stretching is not difficult, but it, too, is a form of exercise, and it can do harm if done incorrectly. It should be relaxing,

Stretching Your Calves

- Stand far enough away from a rock or tree (or wall) so that you have to lean forward to rest your hands against whatever object you have chosen.

- Keep your toes pointing straight toward the object.

- Flex one knee and shift that foot toward the object. Your back leg should be straight out with your heel flat.

- Without changing foot positions, shift your hips forward until you feel the stretch in the calf of your back leg.

Stretching Your Hamstrings

- Sit down with your legs straight out in front of you and close together. Keep your toes pointing skyward.

- You are going to bend forward from your hips, keeping your head in neutral alignment and your lower back straight.

- Do not lock your knees. Keep them slightly flexed, and keep your thigh muscles relaxed.

- Bend forward until you feel the stretch in your hamstrings.

216

so you'll need a quiet place and loose, comfortable clothing.

Muscle fibers, the main things you're stretching, have a built-in stretch reflex: You can pull them just so far, and then they contract involuntarily for protection. Stretching too far too fast will actually counteract the beneficial effect you are after. The correct way to stretch is a relaxed, sustained movement with your attention focused on the muscles being stretched, on where you feel the tension. The incorrect way is to bounce up and down with your mind wandering and/or stretching to the point of pain.

When you begin any stretch, you will soon reach a point of mild tension. Stop, and hold at that point for ten to thirty seconds. This easy beginning will reduce muscular tightness and prepare tissues for the developmental part of each stretch. As you feel the tension ease off, move further into the stretch, and when tension returns, hold the new position for ten to thirty seconds. Try counting the seconds softly to yourself as you hold each stretch.

Stretching Your Buttocks

- Stand on one foot with the other foot resting on a log, tree stump, or rock at about the level of your waist or a bit lower.

- Reach slowly for your toes on the leg at about waist level.

- This will stretch your buttocks as well as your inner thigh and hamstrings.

- Remember: Do not force a stretch. When you feel the tension, hold that position until you can relax further into the stretch.

Stretching Your Groin

- Sit with the soles of your feet together. Hold them there with your hands and pull your heels gently in toward your groin until you feel the first bit of tension.

- Keep your lower back straight, not rounded, and keep your head up.

- Slowly pull your upper body forward until you feel the stretch in your groin. You can also push your knees gently toward the ground.

- This will also stretch your inner thighs and lower back.

FIT FOR THE TRAIL

STRETCHING THE UPPER BODY
Stretching improves performance, balance, and peace of mind on the trail

Done properly, stretching is a period of quiet after a bout of hard exercise or a hard day, and it brings relaxation to your body and your mind. Yes, fitness is about attitude as well as physical performance.

As mentioned earlier, you can't stretch properly unless your mind is thinking "relax" as your body eases into each move-

ment. To help in relaxing, stay aware of your breathing. Exhale as you move gently into each stretch. During the period of stretch-holding, breathe slowly and rhythmically.

To maximize the developmental aspect of each stretch, gently flex the muscles being stretched before moving to the next point of tension. When, for instance, you've reached

The Shoulder Shrug

- Stand erect with your arms dangling straight down and relaxed at your sides, and pull your shoulders up toward your ears.

- Roll your shoulders forward, then down, then back, and then back up to where they started. Keep your arms relaxed.

- After a few forward rolls, reverse the order, rolling your shoulders back first.

- As long as you are moving slowly, it is difficult to over-stretch and hurt yourself with this exercise.

The Swim

- After the shoulder shrug, your shoulders will be loose and ready for the swim.

- Standing erect, swing your arms gently in large circles, as if you were swimming.

- Do not fling your arms. Keep them under your control.

- This is not an arm exercise but rather a shoulder exercise. Keep your attention on your shoulders, keep them relaxed, and roll them through a full range of motion.

a point of tension in your shoulders, and you've held it for ten to thirty seconds, flex your shoulder muscles for three to six seconds before moving to the next point of tension. This brief contraction of the muscle being stretched causes the muscle to relax even more during the next phase of the stretch. The brief flex helps overcome the muscle's involuntary stretch reflex (see page 217).

Your flexibility will improve faster if you do more than simply stretch. Several aspects of stretching are at least as important to you as becoming more limber: Keep all your muscles relaxed, not just the one you're working on, during the stretch. Remember your body will not be exactly the same on any two days. It will vary even between morning and night. Adjust your stretch to the way your body presents itself. Never try to force it to be the way it was the last time you stretched. Keep your body properly aligned during a stretch, sort of like maintaining good posture. Learn to get the right "feel" out of a stretch instead of seeing how far you can bend or contort your muscles.

The Shoulder Stretch

- Standing erect, reach behind your back and clasp your hands together.

- Keep your arms slightly flexed but almost straight, and keep your hands relaxed, not tightly clasped together.

- Lean forward slowly from your hips while lifting your hands slowly toward the sky until you feel the stretch. Hold that position until you can move further into the stretch.

- This exercise also stretches your arms and chest.

Tips for proper stretching:

- Be sure your clothing fits loosely.

- Relax your mind as well as your body.

- Take a deep breath and breathe out slowly as you move into a stretch.

- While maintaining a stretch, take shallow breaths.

- Hold at the point of tension and concentrate on relaxing the muscles being stretched.

CARDIOVASCULAR TRAINING: PART 1
To be fit, you have to put your heart into it

Endurance on the trail is a result of cardiovascular fitness. Cardiovascular fitness (sometimes called "cardiorespiratory endurance") is a measure of the efficiency of your heart, lungs, and vascular system in delivering oxygen to working muscles in order to prolong muscular activity. It's all about getting out there and doing something that gets your heart rate up

and keeps it up—walking, running, biking, swimming, cross-country skiing, snowshoeing, rowing.

With every workout, your heart grows more efficient, pushing more blood with every beat and pumping it more easily. Capillaries, where oxygen and nutrients pass from the blood into muscle cells, increase in number, and the cells them-

Step 1: Walk on Flat Terrain

- Nothing prepares you better for a long hike than a long hike. Get out there and walk.

- Start on flat terrain: around town, around a city park, along roads.

- Start without a pack. Wear the footwear you intend to hike trails in.

- When you can walk 2 miles in a half hour or less, without coming home exhausted, you are ready for the next level of training.

Step 2: Walk on Uphill Terrain

- You can increase the intensity of a walk by walking faster, but your goal is to be able to walk longer distances.

- As you increase the distance you walk, maintain the same pace as before, a pace of 2 miles per half hour or faster.

- Begin to add uphill terrain as a part of your workout.

- Slow down when you first add uphill terrain, but your goal is 2 miles in a half hour while walking uphill.

selves grow better at utilizing the fuel you are sending their way. And those benefits start as soon as you get going.

No exercise gets you ready for long walks better than walking, and no exercise gets you fit for hiking with a pack better than hiking with a pack. But there are many types of cardiovascular training to make your body trail-worthy. And, yes, you can hit the trail without being fit and often perform well enough to get there and back. You will also come home sore, tired, and possibly limping. Maybe even worse, you will have had less fun.

Those who start walking to train can usually make 2, sometimes 3 miles in an hour. When you can walk 2 miles in a half hour or less, you are ready to bump up the intensity of your exercise (see page 222). You can increase intensity by walking longer distances, walking a more difficult route, such as uphill, walking with a pack, or a combination. Avoid, however, trying to do too much too soon, which is the route to debilitating soreness and injury. Build intensity into your workouts slowly.

Step 3: Walking with a Pack

- When you are comfortable at a steady uphill pace, you're ready to add a pack to your back.

- Wear the pack you intend to use backpacking, and start with a very light load in your pack, no more than a few pounds.

- As your fitness improves, add weight to the pack.

- You can walk every day with an occasional rest day, but three or four walks per week will soon have you ready for the trail.

Treadmill

- If the weather is inclement or if you just have no handy place you want to walk outdoors, you can achieve the cardiovascular results you want on a treadmill.

- For the best results, the treadmill should allow you to increase the incline at which you walk.

- A good treadmill tells you the distance you walked and the time it took you.

- You can fight the boredom by watching TV during your workout.

CARDIOVASCULAR TRAINING: PART 2

With so many choices, it may be difficult to choose a type of training

If you work toward intensity gains, you will improve your cardiovascular fitness, no matter the type of training. Intensity is determined by how often your heart beats during exercise. Adequate gains will be made when you exercise at an intensity level of about 60 to 70 percent of your maximum heart rate. One way to find your maximum heart rate, approximately, is by subtracting your age from 220. Though not a precise formula, it does give you a good idea of how hard you can safely work out and still achieve the best cardiovascular results.

If you're starting with a low level of fitness, and/or if you're not young in body, consider starting with a checkup for safety's sake. Then do no more than one short, intense workout a week combined with two or three days of light exercise per

Running

- There is no perfect training program for runners every runner is different. Each runner, does benefit from having three elements in his or her training program.

- One element is a long-distance run. Once a week plan on running farther than you usually run.

- Another element is hill running. To get the best training results, choose a route that includes some uphill work but not every day.

- Finally, every runner needs to get plenty of rest in between runs.

Biking

- Biking, unlike running, is a nonimpact exercise. It doesn't punish your joints. You recover faster after exercising, and you get injured less.

- You can bike on roads with any bike and on trails with a mountain bike.

- To train for hiking, choose a biking route with rolling hills but no long climbs or descents.

- You want to vary pushing yourself hard for an interval of time with cruising at a steady pace for an interval.

week. Increase the level of intensity as you feel more capable. The two simplest ways to increase intensity are to go longer or go faster. When you can do one thirty- to forty-minute workout at high intensity (at 60 to 70 percent maximum heart rate), start building toward a second one in one week, with at least one rest day (no workout) in between.

The hardest part of any training regimen is getting out of the chair and opening the front door. Here are a few ideas to help with that.

Find a partner. It's almost always easier to get going if someone is waiting for you.

Add spice with variety. Vary the route you walk, run, bike, or ski. Vary the people you work out with. Mix running with biking.

Do not train intensely on two back-to-back days. A possible regimen, as an example, could include a hard workout, light workouts on the next two days, and then a complete rest day.

Swimming

- For cardiovascular training, swimming has advantages over running and biking.

- You can do it year-round in a controlled environment, so your workouts are consistent, and you use more muscles than any other sport except cross-country skiing.

- On the downside, learning to swim well is much harder than learning to run or bike well, and your upper body gets more of a workout than your legs.

- When training for the trail, swimming is best used in combination with walking, running, and/or biking.

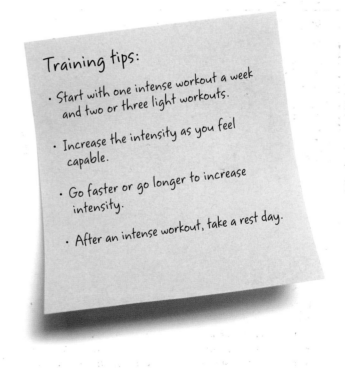

Training tips:

- Start with one intense workout a week and two or three light workouts.

- Increase the intensity as you feel capable.

- Go faster or go longer to increase intensity.

- After an intense workout, take a rest day.

WEIGHT TRAINING: UPPER BODY
Muscles are about a lot more than just looking good

Your strength, the third area of fitness, improves with any exercise, but training with weights is the only way to focus strength gains in the muscle groups you use on the trail. Weight training is especially important after you reach approximately thirty-five years of age, when muscle loss starts regardless of your level of fitness in other areas. Most people think muscles look good, but strength also allows you to stand and move with better posture, reducing the chance of back problems, a bane of backpackers. Strong hikers, too, have better balance and fewer accidents on the trail, and if they do have an accident, they are less likely to be seriously hurt. More than just moving heavy things around, weight training should be approached correctly.

Under a pack, your legs and hips receive quite a bit of stress.

Abdominal Crunches

- The old-fashioned sit-up is usually done incorrectly and can be dangerous to your lower back.

- Crunches work the upper abdominal wall primarily and the lower wall secondarily. They're easy to do right, and you can't hurt yourself.

- Lie on your back with your legs bent and your hands behind your head. Raise your head toward your knees, curling your spine as far as you comfortably can. Hold, and then lower.

- Do leg raises to work the lower abdominals.

Bench Press

- For overall chest development, bench presses work well, although there is emphasis on the lower chest.

- Lie flat and centered on the bench with your hands on the bar spaced a few inches wider than your shoulders.

- Lower the bar, under control, until it touches your mid- to upper chest. Press the bar up until your elbows are almost fully extended.

- Incline the bench at 45 degrees to emphasize the upper chest.

Your knees and ankles are pounded by flat and uphill terrain, and much more so by downhill terrain. Your abdominals are in constant use holding your back in line. You also use your chest, back, arms, and shoulders to lift, support, and move the pack down the trail and your gear around camp. Your weight-training routine needs to emphasize these muscles groups.

Although three workouts per week are often recommended, the amount of muscle gained from two days per week will be enough for most people. Lifters who work out three times a week, in fact, see surprisingly little gain over those who work out twice a week.

When you use dumbbells or plates you add to or take off bars, you are using "free weights" as opposed to a weight machine. Which is best? The strength you gain will be the same. Free weights probably add more to your balance, and a weight machine gives you less opportunity to use poor form. The choice is yours.

Shoulder Press

- Space your hands on the bar several inches wider than your shoulders.

- Lower the bar, under control, until it touches the base of your neck.

- Press the bar up until your elbows are almost fully extended. Keep your shoulders in a natural position, not shrugged up toward the bar.

- You can do the same exercise with two dumbbells. It is a little more difficult to balance the weight.

Dips

- Dips can work the triceps on the backs of your upper arms or your chest.

- If you keep your head up during a dip, you will concentrate the workout on your triceps.

- If you roll your upper body forward, chin to chest, you will work your chest muscles.

- Do not lower yourself so far down between the bars that you cannot press yourself back up to almost fully extended arms.

WEIGHT TRAINING: LOWER BODY
Muscle strength is necessary to complete the fitness of a hiker

When you lift a weight once, it's called a "repetition" (rep), and reps are grouped into sets. Start your weight-training with a weight that allows you to do at least eight reps in one set. After two to three sets, it's usually time to move to another muscle group, but there's nothing wrong with more sets.

When you can do twelve reps in one set, it's time to add weight, if strength gain is your primary goal. Doing longer sets, even up to thirty reps, increases the aerobic capacity of your muscles faster. Strength gains mean you can lift heavier and heavier weights, and aerobic capacity gains mean you can work the muscles for longer periods of time—and on the trail there are benefits from both.

Weight training, when done properly, does not consume a large amount of time. If you take an appropriate rest, about

Leg Extensions

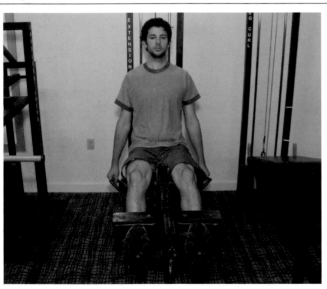

- The front of your thighs, from the knee to the hip, are worked by leg extensions. You will be strengthening some of the muscles that support your knees.

- You'll be sitting, and you start with your knees fully bent, feet pointing slightly down.

- Fully extend your legs until your ankles, knees, and hips are in a line, and your toes are pointed up.

- Movement up and down should be smooth and controlled with no bouncing on either end of the movement.

Leg Curls

- You will strengthen your hamstrings, the backs of your upper legs, with leg curls.

- You start face down with your feet hooked under the pads of the machine and your knees straight.

- Flex your hamstrings and bend your knees, curling your feet up toward your buttocks as far as they will go. The pads of the machine will roll up your legs.

- Lower your feet back down under control. Do not drop them.

forty-five seconds, between sets, you can complete two sets of eight to ten different exercises in less than twenty-five minutes.

Although you can work out at home, it's not a bad idea to join a gym, especially if you're new to weight lifting. A gym's trainer can coach you, making sure you're using the proper form with each exercise. Gyms also have mirrors that allow you to monitor your form. Good form involves controlling the weight, not jerking or snapping it but moving it slowly through most of the range of the muscles being worked. You

stop movement before completely extending your arms or legs. When you reach the end point of movement, the weight should be lowered slowly back to the starting point.

If you're lifting the right amount of weight, a weight no more than you can lift correctly, a warmup is not necessary. Some lifters, however, prefer a few minutes of brisk walking or jogging prior to weight training.

Squats

- Squats work the thigh muscles as well as the muscles of the hips and buttocks.

- Your feet should be somewhere between 12 and 15 inches apart. Your knees and hips bend as you lower the weight toward your buttocks.

- Your knees and hip joints straighten as you bring the weight back up.

- If you use a bar instead of a machine, balance the bar evenly across both shoulders before beginning.

Tips for weight training:

- Use a weight that you can control.

- At the top of each movement, lower the weight, do not drop it.

- At the bottom, lift the weight, do not throw it.

- Do not hold your breath.

- If using heavy weights, work out with a partner.

TRIP PLANNING

The better planned your hike, the greater the chance of success on the trail. The longer your trip, of course, the more involved your plan. A plan starts with where you're going to go in general, and, when you know, you'll need to choose your specific route (see page 232). Then you'll choose when to go, and, somewhere along the line, you'll know who is going with you (see below). Once those things are known, you can get down to the nitty-gritty: a checklist of gear and clothing and a food plan. You need to decide how you're going to get there. If you're driving, you'll need to know the roads to take and where you'll park the vehicle. A trip plan is all about gathering information and then making informed choices. For most hikers, the planning, and the anticipation it generates, is a great part of the adventure.

As you think about where to go, remember that some environments may require quite a bit more preparation than others. You could be well-prepared gearwise for a hike into hot climes, but a journey to some place cold could involve acquiring a different set of gear. If you live where the temperatures sink low, a trip into a desert region will involve additional time for your body to adjust to the heat. And a hike to high altitude will likewise necessitate some additional time for acclimatization to thin air.

Forested regions are, generally speaking, the most forgiving of environments. If you are new to hiking, consider a woodland destination—and a summer month (see page 34).

On the even-easier side of hiking, consider hut-to-hut hiking. Hut-to-hut trips take much of the stress off of foot travel. Your pack is light, and each night's destination provides accommodations that range, depending on the trail, from rustic shacks to lavish lodges with comfortable beds and fine meals.

Where to Go

The United States is astoundingly rich in public areas to hike: state parks and forests, national parks and forests, Bureau of Land Management areas—millions of acres, thousands of miles of trails. You may already know the area you want to hike, maybe even the specific trail, and you can concentrate your gathering of information. Or you might start by gathering data about a general area or, even more basically, about a general environment—mountains, deserts, canyons, beaches—and then, info in mind, begin to narrow a plan down to specifics.

When to Go

Sometimes the "when" of a trip is dictated by powers beyond your control—or at least partially beyond your control, such as holidays and your vacation schedule. More often, however, you are the deciding factor, and there are numerous considerations worthy of thought.

Do you want at least a bit of solitude? When you know an area's busy season, you might want to choose another time of year. Trails near dense population centers tend to be crowded, especially on weekends and holidays. And the crowds

could be nonhuman. If mosquitoes are thick in summer at your destination, you'll probably be happier in the fall.

One piece of research you do not want to fail to do involves permits and regulations for land managed by agencies of the government. Some areas, national parks being a notable example, require permits to backpack, sometimes permits to simply hike. (They are often free, but there may be a fee attached.) Many trails have a limited number of permits available, and they may be all issued months in advance. If you cannot get a permit for the days you want to be there, you cannot go there. Regulations typically tell you what activities are not allowed (such as fishing) or what measures are required (such as setting camp a specific distance from water). But some regulations close trails for important reasons: during the breeding season of wildlife, during a period of time that allows the area to recover from overuse. Although they may seem bothersome, permits and regulations serve an important purpose. You need to follow the rules.

Weather patterns and predictions are important factors when choosing a time to hike, but weather history should also be taken into consideration. A trail, for example, that runs free and clear in July may be choked with last winter's snow well into June, making later in the summer a better "when."

Companions

There remains what some would call the most important decision of all: Who will you hike with? The most common reason solo hikers give for going out alone is this: There is nobody to complain about the slowness of the pace, or the rapidity of the pace, or the smell of unwashed bodies, or the rain, wind, snow, sleet, hail, dark of night, or the taste of freeze-dried macaroni and cheese. There are, in other words, few, if any, things that can spoil a walk in the wilderness as fully as an un-companionable companion. However, all the wonders of the trip, small and great—the sunsets, the vistas, the smells and sounds—will live longer and more richly if they are shared with someone you consider worth the sharing.

There is no greater predictor of a successful hike with someone than a history of having one or more successful hikes with that same someone. If you are contemplating a long backpacking trip with someone (or more than one person), your best chance of having a wonderful time is to take a shorter hike with the same companion or companions first. As with all rules, there are exceptions. It may be more important to travel with your family, despite the whining kids, because you love them, than to travel in relative peace and quiet with old friends. "The trail," wrote Robert Service, "holds its own stern code," and that includes doing your best to make every hike memorable in a positive way. Why make it a chore? Put at least as much thought into your companions as you do any other trail decision.

229

Sources of Information for Trip Planning

The best sources of information are people who have been there and done it. You can reach them by visiting local land management offices, local outdoor specialty stores, and hiking organizations. You can also phone or e-mail for information.

Rangers, state and federal, especially backcountry rangers, are often the most up-to-date sources of information about what to expect in a specific area. They may be able to direct you to or even provide other sources of information, such as maps and brochures. They can tell you if a permit is necessary and give you info on local regulations.

Guidebooks and how-to books are sort of like extended interviews with people and are often sources of excellent info. Be sure to check the publication dates on guidebooks. Five years ago things could have been quite a bit different where you're headed.

The Internet is a never-ending, at-your-fingertips source of information for hikers and backpackers.

Federal Land Management Agencies

Bureau of Land Management (BLM), 1849 C Street NW, Washington, DC 20240; (202) 208-3801. www.blm.gov. Search for a specific area.

National Park Service (NPS), 1849 C Street NW, Washington, DC 20240; (202) 208-6843. www.nps.gov. Search for a specific park.

U.S. Forest Service (USFS), 201 14th St. SW, Washington, DC 20024; (202) 205-8333. www.fs.fed.us. Search for a specific forest.

Hiking Organizations

Adirondack Mountain Club (ADK), 814 Goggins Road, Lake George, NY 12845; (518) 668-4447 or (800) 395-8080. www.adk.org.

American Hiking Society, 1422 Fenwick Lane, Silver Spring, MD 20910; (301) 565-6704. www.americanhiking.org.

Appalachian Mountain Club (AMC), 5 Joy Street, Boston, MA 02108; (617) 523-0636. www.outdoors.org.

Colorado Mountain Club, 710 Tenth Street, No. 200, Golden, CO 80401; (303) 279-3080. www.cmc.org.

Green Mountain Club, 4711 Waterbury-Stowe Road, Waterbury Center, VT 05677; (802) 244-7037. www.greenmountainclub.org.

Sierra Club, 85 Second Street, Second Floor, San Francisco, CA 94105-3441; (415) 977-5500. www.sierraclub.org.

Education

Leave No Trace Center for Outdoor Ethics, P.O. Box 997, Boulder, CO 80306-9816; (800) 332-4100 www.LNT.org.

National Outdoor Leadership School (NOLS), 284 Lincoln Street, Lander, WY 82520-2848; (307) 332-5300. www.nols.edu.

Weather

National Weather Service. http://weather.noaa.gov/weather/ccus.html.

Books

The Globe Pequot Press, 246 Goose Lane, P.O. Box 480, Guilford, CT 06437; (203) 458-4800. www.globepequot.com.

Guidebooks and how-to books covering all aspects of hiking and backpacking.

Jacobson, Cliff. *The Basic Essentials of Map and Compass*. Guilford, CT: The Globe Pequot Press, 1988. Expert advice on navigation.

Lanza, Michael. *Ultimate Guide to Backcountry Travel*. Boston, MA: Appalachian Mountain Club Books, 1999. Covers all the basics.

Lyle, Katie Letcher. *The Complete Guide to Edible Wild Plants, Mushrooms, Fruits and Nuts*. Guilford, CT: The Lyons Press, 2004. When you want to eat wild.

Tilton, Buck. *Cooking the One Burner Way, Second Edition*. Guilford, CT: The Globe Pequot Press, 2000. How to do it all from planning to boiling, frying, and baking.

Tilton, Buck. *Wilderness First Responder, Second Edition*. Guilford, CT: The Globe Pequot Press, 2004. How to handle any emergency.

CHOOSING THE ROUTE

"Route planning" refers to the specific trail or trails you plan to hike and how you will connect trails, if you need to, if they have no meeting or crossing point. You will need accurate maps and, once again, up-to-date info. As you choose your specific route, you want to keep several factors in mind: how far you'll travel, how much time it will take you, and what you'll find when you get there.

Distance and time: How far can you go, and how long will it take you? A rule of thumb says a fit hiker with a reasonable load in the pack can cover about two trail miles an hour. An average hiker with a full load on moderate terrain, says another rule, can cover 5 to 10 miles per day. But the only thing that really matters is what you can do, and only experience can finally answer that question. If you haven't hiked recently, or ever, with or without a pack, you will want to plan on fewer miles and more time to cover them until you learn your own trail ability.

Terrain: The lay of the land. More than distance, the ground you'll be walking on will determine your speed. Firm, flat trails

are "easy," and you should make good time. "Moderate" trails will involve some elevation gain and loss, maybe some rocks or mud to cross, and you'll slow down. "Hard" trails might mean steep ground and/or rough ground—bogs, talus, boulders, river crossings. Hard trails, and just about anything off-trail, can cut your miles per hour in half or more. Another rule of thumb: For every 1,000 feet you gain in elevation, you add an hour to your estimated travel time compared with the same distance on flat ground.

High altitude: Thin air. If you live around sea level, you will notice that additional effort—and time—is required to hike starting as low as 5,000 feet elevation. Almost everyone, the well-acclimated being an exception, will move at a slower pace by the time he or she reaches 7,000–8,000 feet. You need to plan your distance and time accordingly.

Campsites/Water sources: Where to stop. As you plan your specific route, consideration as to where you will camp and refill your water bottles will be of the utmost importance, more important than distance and time. Study the maps, ask the right people, check the guidebooks, and pick a route that promises acceptable campsites and sources of water.

Communication

In terms of communication from your chosen route, one thing, at least, is inarguably true: Vast advances in technology have made it much easier to relay information to and from the trail. But, all that technology considered, you simply cannot assume that your cell phone, satellite phone, or other device conceived to work wirelessly and wondrously will work from where you stand out there.

A cell phone (or, more accurately, a cellular phone) is, for all its sophistication, a radio. As with all radios, a cell phone might be out of range. Cell phones use cell sites on the ground to bounce messages back and forth, while satellite phones use satellites high in the sky to do the same basic job. Peaks, valleys, and other geophysical formations may block the message of a satellite phone, or you may be in a spot with no satellites spinning overhead. In either case, or any case involving communication from the trail, what you think might work might not.

There is definitely a positive side to modern means of communication because when it works it's great. On the negative side, cell phones and such can give you a false sense of security that would be much better replaced with the skills and gear to manage emergency situations confidently and with self-reliance. Another negative side to wireless communication concerns numerous incidents when someone in the backcountry has needlessly called for help, endangering the well-being of rescuers who would have been better served staying home.

The choice of whether or not to carry electronic communication devices is entirely personal. If you do carry, say, a radio, you must also carry the skills to use it, the knowledge of when to use it, and an understanding of its limitations.

Sources of Information for Route Planning

Many of the same sources of information you used to plan your trip will serve to help you choose your route.

Books

FalconGuides, 246 Goose Lane, P.O. Box 480, Guilford, CT 06437; (203) 458-4800. www.falcon.com. Guidebooks to every accessible hiking area.

Maps

DeLorme, (800) 561-5105. www.DeLorme.com.

Trails Illustrated and National Geographic, (800) 962-1643. maps.nationalgeographic.com.

USGS Map Sales, Federal Center, P.O. Box 25286, Denver, CO 80225. http://mcmcweb.er.usgs.gov

Websites

http://gorp.away.com. Trail information for state and federal land.

www.trails.com. Specific information on thousands of trails.

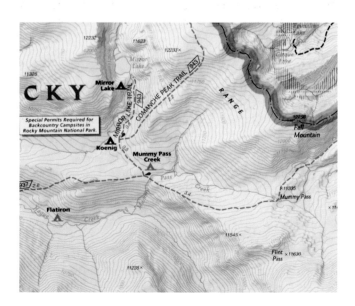

INDEX

INDEX

INDEX

HILLSBOR
H
Member of Washington County
COOPERATIVE LIBRARY SERVICES